TEPS in TEPS

990 독해

박기혁

서울대학교 졸
(현) 메가스터디 어학센터 TEPS 강사
(현) SLA 학원 TEPS 대표 강사
(현) 중앙일보 영자 신문 중앙 데일리 교육 분야 객원 논설위원
(현) 한국 생산성 본부 영어 전임 강사
(현) PTT(Park's TEPS Teacher's Group) 대표 강사
– TEPS의 최고를 지향하는 강사들의 모임

TEPS in TEPS 990 독해 2nd Edition

저자	박기혁
초판 1쇄 인쇄	2009년 8월 4일
개정 2쇄 발행	2012년 1월 25일
발 행 인	박효상
영　　업	이종선, 이태호, 이전희
기획, 진행	강성실, 모희진, 이종만
출판등록	제 10-1835호
발 행 처	사람in
주　　소	121-839 서울시 마포구 서교동 378-16 4F
전　　화	02)338-3555(代)
팩　　스	02)338-3545
E-mail	saramin@netsgo.com
Homepage	www.saramin.com

Special Staff

디자인 표지		장선숙
	내지	홍수미
편　집		조현진
조　판		김선자

※ 책값은 표지 뒷면에 있습니다.
※ 파본은 교환해 드립니다.

ⓒ박기혁 2009

ISBN 978-89-6049-181-6 13740
ISBN 978-89-6049-175-5 (세트)

TEPS in TEPS

990 독해

박기혁

사람in
saram
in.com

Preface

영어 시험을 둘러싼 여러 가지 환경 변화에 의해서 TEPS의 중요성은 나날이 강조되고 있고 그 특징 또한 뚜렷이 변화를 겪고 있다.

첫째, 갈수록 문제가 다양화되고 있고 더욱더 세련되어지고 있다.
둘째,　시험을 치르는 대상 연령층이 자꾸 낮아지고 있다.
셋째, 특목고나 외고, 로스쿨이나 의학전문대학원 진학 등 그 쓰임새가 더욱 광범위해졌다.

이러한 세 가지 변화에 발맞추어, TEPS 교재도 다양화되고 진화되어야 하는데, 현재의 교재 시장은 그러한 가시적인 변화에 능동적으로 대처하지 못하는 것이 사실이다. 이에, 이번 TEPS in TEPS 시리즈를 통해서 진화하는 TEPS에 가장 적합한 패러다임을 제시하고자 한다.

TEPS는 참으로 복잡하고 미묘한 시험이다. TOEFL처럼 학문적인 점에 초점을 맞추는 것도 아니고, TOEIC처럼 실용 언어적인 측면만을 강조하는 시험도 아니다. 어쩌면 이 둘의 장점만을 모아 놓은 시험이라 할 수 있겠다.

학문적인 내용들을 풀어가되 좀 더 현실성을 부여하여 실용적으로 쓰이는 영어들을 묻는 것이다. TEPS가 최근 시험 시장에 지각 변동을 일으키고 있는 이유는 이런 장점이 토대가 되었다고 볼 수 있다.

TEPS는 실제로 회화를 하다가 혹은 네이티브가 보는 외국 신문 등을 읽다가 느끼는 애로사항을 잘 해결해 줄 수 있는 시험이다. 어휘력의 측면에서 보아도 실생활에서 우리는 이런 어려움을 겪는다. ‘단어 하나하나의 해석은 되는데 왜 전체적으로는 독해가 안 되고 해석이 안 될까?’ , ‘이 상황에서 저 말은 대체 무슨 뜻으로 쓰이는 걸까?’

그것은 바로 간단한 단어라도 초보적으로 배웠던 사전적 지식 외에 실생활에서는 다양한 뜻으로 활용되기 때문이다.

이처럼 네이티브와의 가장 적절한 의사소통에 초점을 둔 TEPS는 지극히 영어수험과 영어실용의 접목이라는 공인영어시험의 목적에 가장 합당한 인증시험이라 하겠다.

TOEIC이 점수 인플레로 상위권 수험생의 변별력을 상실했다는 비판이 많다. TEPS는 TOEIC과 같은 패턴의 지속적인 반복만으로는 해결할 수 없는 시험이다. 이에 학습자들도 이런 TEPS에 대한 관심과 욕구가 더욱 늘어나고 있는 현실이다.

필자는 좀 더 실용적이고 영어 실력 향상에 도움이 되는 TEPS에 대한 관심이 높아지고 있는 것은 고무적인 일이라 생각한다. 그리고 그런 TEPS를 연구하고 학습하는데, 이 'TEPS in TEPS 시리즈' 가 선구자적인 역할을 하길 진심으로 바라는 마음으로 문제 하나 설명 하나에 세심한 신경을 쓰면서 작업에 임하였다.

혼자서는 할 수 없었던 작업에 언제나 도움이 되었던 분들께 감사의 마음을 전할까 한다. 늘 미안한 마음이 드는 가족들과, 사람인 출판사의 박효상 사장님, 김상호 팀장님, 조승주 대리님 그리고 이 책의 출간에 물심양면으로 도움을 주신 류건 선생님, 신일섭 조교, 윤이랑 조교에게도 아울러 감사의 뜻을 표하고 싶다.

PTT(Park's TEPS Teacher's Group) 대표 강사

박기혁

TEPS in TEPS

학생들의 자습서와 학원 교재의 성격을 둘 다 가질 수 있게 만들었다. 그래서 학원에서의 강의는 물론 독학용으로 사용하도록 준비했다.

1. 상세한 해설을 통해 정답을 공략하는 법과 함께 오답을 피할 수 있는 Skill들을 제시하여 좀 더 높은 점수로의 도약이 가능하게 하였다.

2. TEPS의 4대 영역(독해, 어휘, 청해, 문법)과 기준 점수대별로 학습 목표와 가장 효율적인 방법들을 제시하여 좀 더 전문적이고 체계적인 학습자 맞춤형 학습이 가능하도록 하였다.

3. 애매모호한 이론이나 군더더기 설명을 최대한 배제하여 학습 시간 대비 효율성을 극대화하도록 구성하였다.

TEPS in TEPS

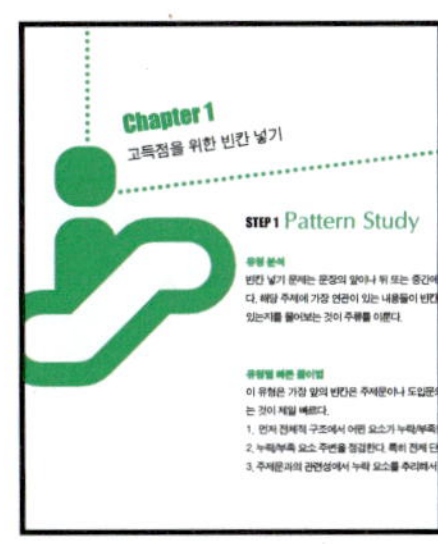

1. TEPS 약점 유형을 집중 보강한 Part 1

TEPS 약점 유형 5가지를 집중적으로 분석하고 이에 따른 빠르고도 정확한 해결법을 제시하였다. 출제 패턴을 철저히 분석하고 올바른 풀이법을 적용할 수 있는 다이어그램을 제시하여 정확성과 시간 모두를 잡을 수 있도록 하였다.

2. TEPS 고득점 테마를 세밀히 분석한 Part 2

TEPS 독해에 잘 나오는 소재들을 테마별로 나누어서 분석하고 해결법을 제시하였다. 고득점에 가장 필요한 BEST 테마별로 독해에 적용할 수 있는 필수 표현들을 챙겨 익히도록 하여 TEPS에 가장 적절한 독해법을 완성하였다.

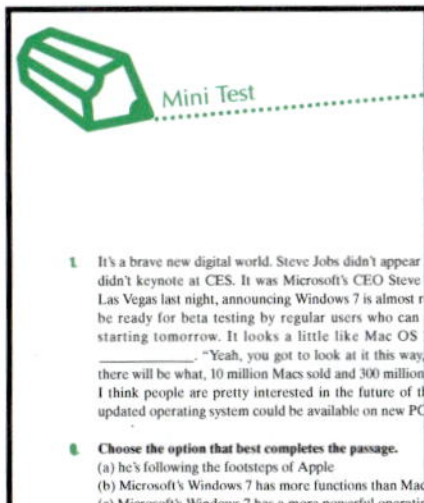

3. 자신만의 해결 노하우를 만들어가는 Mini Test

TEPS 유형에서 고난이도의 문제들만을 엄선하여 풀어보도록 하였다. 좀 더 어려운 난이도의 문제들을 통해서 고득점으로 가는 자신만의 문제풀이 비법을 완성하도록 하였다.

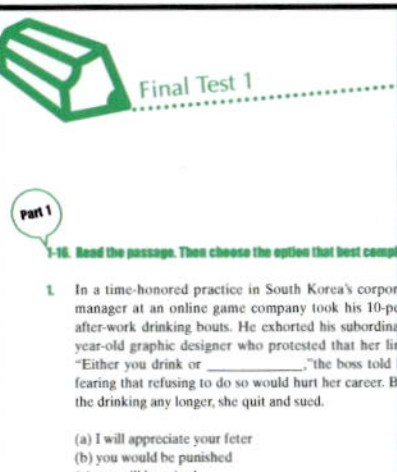

4. 실전보다 더 실전 같은 Final Test

TEPS와 가장 가까운 문제들만 엄선하여 학습자로 하여금 실전 감각을 최고조에 이를 수 있도록 하였다. 기존의 TEPS 문제들을 철저하게 분석함은 물론 앞으로 출제가 예상되는 부분까지 반영하여 어려운 문제가 나오더라도 자신감 넘치게 대처할 수 있도록 하였다.

Final Test

Part 1

고득점을 위한 패턴별 독해

STEP 1 Pattern Study

유형 분석

빈칸 넣기 문제는 문장의 앞이나 뒤 또는 중간에 빈칸을 넣어서 그 내용을 채워 넣는 유형이다. 해당 주제에 가장 연관이 있는 내용들이 빈칸으로 제시되어 학습자가 대의를 잘 파악하고 있는지를 물어보는 것이 주류를 이룬다.

유형별 빠른 풀이법

이 유형은 가장 앞의 빈칸은 주제문이나 도입문의 경우이므로 다음과 같은 순서로 답을 구하는 것이 제일 빠르다.

1. 먼저 전체적 구조에서 어떤 요소가 누락/부족한지를 파악한다.
2. 누락/부족 요소 주변을 점검한다. 특히 전체 단락에서의 주제문의 위치를 체크한다.
3. 주제문과의 관련성에서 누락 요소를 추리해서 답을 찾는다.

Sample

As to goodness of character in general, Aristotle says that we start by having a capacity for it, but that it has to be developed by practice. How is it developed? By doing virtuous acts. _______________. Aristotle tells us that we become virtuous by doing virtuous acts, but how can we do virtuous acts unless we are already virtuous? Aristotle answers that we begin by doing acts which are objectively virtuous, without having a reflex knowledge of the acts and a deliberate choice of the acts as good, a choice resulting from an habitual disposition.

Q. **Choose the option that best completes the passage.**

(a) At first sight this looks like a vicious cycle.
(b) It is then virtuous in this respect.
(c) The acts of truth-telling develop gradually out of correct habits.
(d) It appears that goodness is innate.

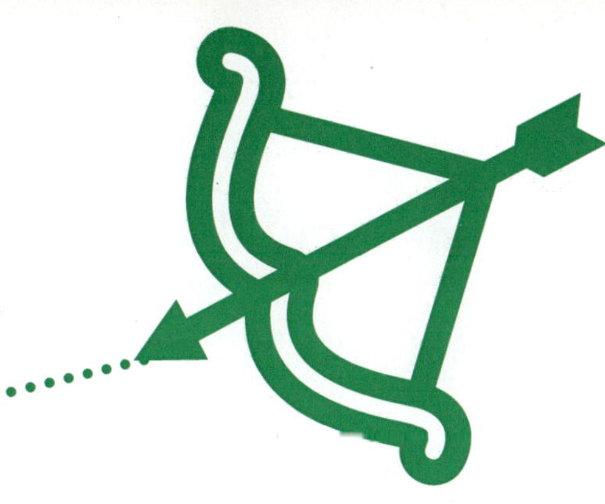

이런 유형의 문제를 풀때 유념해야 할 것은 중심 주제와의 관련성이다. 중심 주제를 빨리 파악하면서 빈칸에 들어갈 말을 생각해서 답을 찾아내야 한다. 글의 전반적인 주제가 덕이 있는 행동이고, 빈칸에는 그에 따른 주제를 강조하기 위해서 언뜻 보기에는 납득이 가지 않는 모습을 나타내는 문장이 들어가야 한다. 악순환처럼 말이다. 다시 말해서 덕이 있으려면 덕이 있는 행동을 하라고 했으니까, 이것은 단순한 반복 논리가 된다. 따라서 정답은 (a)이다.

풀이 적용 다이어그램

누락 요소 점검	누락 요소 주변 점검	빈칸 주변의 내용 파악
문단의 중간에 누락 요소가 있다.	빈칸 앞의 의문문의 제시로 볼 때, 빈칸은 주제나 주제 의식의 보강이 된다.	반복 논리의 예로 제시된 문장 다음에 빈칸이 있으므로 악순환처럼 보일 것이라는 부연 설명이 정답

Translation

아리스토텔레스는 사람의 일반적 품성의 선함에 관하여, 인간은 가능성을 가지고 인생을 시작하지만, 그 가능성은 실천에 의해 발전시켜야 한다고 말한다. 가능성을 어떻게 개발시킨다는 것인가? 덕망 있는 행동을 함으로 개발시킬 수 있다. 언뜻 보면 이 말은 악순환의 반복 논리처럼 보인다. 아리스토텔레스가 우리에게 말하는 것은 덕망 있는 행동을 함으로써 덕이 있게 된다는 것인데 우리가 이미 덕이 있지 않다면 어떻게 덕망 있는 행동을 하겠는가? 아리스토텔레스는 우리가 행동에 대한 무의식적인 반응이나 착한 행동으로서 의도적인 선택, 즉 습관적인 기질에 의한 선택을 하지 않고 객관적으로 덕망 있는 행동을 시작할 수 있다고 대답한다.

Words

capacity 가능성
virtuous 덕망 있는
objectively 객관적으로
habitual disposition 습관적인 기질

1.

There are several factors in the radio and television industry which work against balanced schedules and tend to lower the quality of the programs offered. Of these, one of the most important factors is the fierce competition among stations. Program producers are under constant pressure to reach larger and larger audiences. To achieve this end, stations resort to producing more and more of one type of program that happens to have a wide popular appeal at the moment. As a result, ______________.

Q. **Choose the option that best completes the passage.**
   (a) various types of programs are produced, following a trend
   (b) variety is ignored and sameness prevails
   (c) balance is achieved in schedules
   (d) the quality of the programs offered improves

2.

In most parts of the United States the weather is either fair or foul. It rains or shines with a businesslike intensity. ______________. Westerly winds reach across continent, without the moisture and the tempering of the Atlantic. North-west winds prevail in the winter, and south-west winds in summer. Consequently the summers are everywhere hotter than in the British Isles, and the winters, north of Virginia, colder; the extremes of heat and cold in the same season are greater; the rainfall less, although adequate for animal and plant life.

Q. **Choose the option that best completes the passage.**
   (a) In comparison, the weather of the British Isles is perpetually unsettled
   (b) The climate is in many respects different from Europe
   (c) Compared with France, the entire country is one vast forest
   (d) Like western Europe, the area lies wholly within the northern temperate zone

3.　⬚ 고난이도

The World Bank Tuesday said Asia was plunging into a depression and called on Japan to help pull the region out of its economic nosedive. A World Bank senior regional expert said Asia was on the threshold of a deep and long depression and warned a global economic slump could be just months away. "We are probably at the end of the first cycle of the crisis and we are entering into a deep recession; you could even ______________," he told a major trade and investment conference in Australia.

Q.　**Choose the option that best completes the passage.**
(a) use the term "panic"
(b) speak of warlike scenario
(c) refer to it as the status quo
(d) boost economic recovery

Section Switch

☐ **resort to** (어떤 수단, 방법에) 의존하다, 호소하다, ~을 쓰다
☐ **prevail** 우세하다
☐ **foul** 몹시 나쁜
☐ **businesslike** 실제적인
☐ **perpetually** 끊임없이
☐ **rainfall** 강우량
☐ **plunge into depression** 경기 침체에 빠지다
☐ **call on Japan to** 일본에게 ~하도록 요구하다
☐ **nosedive** 곤두박질, 폭락
☐ **be on the threshold of** 이제 막 ~하려고 하다, ~이 임박해오다
☐ **status quo** 현재 상황, 현상 유지

Chapter 2
고득점을 위한 일치/불일치 찾기

STEP 1 Pattern Study

유형 분석

일치/불일치 문제는 관점에 따라서 상당히 난해한 유형일 수도 있다. 그러나 각 설문의 요점에 유념해, 그 대상에 대한 서술의 긍정/부정 성격을 파악하면서 읽어낸다면 반드시 답을 구할 수 있다.

유형별 빠른 풀이법

일치/불일치 문제는 가장 시간이 많이 걸리는 문제 유형이기는 하지만 다음과 같이 풀면 빨리 풀린다.

1. 빠른 속도로 본문을 읽어서 대략적인 대의를 빨리 파악한다.
2. (a), (b), (c), (d)에서 묻고 있는 것을 긍정/부정의 시각으로 구분하여 빨리 본문에서 찾아낸다.
3. 주로 오답과 정답으로 나오는 전형적인 표현들에서 빨리 힌트를 찾으려고 노력한다.

Sample

The politics of the Joseon Dynasty, which ruled Korea from 1392 to 1910, were governed by the reigning ideology of Neo-Confucianism. Political struggles were common between different factions of the literati. Purges frequently resulted in leading political figures being sent into exile or condemned to death. The political system of this period was dominated by a Neo-Confucian bureaucracy. The power of the bureaucrats often eclipsed that of the central authorities, including the monarch. For much of the dynasty, a complex system of checks and balances prevented any one section of the government from gaining overwhelming power.

Q. **Which is correct about the Joseon Dynasty according to the passage?**

(a) The politics of the Joseon Dynasty was dominated by male chauvinism.
(b) The power of the king was supreme during the period of Joseon Dynasty.
(c) There were lots of political fights between different political parties.
(d) Political figures were sent to prison in regular purges.

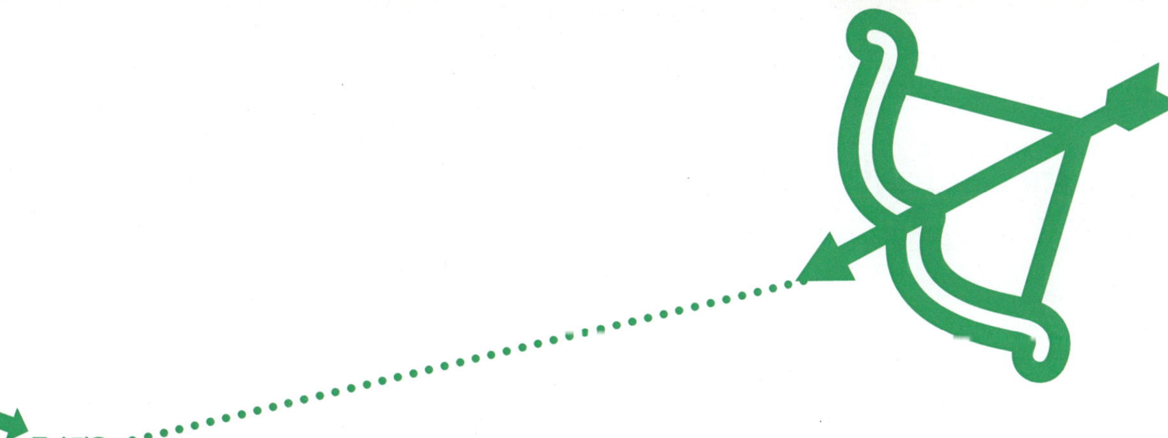

글의 전반적인 주제는 조선시대의 정치적인 분쟁이고, 끝부분에서 그러한 분쟁의 결과, 정부의 한 구성 부분이 권력을 독점하는 것을 막았다는 서술이 있다. 따라서 (c)의 여러 정파 사이에서 정치적 싸움이 많았다고 하는 부분이 중심적 내용이 된다. 본문에 나와 있는 설명에 근거하여 답을 찾는 것이 중요하다. 본문 둘째 문장에 근거하여 (c)의 답안을 고를 수 있다. (a)는 알 수 없으며, 다섯 번째 문장에서 (b)가 틀렸음을 알 수 있다. (d)에서는 prison의 표현이 틀렸다.

풀이 적용 다이어그램

전반적 대의 파악	긍정/부정의 시각에 의한 보기 점검	오답으로 이끄는 전형적 보기 찾기
조선 왕조의 왕권과 관료의 관계	역학관계가 상황에 따라서 변했으므로 (b)의 supreme during은 틀림	(d)의 맨 마지막 단어 prison이 틀렸음

Translation

한국을 1392년부터 1910년까지 지배했던 조선 왕조의 정치는 신유교의 지배 이념에 따라 통치되었다. 정치적 투쟁은 지식계급의 여러 당파 사이에서 빈번했다. 숙청은 자주 정치적인 인물들이 유배당하거나 사형에 처해지는 결과를 낳았다. 이 시기의 정치적인 체계는 신유교의 관료 제도에 의해 지배되었다. 관료들의 권력은 종종 군주를 포함한 중앙 권력을 능가하였다. 왕조의 상당 기간 동안 견제와 균형의 복잡한 체계는 정부의 어떤 한 구성 부분이 압도적인 권력을 얻는 것을 방지하였다.

Words

politics 정치
confucianism 유교
faction 당파
purge 숙청
dominate 지배하다
eclipse 그늘지게 하다, 능가하다

reigning 군림하는, 널리 퍼져 있는
struggle 투쟁
literati 지식계급, 문학자
exile 추방
bureaucracy 관료제도

1.

In American society, it is common to hear people talk about a Catch-22 situation. The term comes from a popular novel with that title and describes a series of the situations of the following nature: A cannot be corrected until B is corrected, but B cannot be corrected until C is corrected, and C cannot be corrected until A is corrected. As a result, none of the situations is ever realized. Foreign students coming to the U.S. very often find themselves in a Catch-22 situation. For instance, if a male foreign student wants to marry an American woman, he might find that the parents would like him to have a job before he gets married. But he can't get a job because the U.S. government will not let him work. So he can't get married.

Q. **Which of the following is correct according to the passage?**
(a) A Catch-22 is the title of a popular novel.
(b) The victim is unable to escape from the vicious circle.
(c) A foreign student can not work in the U.S.
(d) Having a permanent resident visa in the U.S is ideal.

2.

The term "American dream" had been around for countless decades. The U.S. was once recognized as a country of many opportunities. Indeed, this was quite true until recently. Every year large number of Koreans with passion and dreams of a successful life immigrated to the U.S. for a better future. Well, it now seems that Korea, once considered as having a poor job market and working conditions, is now a better place to be. More and more Koreans are returning from the U.S. as almost every company in the U.S. is downsizing. We can forget about the term "American dream," since as most of you know, the U.S. is now considered as the epicenter of the global financial crisis.

Q. **Which of following is correct according to the passage?**
(a) More and more Korean-immigrants are returning from the U.S.
(b) The U.S. is taking a measure to provide financial support for immigrants.
(c) Many unemployed people are looking for shorter-term contract work.
(d) Most companies are offering more generous early-retirement incentives.

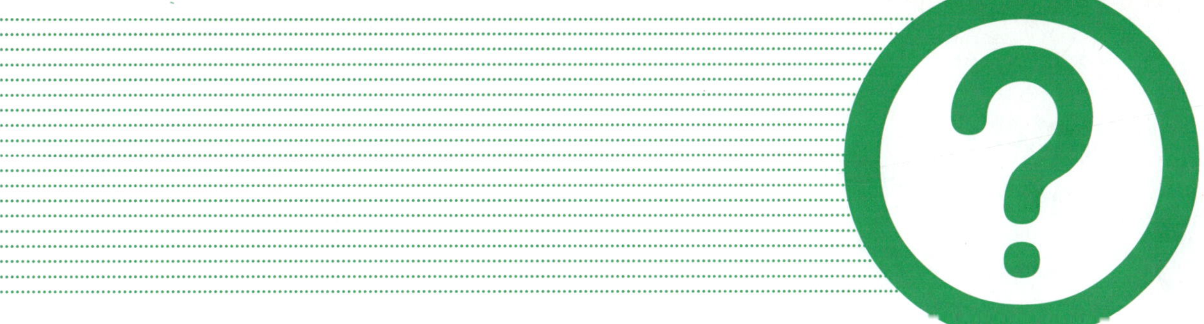

3. 고난이도

Standing at a podium announcing "This is It" Thursday in London's O2 Arena, Michael Jackson posed, waved, smiled, blew kisses to screaming fans, and haltingly announced his first concert since 2001. In the last decade the singer has been buffeted by rumors of failing health and has made more headlines because of his troubled personal life than his music. He was arrested in 2003 on child-molestation charges and acquitted in 2005 after a trial in California. Financial struggles followed and last year he surrendered the deed to his 2,500-acre Neverland ranch in California. He was to auction more than 2,000 personal items from Neverland next month, but on Wednesday filed a lawsuit against Julien's Auction House, saying that the company is not authorized to sell off memorabilia removed from his estate.

Q. **Which of the following is correct about Michael Jackson?**

(a) Michael Jackson was accused of fraud.

(b) Michael Jackson withdrew the complaint against Julien's Auction House.

(c) Michael Jackson was summoned to stand trial for molestation.

(d) Michael Jackson's entire estate was all sold off.

Section Switch

- ☐ **term** 기간; 용어
- ☐ **for instance** 예를 들어
- ☐ **vicious circle** 악순환
- ☐ **downsize** (인력, 규모를) 감축하다
- ☐ **epicenter** (지진의) 발생지, (문제의) 핵심
- ☐ **financial crisis** 금융 위기
- ☐ **podium** 연단
- ☐ **haltingly** 머뭇거리면서
- ☐ **buffet** 사람을 괴롭히다, 못살게 굴다
- ☐ **acquit** ~을 석방하다
- ☐ **ranch** 농장
- ☐ **auction house** 경매 회사
- ☐ **sell off** 헐값에 팔아치우다
- ☐ **memorabilia** 기념품, 기념할 만한 일

Chapter 3
고득점을 위한 제목/요지 찾기

STEP 1 Pattern Study

유형 분석

제목이나 요지, 대의를 찾으라는 문제의 핵심은 주제를 파악하기보다는 한 단계 더 나아가서 중심을 이루는 핵심의 대의를 한두 마디로 분석하는 것이 중요하다. 따라서 빠른 속도로 주제를 찾아서 내용 파악을 하고 그에 맞춰서 제목을 짚어내야 한다. 물론 주제를 파악하고 한번 더 생각해야 하므로 시간은 다소 더 걸리는 유형이다.

유형별 빠른 풀이법

제목이나 대의를 찾는 문제는 지문 전체를 다 읽어야 하는 부담이 있지만 다음과 같은 과정을 따르면 문제를 빨리 해결할 수 있다.

1. 빠른 시간 내에 주제를 찾으려면, 주제를 나타내는 표현을 빨리 찾아내야 한다.
2. 주제가 되는 표현은 역접의 접속사 뒤에 올 수도 있고, 권위자나 연구 결과를 발표하는 부분 등에서 주제가 부각될 수도 있다.
3. 답을 찾고도 혹시 시간 여유가 있다면 주제에 맞춰 글을 썼는지 다시 한번 검토해보도록 한다.

Sample

In what is being called the biggest outbreak of its kind in U.S. history, more than 4,000 people suffered food poisoning from a rare form of E. coli bacteria by eating food prepared by a south suburban Chicago caterer. Health officials say the bacteria, enterotoxigenic E. coli or ETEC, is normally found only in developing countries. They say they still do not know the source of the bacteria found in the potato salad prepared by Iwans Deli & Catering of Orland Park. It is unclear whether the bacteria was in one of the ingredients, whether one of the caterer's employees was ill or whether there was a problem with the water system.

Q. **Which of the following best summarizes the above passage?**

(a) A rare form of bacteria was discovered in a developing country.

(b) There was an outbreak of food poisoning from ETEC near Chicago.

(c) A catering company deliberately infected its potato salad with bacteria.

(d) The source of the ETEC was prepared food infected by the water system.

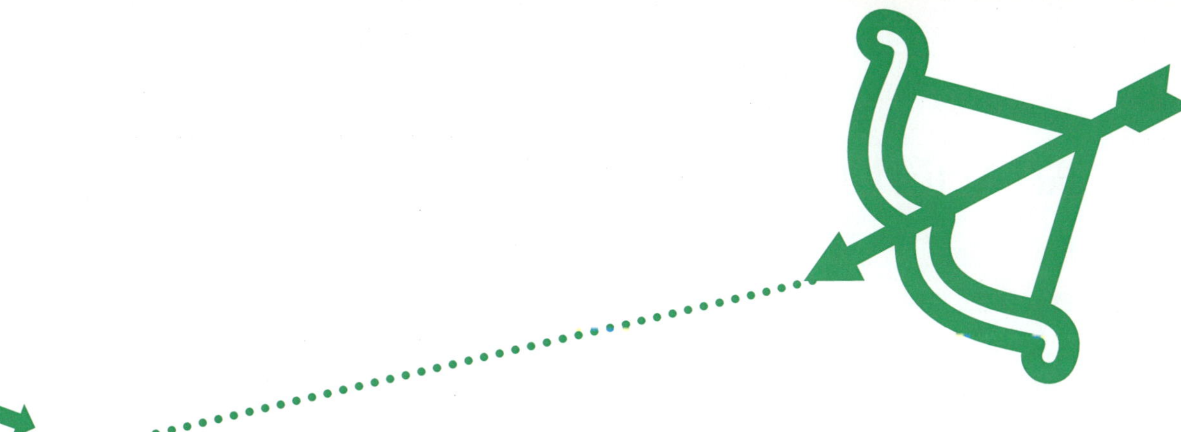

요약된 신문 기사를 통해 대의 파악 능력을 측정하는 문제이다. 특히 보건 당국의 이야기까지 언급하면서 내용을 소개한 것은 병의 위중함과 그 발병을 실감나게 나타내려는 취지일 것이다. 따라서 정답은 (b)가 된다.

풀이 적용 다이어그램

주제가 되는 표현을 찾기 (1)	주제가 되는 표현을 찾기 (2)	보기 확인 검토
단순 소개가 아닌 의문사 what을 동원한 강조 제시	보건 당국의 이야기를 언급해서 서술의 정당성을 확보	(c)에서의 deliberately 는 전형적 오답 요소

Translation

미국 역사상 가장 큰 식중독 사건이라고 할 만한 일이 일어났다. 시카고 남부 교외에 위치한 출장 요리업체가 제공한 음식에 희귀한 E. coli 박테리아가 들어 있어서 이 음식을 먹은 4천 명 이상의 사람들이 식중독을 일으켰다. 보건부 관계자들은 enterotoxigenic E. coli, 혹은 ETEC라고 불리는 이 박테리아가 주로 개도국에서만 발견되는 균이며, 올랜도 파크의 이완스 델리 앤 캐이터링에서 만든 감자 샐러드에 어떻게 이 균이 들어가게 되었는지 아직도 밝혀내지 못했다고 말했다. 균이 재료 속에 있었는지, 혹은 출장 요리업체 종업원이 병에 걸려 있었는지, 아니면 급수 시설이 불결해서 이런 일이 일어났는지는 확실하지 않다.

Words

outbreak 갑작스런 발병, 발작
food poisoning 식중독
caterer 출장 요리업체, (호텔 등의) 연회 업자
ingredient 성분

1.

During the 1960s, people in all the industrialized countries became more and more worried about the effect of man and technology on the environment. Individual people, organizations, even governments grew concerned. One small sign of the times was the naming of a British government ministry as the Department of the Environment. In a time of economic decline, to worry about preserving the environment might have seemed a luxury. The great majority of people were chiefly interested in improving their standard of living, which meant more possessions, more "consumption."

Q. **What is the best title of the passage?**
(a) The Bright Future of the British Economy
(b) Consumer Society in Great Britain
(c) Britain's Economy and Pollution
(d) The Coming of Britain's Nuclear Age

2.

"Peanuts" remained the heart of Schulz's life literally right up until the end. The cartoonist died of cancer on February 12, 2000, the day before his final Sunday strip ran. "Schulz and Peanuts" has meaning unknown to most readers. Author Michaelis draws parallels between Schulz's sometimes contentious first marriage and the relationship between Charlie Brown and Lucy. He observes that a number of character names — Shermy, Linus, even Charlie Brown — had real-life roots. And he goes into Schulz's dark places, from his fear of travel to the death of his mother. "Charlie Brown has to carry Charles Schulz's spears, and the slings and arrows of the world," he said.

Q. **What is the main idea of the passage?**
(a) Cartoon author was depressed about life.
(b) Schulz didn't like overseas trips.
(c) We should be critics of the world and of ourselves.
(d) There is a close relationship between an author and the works.

3. 고난이도

The common scorpionfly has a black and yellow body, with a reddish head and tail. The male has a pair of claspers at the end of its tail (for holding the female during mating), giving it a scorpion-like appearance, although there is no stinger. It has a wingspan of about 35mm. The head is drawn into a prominent, downward pointing beak, with the mouthparts at the tip. The eyes are large. The wings are mostly clear, but have many dark spots or patches.

Q. What is the best title of the passage?
(a) A natural enemy of the common scorpionfly
(b) The habits of the common scorpionfly
(c) Bodily function of the common scorpionfly
(d) A description of the common scorpionfly

Section Switch

- ☐ industrialized country 선진 공업국
- ☐ preserve 보존하다
- ☐ chiefly 주로
- ☐ consumption 소비
- ☐ draw a parallel with/between A and B A와 B를 비교하다
- ☐ spear 창
- ☐ sling 새총
- ☐ arrow 화살
- ☐ reddish 불그스름한
- ☐ clasper 걸쇠, 갈퀴
- ☐ prominent 돌출된
- ☐ beak 부리

Chapter 4
고득점을 위한 추론 문제

STEP 1 Pattern Study

유형 분석

추론 문제는 내용에서 바로 답이 나오는 것이 아니라 그 내용에서 하나가 걸러지는 내용에 대한 물음이다. 지문에 직접 드러난 사실에서 추론해 알 수 있는 내용을 물어본다는 점에서 방심하지 말고 내용을 점검해야 한다.

유형별 빠른 풀이법

추론 문제는 TEPS의 특이한 독해 유형이다. 다음과 같이 풀면 빨리 풀린다.

1. 추론 문제를 풀기 위해서는 빠른 속도로 글의 전체 취지를 이해한다.
2. 흔히 뒤에 있는 내용을 전제로 추론의 정답이 나온다.
3. 따라서 뒷부분에 유념하면서, 앞으로 나올 이야기의 전반적인 내용을 추가로 정리하고, 해당 사실이 확장될 여지에 대하여 검토한다.

Sample

Ostracism was a procedure under Athenian democracy in which a prominent citizen could be expelled from the city-state of Athens for ten years. While some instances were clear expressions of popular anger at the victim, ostracism was often used pre-emptively. It was used as a way of defusing major confrontations between rival politicians (by removing one of them from the scene), neutralizing someone thought to be a threat to the state, or exiling a potential tyrant. Crucially, ostracism had no relation to the justice system. There was no charge or defence, and the exile was not in fact a penalty; it was simply a command from the Athenian people that one of their number be gone for ten years.

Q. **What can be inferred from the passage?**

    (a) Ostracism was used less frequently than expressing popular anger at the victim directly.

    (b) Ostracism was usually used to punish betrayers.

    (c) Ostracism had nothing to do with justice.

    (d) Ostracism was in use throughout the whole period of Athenian democracy.

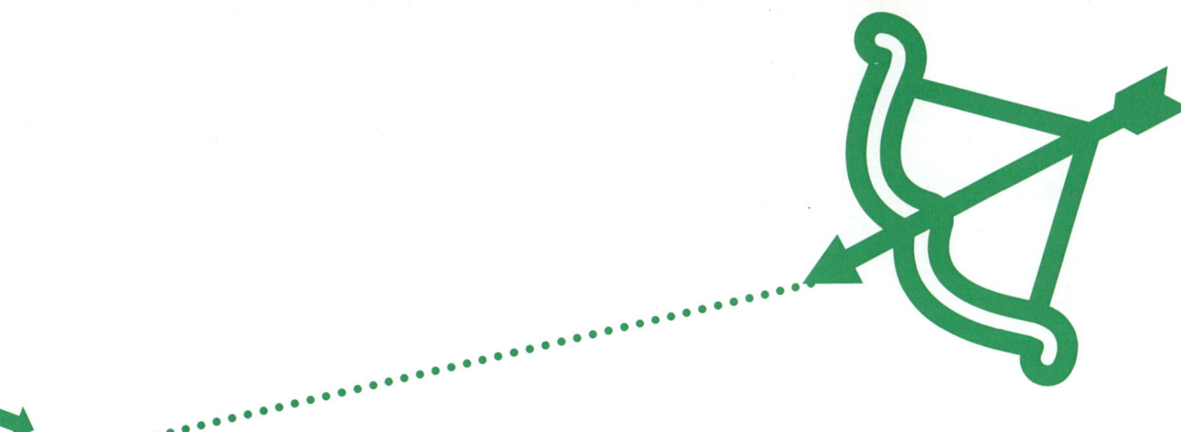

특히 뒷부분에 나온 Crucially, ostracism had no relation to the justice system. There was no charge or defence, and the exile was not in fact a penalty에서의 crucially처럼 말하고자 하는 것을 직접적으로 드러낸 표현을 파악한다면 쉽게 (c)가 정답임을 알 수 있다.

풀이 적용 다이어그램

전체적 취지의 이해		문단의 뒷부분에 유념		뒤에서 획득한 정보에 의한 추론 사실 확정
도편추방제에 대한 설명이 글의 전체적 취지	→	도편추방제는 처벌이 아니었다는 내용 점검	→	도편추방제는 사법 체계와는 무관

Translation

도편추방제는 아테네 민주정치 하에 행해졌던 절차로, 유력한 시민이 도시 국가인 아테네로부터 10년간 추방될 수 있었다. 희생자에 대한 대중의 분노의 표시가 뚜렷한 경우도 일부 있었지만, 대체로 도편추방제는 예방의 목적으로 사용되었다. 도편추방제는 경쟁하는 정치인들 사이에 (한 쪽을 제거함으로써) 주요한 대립의 위험성을 제거하는 방식으로 사용되기도 했고, 국가에 위협이 된다고 여겨지는 인물을 무력화하거나 잠재적인 폭군을 추방하는 용도로 사용되었다. 결정적으로, 도편추방제는 사법 체계와 아무런 관련이 없었다. 기소나 변호도 없었고 추방은 사실상 처벌이 아니었다. 이것은 단지 그들 중 하나가 10년 동안 사라져야 한다는 아테네 시민들로부터의 명령일 뿐이었다.

Words

prominent 저명한
instance 경우
pre-emptively 예방적으로
confrontation 대립
tyrant 폭군

1.

Starwood Hotels offers discounts to Harvard Travelers worldwide. Harvard travelers can now reserve rooms at a 20% discount off the applicable hotel's best available room rate. Starwood Hotels & Resorts Worldwide, Inc. is one of the leading hotel companies in the world with 9 brands (Sheraton, Four Points by Sheraton, St. Regis, Luxury Collection, Le Meridian, W Hotels, Westin, Aloft and Element Hotel) and more than 860 hotels in over 95 countries. To be eligible you must be enrolled in Starwood's loyalty program or the Starwood Preferred Guest (SPG) Program. Enrollment is free, and easy.

Q. What can be inferred from the passage?

(a) Starwood Hotels provides Havard Travelers with a 20% discount off the hotel room rate.
(b) There are 95 branches of Starwood Hotels all over the world.
(c) Sheraton is the main brand of Starwood Hotels and Resorts.
(d) You should pay an enrollment fee to enroll in Starwood's loyalty program.

2.

I enjoy wine, beer, and other spirits. Although many people think that alcohol is harmful, I would not want the government to restrict my right to drink. By the same token, I would not argue that the fact that I like to drink gives me the right to put a little alcohol into everyone's water. Fortunately, when I drink, my alcohol does not escape into other people's glasses, but the same is not true for tobacco. Smokers must understand this and accept the fact that restrictions must be placed on their right to smoke.

Q. Which one of the following most strongly supports the passage?

(a) Nonsmokers also have the right to breathe clean air.
(b) Smokers feel we have gone too far in restricting their right to enjoy tobacco.
(c) The air we breathe can be compared to the water we drink.
(d) We should be free to do what we like as long as we are not harming others.

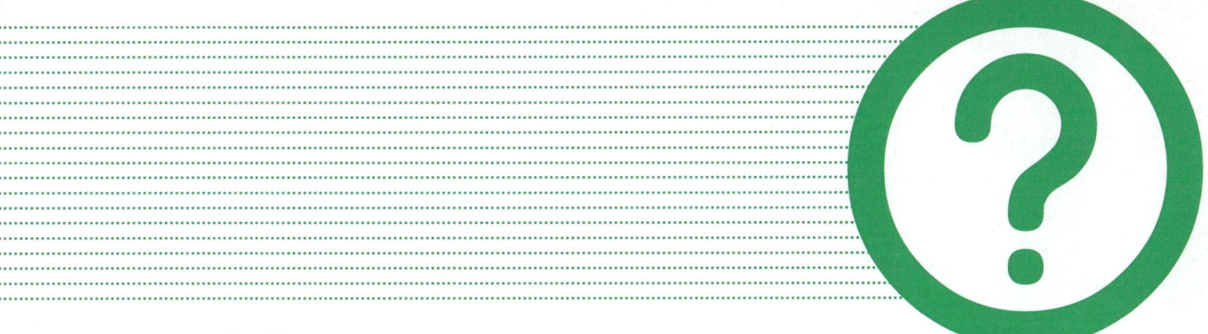

3. 〔고난이도〕

Gustav Klimt, an Austrian-born painter, was founder of the school of painting known as the Vienna Secession. Turn-of-the-century Vienna was obsessed with the aesthetic and the erotic. It was a time of happiness and abandon as well as dazzling intellectualism. Gustav Klimt's art spoke the deep psychological truth of his time, and as is often the case was violently criticized for it. Klimt's work reflected the contradiction of his time. He combined a deliciously sensual mixture of opposites; ecstasy and terror, life and death, austerity and pleasure. The sensual figures in The Kiss, although portrayed in a flat, two-dimensional way are surrounded in gold as if to be immortalized; as if to make the sensual divine.

Q. What's the mood of the passage?
    (a) Jocose
    (b) Meticulous
    (c) Scrupulous
    (d) Informative

Section Switch 

- ☐ **reserve** 예약하다
- ☐ **eligible** 자격이 있는
- ☐ **enrollment fee** 등록비
- ☐ **restrict** 제한하다, 규제하다
- ☐ **spirit** 알코올, 독한 술
- ☐ **by the same token** 같은 이유로
- ☐ **tobacco** 담배
- ☐ **secession** 분리파(1898년 비엔나에 일어난 예술 운동)
- ☐ **obsess** (귀신·망상 따위가) 들리다, 붙다
- ☐ **dazzling** 눈부신, 현혹적인
- ☐ **intellectualism** 주지주의
- ☐ **ecstasy** 무아경, 황홀
- ☐ **austerity** 엄격, 준엄
- ☐ **jocose** 우스꽝스런, 익살맞은(facetious)

Chapter 5

고득점을 위한 문맥상 어울리지 않는 것 찾기

STEP 1 Pattern Study

유형 분석

문맥상 어울리지 않는 것을 골라내는 상당히 난해한 유형이다. 글의 전체 취지를 이해해서 내용을 파악하고 거기에 맞춰서 대의에 어긋나는 부분을 파악해야 한다. 따라서 대의의 긍정적/부정적 방향성을 확인하고 그에 맞춰 내용의 방향에 어긋나는 부분을 찾아내야 한다.

유형별 빠른 풀이법

학습자들이 가장 시간을 많이 잡아먹는다고 말하는 것이 문맥상 어울리지 않는 것을 찾는 유형이다. 다음과 같은 순서로 풀자.

1. 전반적 대의를 빨리 파악해야 한다.
2. 전반적 대의란 하나의 구체적 대상에 대한 긍정적/부정적 서술의 방향이다.
3. 그러한 서술의 방향과 어긋난 서술을 빨리 찾아내면 된다.

Sample

Read the passage. Then identify the option that does NOT belong.

(a) In its State of the World Population Report 2008, the United Nations Fund for Population Activities (UNFPA) severely criticizes the discrimination against women, particularly in developing countries, and warns of serious consequences for the environment and social structure of many countries if more equality isn't shown. (b) The comprehensive report says employment, healthcare, education and equality in the home are the major areas where women are discriminated against. (c) The UNFPA Report, although it doesn't describe anything new, does serve to keep the spotlight on discrimination against women and will hopefully create greater awareness throughout the world of this problem. (d) However, what the report doesn't say is how to break down traditional male prejudices and social practices, some of which are thousand of years old.

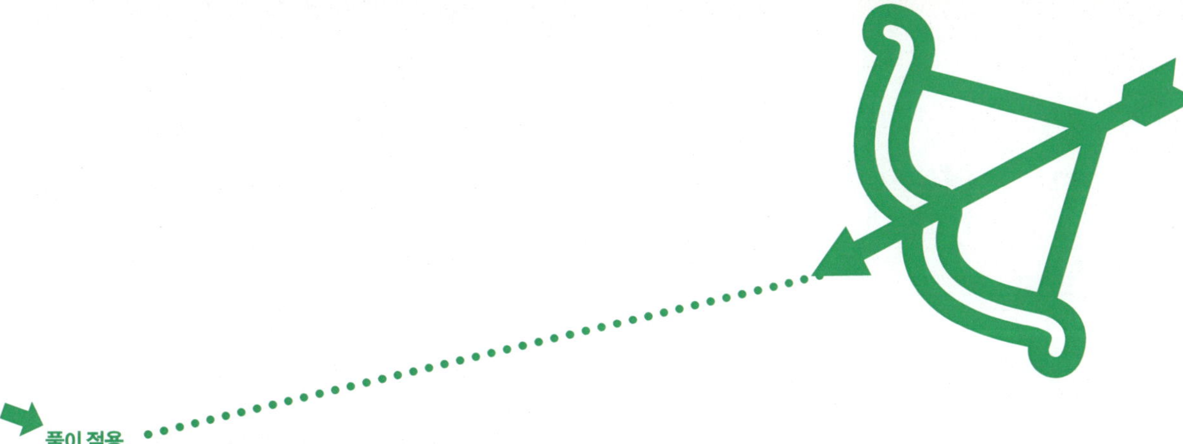

풀이 적용

(c) 'UNFPA 보고서는 새로운 것을 기술하고 있지는 않지만 여성 차별에 초점을 맞추는 데는 성공했으므로 이를 통해 전 세계적으로 이 문제에 대한 더 광범위한 인식을 불러 일으키리라는 희망을 가져볼 수 있을 것이다.' 라는 표현은 보고서의 글 전체적 성격과 장단점 등의 내용에 다소 어울리지 않는다.

풀이 적용 다이어그램

전반적 대의 파악		구체적 대상의 서술 방향		전반적인 방향에 어긋난 서술
UNFPA 보고서의 내용	➡	보고서는 새로운 내용을 담고 있음(특히 여성 문제에 대해서)	➡	새로운 내용 제시에 대비해서 (c)는 새로운 것을 제시하지 않고 있다고 했으므로 오답

Translation

국제연합 안구 기금(UNFPA)은 2008년판 '세계 인구 보고서' 에서 여성 차별, 특히 개발 도상국에서의 여성 차별에 대해 신랄하게 비판하면서, 더욱 더 많은 평등이 보장되지 않으면 많은 국가들의 환경과 사회 구조에 심각한 결과가 초래될 것이라고 경고하고 있다. 이 포괄적인 보고서는 고용, 보건 의료 서비스, 교육 그리고 가정 내의 평등을 여성이 차별받고 있는 주요 분야라고 지적한다. UNFPA 보고서는 새로운 것을 기술하고 있지는 않지만 여성 차별에 초점을 맞추는 데는 성공했으므로 이를 통해 전 세계적으로 이 문제에 대한 더 광범위한 인식을 불러일으키리라는 희망을 가져볼 수 있을 것이다. 그러나 보고서는 인습적인 남성의 편견과 수천 년 지속되어온 사회적 관습들을 어떻게 타파할 수 있는가에 대해서는 언급하고 있지 않다.

Words

discrimination 차별
describe 묘사하다, 언급하다
prejudice 편견
taboo 금기

1. Read the passage. Then identify the option that does NOT belong.

Finally ecological problems are no great respecters of national boundaries. (a) Pollution of the atmosphere and seas can have transnational effects, as vividly illustrated by the legendary penguins of Antarctica with the high concentration of D.D.T. in their tissues. (b) Thus in some instances understanding the problem requires a global perspective. (c) Of course, with numerous nations involved the administrative difficulties of any policy are multiplied. (d) It would, thus, be extremely difficult to gain universal acceptance of a particular pollution tax rate.

2. Read the passage. Then identify the option that does NOT belong.

Latin and Classic Chinese, the languages of the two gigantic intellectual communities of Europe and East Asia, have now passed into disuse. (a) In both areas, if anything has replaced them as the international language, it is English, which has become the language of science so universally that it seems without a peer in the history of our planet. (b) The reasons have little to do with any inherent merits of English itself. (c) Its present position seems to derive primarily from two facts. (d) It is not easier to learn or to use than other languages — indeed it may be harder than most — and it is not any more logical or less ambiguous than the others.

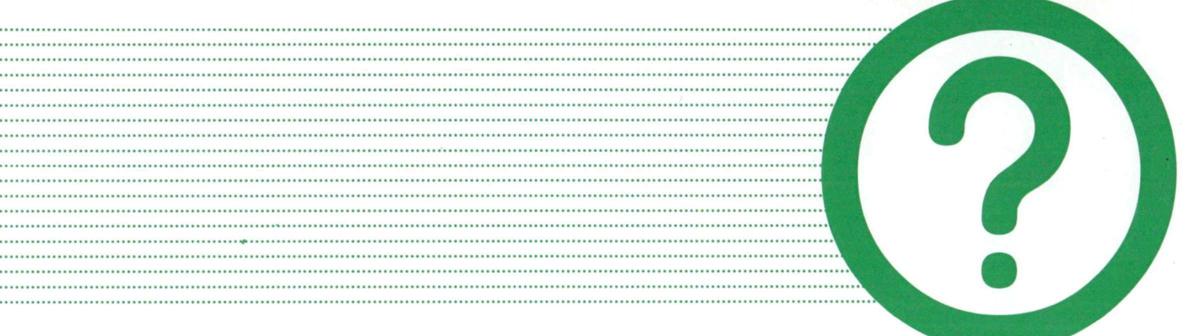

3. 고난이도

Read the passage. Then identify the option that does NOT belong.

The Senate passed a landmark bill that gives consumers new protections in their agreements with credit card companies. (a) The bill imposes an unprecedented set of restrictions on the credit card industry and would curtail retroactive interest rate increases and require advance notice of rate increases. (b) And it prohibits lenders from raising rates when a cardholder is late on a separate debt. (c) The Senate measure, which would go into effect one year after it is signed into law, is also stronger than a set of regulations on credit card practices developed by the Federal Reserve Board. (d) It also would make it more difficult for companies to solicit college-age students for credit cards and prevent companies from charging a fee for paying a bill.

Section Switch

- [ ] **ecological** 생태학의
- [ ] **respecter** (보통 부정문에서) 차별 대우하는 사람, 편파적인 사람(e.g.: be no respecter of persons)
- [ ] **Antartica** 남극대륙
- [ ] **D.D.T.** 방역, 살충제의 일종
- [ ] **perspective** 시각, 조망
- [ ] **gigantic** 거대한, 방대한
- [ ] **disuse** 쓰이지 않음
- [ ] **without a peer** 비할데 없는
- [ ] **inherent** 본래의, 고유의
- [ ] **ambiguous** 애매한, 모호한
- [ ] **unprecedented** 전례가 없는
- [ ] **retroactive** 효력이 소급하는
- [ ] **curtail** 줄이다, 삭감하다

1. It's a brave new digital world. Steve Jobs didn't appear at MacWorld and Bill Gates didn't keynote at CES. It was Microsoft's CEO Steve Ballmer taking the stage at Las Vegas last night, announcing Windows 7 is almost ready for prime time and will be ready for beta testing by regular users who can download and play with it starting tomorrow. It looks a little like Mac OS 10, but Ballmer indicates ______________. "Yeah, you got to look at it this way, you know this year, maybe there will be what, 10 million Macs sold and 300 million PCs, or something like that. I think people are pretty interested in the future of the personal computer." The updated operating system could be available on new PC's within a year.

Q. Choose the option that best completes the passage.
(a) he's following the footsteps of Apple
(b) Microsoft's Windows 7 has more functions than Mac OS 10
(c) Microsoft's Windows 7 has a more powerful operating system than Mac OS 10
(d) he's not obsessing about Apple

2. This is supposed to reassure all parents about the safety of children's vaccines, but it probably won't comfort some. A theory that thimerosal is to blame for autism has been repeatedly discounted in scientific studies. Now, a new study from Italy is adding to the evidence that the mercury-based preservative, once used in many vaccines, doesn't hurt children. Only one case of autism was found when testing the brain function of 1400 children 10 years after thousands of healthy Italian babies got two different amounts of the preservative in a study of whooping cough vaccine. The study was funded by the U.S. Centers for Disease Control and Prevention.

Q. Which of the following is correct about the article?
(a) Children's vaccines are not safe these days.
(b) Scientists have been asserting that thimerosal causes autism.
(c) Thimerosal is a mercury-based antiseptic.
(d) The study was supported by the World Health Organization.

3. Liver damage is probably the most sensationalized of all side effects possible from steroid use. Most anabolic steroids which are ingested orally pass through the liver. When something goes through the liver, it is broken down by various enzymes, and passed along into the bloodstream. Most research on orally administered anabolic steroids focus on the fact that liver enzymes are elevated following ingestion. But does this necessarily mean that the liver is being damaged? The liver functions as the filter for the human body. It's going to be activated whenever something passes through it. Does that mean that steroids damage the liver?

Q. **What can be inferred from the passage?**
(a) Liver damage is one of the side effects of steroids.
(b) Some steroids can cause high cholesterol levels with low HDL and high LDL.
(c) Use of steroids has nothing to do with liver damage.
(d) Liver enzymes could return to the same levels as non users if one stays using steroids.

4. In 1998, Andrew Lloyd Webber released a video version of *CATS*. The video version was directed by David Mallet and recorded in London, the same city where the play first opened in 1981. Other members of the original London cast from the play's 1981 opening include Steven Wayne, John Chester, Sharon Lee Hill, Geraldine Gardner, Brian Blessed and Finola Hughes. The original Broadway cast had fewer members than the original London cast but the core message in the play came across equally as effective. Anyone familiar with the live stage performance knows how physically draining one theatrical production can be. The fact that *CATS* has enjoyed a successful run is nothing short of remarkable. Casting at each of its global venues is making it a treasured part of theatrical history.

Q. **What can be the most proper title of the passage?**
(a) The Musical *CATS* and Record Setting Theatre Performances
(b) The Musical *CATS*' Original Cast and New Film
(c) The Musical *CATS* Sets Live Theatre Records.
(d) The Musical *CATS* opened for the first time in London's West End in 1981.

5. Back in the late 80s, Randy "The Ram" Robinson was a headlining professional wrestler. Now, twenty years later, he ekes out a living performing for handfuls of diehard wrestling fans in high school gyms and community centers around New Jersey. Estranged from his daughter and unable to sustain any real relationships, Randy lives for the thrill of the show and the adoration of his fans. _______________, a heart attack forces him into retirement. As his sense of identity starts to slip away, he begins to evaluate the state of his life, trying to reconnect with his daughter. Yet all this cannot compare to the allure of the ring and passion for his art, which threatens to pull Randy "The Ram" back into his world of wrestling.

Q. **Choose the option that best completes the passage.**
(a) By the way
(b) However
(c) In addition
(d) In the end

6. It is impossible that the economy has developed so rapidly over a long period without women having been to some extent liberated from their traditional domestic tasks, and without their having been permitted to play an important role in society, particularly in the labor market. Viewed in this light, the education of women and the improvement of their social, economic, legal and political status become more than the focus of an emotional crusade for human rights. They must be acknowledged as a prerequisite to national development and given a high priority for strictly practical reasons.

Q. **What can be inferred from the passage?**
(a) The improvement of women's rights has a direct influence on national development.
(b) The role of women has been overlooked for many decades.
(c) Reduction in family size is a precondition for building a significant female work-force.
(d) Women have been educated into submission.

7. Freeman John Dyson, born December 15, 1923, is a British theoretical physicist and mathematician, famous for his work in quantum field theory, physics, and nuclear engineering. He described reductionism in physics as the effort "to reduce the world of physical phenomena to a finite set of fundamental equations," and then he cited the work of Schroedinger and Dirac on quantum mechanics, where they reduced bewildering complexities of chemistry and physics to "two lines of algebraic symbols," as examples representing the triumphs of ______________.

Q. **Choose the option that best completes the passage.**
(a) scientific methodology
(b) reductionism
(c) mathematical elegance
(d) quantum mechanics

8. Any poet worth his or her salt is an individual before all else and consequently the literary terms we apply are never adequate descriptions. But they are serviceable. The Metaphysicals did not know they were Metaphysicals, nor did the Romantics know they were Romantics. But we know what they had in common and where they differed from their predecessors. Likewise the term "Modernist" has been retrospectively applied. Whether it is descriptively very useful hardly matters; what needs to be clear is what distinguishes Yeats and Hardy on the one hand from Eliot and Pound on the other. Of course, Yeats and Hardy are very different, one from the other, as are Pound and Eliot; but their attitude to poetic form determines how they must be paired.

Q. **Which of the following would be the most appropriate title?**
(a) The Metaphysicals and the Romantics
(b) The Uses of Literary Terms
(c) A Comparison among the Four Poets
(d) The Identity of the Poet

9. When one is walking down Fifth Avenue, one does not expect to hear a string quartet playing a Strauss waltz. What one expects to hear while walking down Fifth Avenue is traffic. When one does indeed hear a string quartet playing a Strauss waltz while one is walking down Fifth Avenue, one is apt to become confused and imagine that one is not walking down Fifth Avenue at all but rather that one has somehow wound up in Old Vienna. Should one imagine that one is in Old Vienna one is likely to become quite upset when one realizes that in Old Vienna there is no sale at Charles Jourdan. And that is why when I walk down Fifth Avenue I want to hear traffic.

Q. **What is the tone of the passage?**
(a) Cynical
(b) Fatuous
(c) Preposterous
(d) Perilous

10. **Read the passage. Then identify the option that does NOT belong.**

NAFTA eliminated the majority of tariffs on products traded among the United States, Canada, and Mexico. (a) It gradually phased out other tariffs over a 15-year period. (b) Restrictions were to be removed from many categories, including motor vehicles, computers, textiles, and agriculture. (c) NAFTA was initially pursued by politicians in the United States and Canada supportive of free trade. (d) The treaty also protects intellectual property rights (patents, copyrights, and trademarks), and outlines the removal of investment restrictions among the three countries.

Part 2

고득점을 위한
BEST 분야별 독해

STEP 1 Theme Best

출제 경향 파악

예술 분야(음악과 미술은 독립 분야로 다룬다)는 예술의 일반, 그리고 예술의 본질로부터 출발해서 음악과 미술 외에 기타 무대 예술이나 영화 예술 등을 다루는 분야로서 최근 TEPS에서 다음과 같은 내용들이 출제되었고, 또한 출제될 것이다.

1. 예술이라는 말의 유래
2. 공연 - 뮤지컬/연극
3. 르네상스의 예술
4. 레오나르도 다빈치 - 다빈치 코드 / 모나리자
5. 희곡 - 희곡과 일반 소설이 다른 점
6. 영화 - 타이타닉
7. 만화(영화) - 미키 마우스 / 딕트레이시 / 인어공주 등 디즈니 시리즈

Sample

A number of further methodological considerations have guided my approach and contributed to my conclusions. These considerations are tied to a governing concern with what constitutes sufficient evidence for certain conclusions. I note here three aspects of my method that will receive special attention: the repetition of the same inner conflict in successive works by the artist; the basis for the artist's choice of a specific work from antiquity as inspiration for the formal structure of a particular creation; and the interpretation of the artist's unconscious motives that contribute to his distinctive creative solution.

Translation

여러 차례에 걸쳐 더욱 깊은 방법론적 고찰이 나의 연구의 지침이 되었으며 나의 결론의 도달에 공헌했다. 이러한 고찰은 어떤 결론에 도달하기 위한 충분한 증거에 대한 지배적 관심과 연결돼 있다. 나의 방법 중 특히 주의를 기울이게 될 세 가지 측면을 언급한다. 즉, 이 예술가의 일련의 작품에 동일한 정신적인 갈등이 되풀이되어 나타난다는 것, 이 예술가가 어떤 창작품의 구상을 얻기 위한 창조적 자극으로서 고대의 특정한 작품을 선택하는 근거, 그리고 그의 특유의 창작상의 문제 해결에 기여하는 예술가의 무의식적인 동기의 해석이다.

Words

methodological 방법론적
antiquity 고대 (여기서는 그리스 시대)

테마별 주요 표현 BEST

1. aesthete　　　　＿＿＿＿＿＿＿＿＿＿
2. aesthetic　　　　＿＿＿＿＿＿＿＿＿＿
3. appreciation　　＿＿＿＿＿＿＿＿＿＿
4. cinematography　＿＿＿＿＿＿＿＿＿＿
5. piracy　　　　　＿＿＿＿＿＿＿＿＿＿
6. star-studded　　＿＿＿＿＿＿＿＿＿＿
7. vandal　　　　　＿＿＿＿＿＿＿＿＿＿
8. connotation　　＿＿＿＿＿＿＿＿＿＿
9. artisan　　　　　＿＿＿＿＿＿＿＿＿＿
10. protagonist　　＿＿＿＿＿＿＿＿＿＿

Answers

1. 유미(심미)주의자
2. 미의, 심미적인, 미적 감각이 있는
3. (예술품의) 평가, 이해
4. 영화촬영법
5. 불법 복제
6. 유명인이 다수 출연한
7. 예술 · 문화를 파괴하는
8. 함축, 내포
9. 장인
10. 주인공

1.

The word "art" derives from the Latin root meaning "to fit" and shows up in such words as article, artisan, and artifact. The history of the word clearly indicates that, in earlier times, there was no separation between art and the rest of life. Thus, an artifact is something made to fit in both an aesthetic and a practical sense. Today, however, a work of art is generally judged as "fitting" in the aesthetic sense alone and this indicates the current state of fragmentation between art and other areas of life.

Q. **Which of the following is true according to the above passage?**

(a) The meaning of the word art includes article, artisan, and artifact.

(b) In old times, the word art was used in both an aesthetic and practical sense.

(c) Today a close relationship exists between the aesthetic and practical areas of our lives.

(d) As time passes, art is increasingly playing an essential role in human life.

2.

Rent, which won a Tony Award for Best Musical and a Pulitzer Prize, among other awards, was one of the first Broadway musicals to feature homosexual and bisexual characters. In addition, its cast was unusually ethnically diverse. *Rent* brought controversial topics to a traditionally conservative medium, and it helped to increase the popularity of musical theater amongst the younger generation. "*Rent* speaks to Generation X the way that the musical *Hair* spoke to the baby boomers, or those who grew up in the 1960s, calling it "a rock opera for our time, a *Hair* for the 90s."

Q. **What is the best title of the passage?**

(a) Comparison between the musicals *Hair* and *Rent*

(b) The concept of the musical *Rent*

(c) The musical *Rent* as a both popular and controversial topic

(d) The musical *Rent*'s success

3. 고난이도

The Italian arts minister, Sandro Bondi, has hinted that there may be a return to a controversial proposal of ______________, with La Scala and the Accademia di Santa Cecilia in a kind of premier league and other venues being relegated to a minor position — an idea already strongly criticised by leading musicians including Muti and Zubin Mehta. So many artists oppose this proposal, with very few in support of it.

Q. **Choose the option that best completes the passage.**
(a) supporting staff based on efficiency
(b) rebuilding venues based on local tax
(c) raising ticket prices based on income
(d) arts funding based on excellence

Section Switch

- [ ] **artisan** 장인
- [ ] **artifact** 공예품
- [ ] **aesthetic** 미적인
- [ ] **fragmentation** 분열, 파쇄
- [ ] **homosexual** 동성애의
- [ ] **bisexual** 양성애의
- [ ] **ethnically** 인종적으로
- [ ] **conservative** 보수적인
- [ ] **controversial** 논란의 여지가 많은
- [ ] **minister** 장관, 수상, 성직자
- [ ] **venue** 재판지, 범행지, 사건 발생지, 개최 예정지
- [ ] **relegate** 분류하다, 격하시키다

STEP 1 Theme Best

출제 경향 파악

미술 분야는 각 미술 사조를 기본으로 취급하고 그 사조에 따른 화가들의 에피소드 등을 주로 다룬다. 이 분야에서는 최근 TEPS에서 다음과 같은 내용들이 출제가 되었고, 또한 출제가 될 것이다.

1. 르네상스와 고전주의 - 미켈란젤로, 렘브란트, 루벤스
2. 인상파 - 고흐, 세잔
3. 입체파 / 근대주의 - 피카소
4. 현대화가 - 클림트
5. 미술의 후원자들 - 메세나 활동 등

Sample

Dante Gabriel Rossetti was the son of an Italian patriot whose political activities had led to his being exiled to England. The Rossetti household in London was one in which liberal politics and other controversial topics were hotly debated, but the son did not catch the infection. Displaying extraordinary early promise both as a painter and as a poet, Rossetti confined his interest to art. The beauty of colors and textures, above all the beauty of woman's face and figure, made up his own inner world, isolated from the Victorian scene.

Translation

단테 가브리엘 로제티는 정치적인 활동으로 인해 영국으로 망명하게 된 이탈리아 애국지사의 아들이었다. 런던의 로제티 가정에서는 자유주의적 정치와 기타 논쟁적인 화제를 놓고 열띤 토론이 벌어지곤 했지만, 그 아들은 거기에 물들지 않았다. 일찍부터 화가와 시인으로서 남다른 가능성을 보였던 로제티는 오로지 예술에만 관심을 쏟았다. 아름다운 색채와 질감 그리고 무엇보다 아름다운 여인의 용모와 자태는 그에게 빅토리아조의 풍경과는 동떨어진 그 자신의 내면 세계를 만들어 주었다.

Words

patriot 애국자
household 가정, 가족

테마별 주요 표현 BEST

1. abstract painting   __________________
2. avant-garde   __________________
3. mural/wall painting   __________________
4. still picture   __________________
5. lithograph   __________________
6. luminous   __________________
7. illustration   __________________
8. emboss   __________________
9. retouch   __________________
10. profile   __________________

Answers

1. 추상화
2. 전위적인
3. 벽화
4. 정물화
5. 석판화
6. 빛을 내는
7. 삽화
8. (무늬 도안을) 양각으로 하다, 돋을무늬로 하다
9. 가필
10. 옆얼굴, 반면상

1.

The fact that Pablo Picasso dominated Western art in the 20th century is, by now, common knowledge. Before his 50th birthday, the little man from Malaga had become the very prototype of the modern artist as a public figure. No painter before him had _______________ in his own lifetime. That is, Picasso's followers — meaning people who had heard of him and seen his work, at least in reproduction — were in the tens, possibly hundreds, of millions. He and his work were the subjects of unending analysis, gossip, dislike, adoration and rumor.

Q. **Choose the option that best completes the passage.**
  (a) had a mass following
  (b) had his statue made
  (c) taught as many disciples
  (d) made a fortune

2.

Have you ever heard about Gustav Klimt? You might have seen his paintings once even if you don't know about him exactly. Gustav Klimt (July 14, 1862 — February 6, 1918) was an Austrian Symbolist painter and one of the most prominent members of the Vienna Art Nouveau (Vienna Secession) movement. His major works include paintings, murals, sketches, and other art objects, many of which are on display in the Vienna Secession gallery. Klimt's primary subject was the female body, and his works are marked by a frank eroticism — nowhere is this more apparent than in his numerous drawings in pencil.

Q. **Which is correct according to the passage?**
  (a) Gustav Klimt's main theme was the male body.
  (b) Gustav Klimt participated actively in the Vienna Secession movement actively.
  (c) Klimt's works are characterized by hints of eroticism.
  (d) Klimt's works were the only paintings focusing on eroticism.

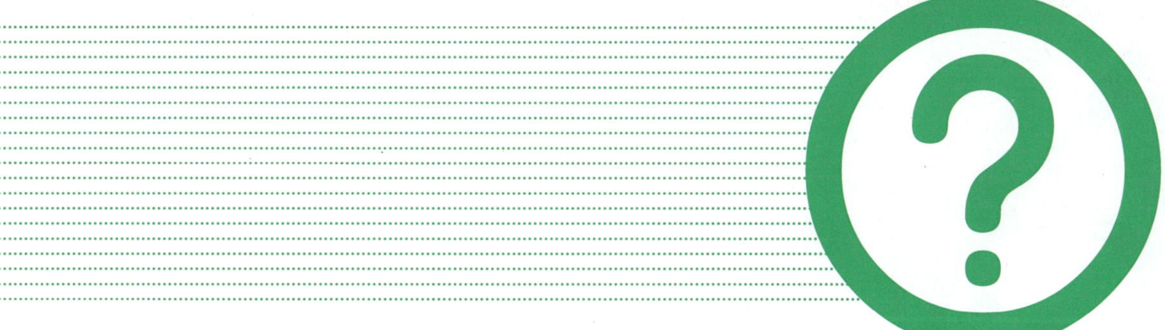

3. 고난이도

Mosaic is an ancient and contemporary art form which uses individual pieces of materials placed together to create a unified whole. The materials commonly used are glass, ceramic, marble, pebble, mirror, shells and china. The term for each piece of material is tessera (plural: tesserae). The term for the spaces in between where the grout goes is the interstices. Andamento is the word used to describe the movement and flow of tesserae. The opus, the Latin for "work", is the way in which the pieces are cut and placed.

Q. **Which is correct according to the passage?**
(a) The term "tessera" indicates the spaces in between where the grout goes.
(b) Mosaic is not a modern but an ancient art form.
(c) Mosaic uses glass, gravel, shells, etc.
(d) Andamento is the term for individual pieces of material.

Section Switch

- [ ] **by now** 이제는
- [ ] **prototype** 원형, 전형
- [ ] **tens, possibly hundreds, of millions** 수천만의, 아니 아마도 수억의
- [ ] **adoration** 찬미, 아주 좋아함
- [ ] **have a mass following** 대단히 많은 추종를 거느리다
- [ ] **symbolist** 상징주의자
- [ ] **prominent** 저명한
- [ ] **secession** 탈퇴, 분리
- [ ] **mural** 벽화
- [ ] **numerous** 수많은
- [ ] **ancient** 고대의
- [ ] **contemporary** 현대의
- [ ] **unified** 통합된
- [ ] **pebble** 조약돌
- [ ] **grout** 시멘트 풀

Chapter 3

문학

STEP 1 Theme Best

출제 경향 파악

문학 분야는 문학의 본질, 즉 글을 쓴다는 것이 인간에게 가지는 의미부터 시작해서 각 글쓰기 장르의 특징, 그리고 비평의 영역까지 다룬다. 이 영역에서는 최근 TEPS에서 다음과 같은 내용(문학 소재)들이 출제되었고, 또한 출제될 것이다.

1. 추리 소설 - 탐정 소설
2. 미스테리 소설
3. 한국 문학의 번역
4. 문학 비평가 - 바람직한 상 / 해야 할 일
5. 독서 - 독서의 종류 / 책을 읽는 방법

Sample

Nonetheless, attracted irresistibly by the example of their idolized Shakespeare, all the greatest Romantic poets, and many minor ones, tried their hand at poetic plays. Some of these were written as closet drama — Byron's *Manfred* and Shelly's *Prometheus Unbound*, for example — but others were expressly written for the stage. The poets, however, lacked experience with the hard necessities of practical theater, and they were for the most part unable to throw off the artifice of an archaic style dominated by Elizabethan and Jacobean models.

Translation

그럼에도 불구하고 많은 군소 시인들과 더불어 모든 위대한 낭만주의 시인들이 그들의 우상인 셰익스피어의 본보기에 어쩔 수 없이 매혹되어 시극에 손을 대었다. 이러한 극들 중 일부, 예를 들면 바이런의 〈만프레드〉나 셸리의 〈사슬에서 풀려난 프로메테우스〉 등은 처음부터 레제 드라마로 쓴 것이지만 그 밖의 것들은 무대용으로 쓰인 것이 분명하였다. 그러나 이 시인들은 실제로 무대에 올리기 위한 여러 가지 까다로운 요건에 대해서는 경험이 부족하였으므로 엘리자베스여왕과 제임스 1세 시대의 전형적 인물들이 지배했던 고풍스러운 기교를 구사할 수 없었다.

Words

closet drama 레제 드라마 (공연보다 읽을거리로 더 적합한 희곡)
Jacobean (영국왕) 제임스 1세 시대의

테마별 주요 표현 BEST

1. anecdote　　　　______________
2. annotation　　　 ______________
3. anthology　　　　______________
4. synopsis　　　　 ______________
5. euphemism　　　 ______________
6. censorship　　　 ______________
7. cliche　　　　　 ______________
8. connotate　　　　______________
9. pedantic　　　　 ______________
10. literacy　　　　 ______________

Answers

1. 일화	2. 주석
3. 시선집, 전집	4. 줄거리
5. 미사여구	6. 검열
7. 클리세이, 진부한 표현	8. 암시하다
9. 현학적인	10. 읽고 쓰는 능력

1.

In mysteries, love, and sporting events, not knowing the eventual outcome is exciting, and most of the time, desirable. Surprises and unexpected turns are what keeps you alert, interested, and involved in the unfolding story, relationship, or game. How much fun would a Sherlock Homes book be if you knew exactly who killed the victim and how and when and why? It wouldn't be fun at all. You wouldn't need a detective at all. You also wouldn't keep reading if you knew the outcome.

Q. **Which of the following is the best title of the above passage?**
(a) Aspects of Story Writing
(b) Suspense and Readers' Involvement
(c) Sherlock Homes as a Detective
(d) The Shock of Unexpected Outcomes

2.

It's a literary critic's duty to be able to feel the impact of a work of art in all its complexity, something which few critics can. A man with a paltry, impudent nature is never capable of writing anything but paltry, impudent criticism. And an emotionally educated man is rare as a phoenix. The general tendency is that the more scholastically educated a man is, the more he is emotionally poor.

Q. **Which of the following is true according to the above passage?**
(a) Few critics can capture all the complex qualities of a literary work.
(b) A paltry or impudent man can never become a literary critic.
(c) The emotional sensitivity of a man has little to do with literary taste.
(d) Scholastic education is the core of a critic's artistic sensibility.

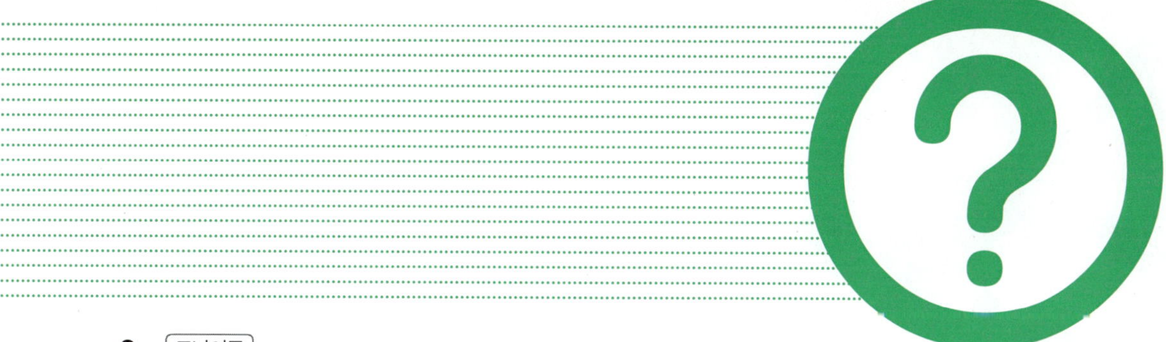

3. 고난이도

Aptronym, a word allegedly coined by United States newspaper columnist Franklin P. Adams, refers to a name that is aptly suited to its owner. Fictional examples of aptronyms include Mr. Talkative and Mr. Worldly Wiseman in John Bunyan's *The Pilgrim's Progress*. A smith is a person involved in the shaping of metal objects. In pre-industrialized times, smiths held high or special social standing since they supplied the metal tools needed for farming (especially the plough) and warfare. The word smith is a cognate with the somewhat archaic English word, "smite," meaning "to hit" or "to strike." Originally, smiths practiced their crafts by forming metal with hammer blows. As an English suffix, -smith also connotes a meaning of specialized craftsmen. For example, wordsmith and tunesmith are words used to describe the skill of a writer or a songwriter, respectively.

Q. **What should not be inferred according to the passage?**
(a) Mr. Locksmith is a person involved in the shaping of locks and keys.
(b) President Truman was likely an honest person.
(c) Dr. Armstrong seems very healthy.
(d) Mr. Talkative is a wise man.

Section Switch

☐ **keep ~ alert** 계속 정신을 집중하게 만들다
☐ **detective** 탐정, 형사
☐ **unexpected outcomes** 예상 밖의 결과
☐ **paltry** 하찮은, 보잘 것 없는
☐ **impudent** 뻔뻔스러운, 철면피의
☐ **phoenix** 불사조, 대천재
☐ **scholastically** 현학적으로
☐ **coin** 신어나 표현을 만들어내다
☐ **cognate** 같은 어원의
☐ **connote** 내포하다

Chapter 4
문학가

STEP 1 Theme Best

출제 경향 파악

문학가 분야는 각 나라별로, 그리고 각 장르별로 유명한 대표 작가를 소개하는 분야로서 여기에서는 최근 TEPS에서 다음과 같은 내용들이 출제되었고, 또한 출제될 것이다.

1. 러시아의 문호 - 톨스토이, 도스토예프스키
2. 미국의 문호 - 헤밍웨이, 스타인벡, 마크 트웨인
3. 유럽의 문호 - 브론테 자매, 서머셋 모옴
4. 노벨 문학상 - 수상자의 선정, 수상(자)
5. 동화, 우화 - 이솝, 안데르센, 그림 형제

Sample

It is probably safe to say that no modern Korean writer is more deeply or widely venerated in Korea than Park Kyung-ni. Veneration is surely an appropriate term, because, more than almost any other novelist, her life and her work have been inextricably intertwined, while both giving expression to the essential Korean value of dignified humanity amidst suffering. Her works carry a message that is relevant now as much as ever, wherever women bear the burden of providing for and nurturing life. She was, in that way, a truly universal writer for our times.

Translation

한국에서 박경리보다 더 깊이, 또는 더 넓게 존경받는 현대 한국 작가는 없다고 해도 과언이 아닐 것이다. 존경이란 단어가 확실히 적당하다. 거의 모든 작가들보다도 더 그녀의 인생과 작품이 언제나 조화를 이루었고, 인생과 작품 모두 고통 속에서도 굴하지 않는 인간성이라는 한국인의 본질적 가치를 표현하기 때문일 것이다. 그녀의 작품들엔 여성들이 가족을 부양하고 양육하는 부담을 감내해야만 하는 여러 곳이면 어디서나 여전히 의미 있는 메시지를 전달한다. 그러므로 박경리는 진정으로 우리 시대의 세계적인 작가이다.

Words

venerate 존경하다, 숭상하다
intertwine 한데 얽어 넣다
dignified 위엄 있는, 고귀한

테마별 주요 표현 BEST

1. innuendo   _______________
2. jargon   _______________
3. whodunit   _______________
4. saga   _______________
5. hyperbole   _______________
6. protagonist   _______________
7. pseudonym   _______________
8. narrative   _______________
9. fable   _______________
10. tale   _______________

Answers

1. 암시, 풍자, 빈정거림
2. 특수 용어, 은어
3. 추리 소설
4. 무용담
5. 과장법
6. 주인공, 주역
7. 익명, 필명, 가명
8. 이야기, 소설
9. 우화, 지어낸 이야기
10. 이야기, 설화

1.

Tolstoy objected to too much cleanliness on the grounds that to be too clean is a badge of class. It is only the rich who can afford the time and money to wash their bodies and change their linen frequently. The laborer who sweats for his living, whose house contains no bathroom, and whose wardrobes has no superfluous shirts, must stink. It is inevitable, and it is also right and proper that he should. Work is prayer. Work also leads to stinking. Therefore stinking is prayer. So, more or less, argues Tolstoy, who goes on to condemn the rich for not stinking, and for bringing up their children to have a prejudice against all human smells however natural and even honorable.

Q. **What can be inferred from the passage?**
  (a) Tolstoy's remedy is that we should all stink together.
  (b) We find it hard to tolerate twice-breathed air and all the odors.
  (c) We have to overcome certain physical repugnances.
  (d) The clean person's prejudice against stinking is largely a class prejudice.

2.

Translator Barkley Cels from the University of Sao Paulo mentioned that some Korean works were too lyrical and when translated, tend to be a bit childish. Professor Bruce Fulton from the University of British Columbia mentioned that one of the problems in teaching translations of Korean literature overseas was that "Korean literary tradition puts emphasis on the importance of short stories rather than full length novels" and that it is rare for publishing companies in the United States to only work on short stories. But for Yoon, Ji-kwan, the director of The Korea Literature Translation Institute, none of these were the greatest hindrance in the local literature translation scene.

Q. **Which of the following is most likely to follow this passage?**
  (a) Pointing out the intellectual and full-length Korean novels
  (b) Introducing various Korean literary tradition
  (c) Proving difference between Korean literature and foreign literature
  (d) Illustrating another problem of Korean literature translation

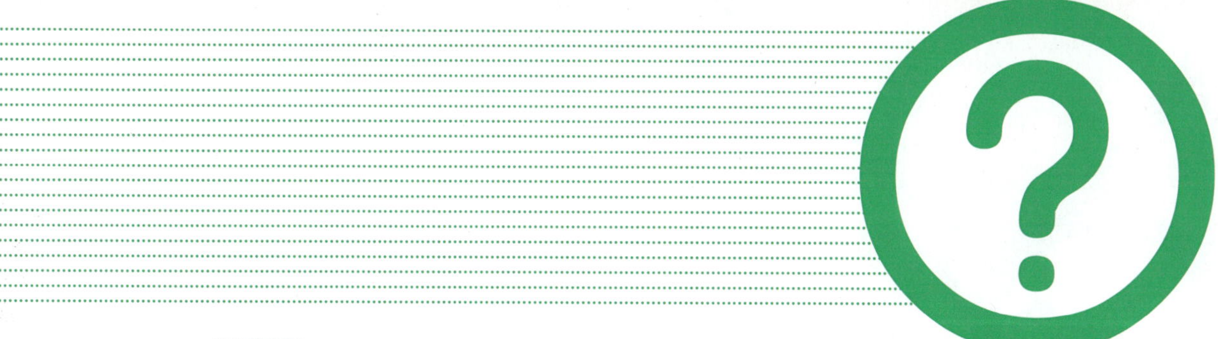

3. 고난이도

Richard Doddridge Blackmore was born in a small village in England in 1825. Like most great writers, little Richard had a rough childhood. His mother passed away when Richard was only a few months old. He was then sent to live with his aunt. Although he had poor health as a child and was often bullied at school, he did extremely well when he began studying classical literature at the prestigious Oxford University. At the age of 22, Richard graduated with honors. At first, he dreamt of a career in law. Yet, his poor health prevented him from entering the field. With his health continuously limiting him from doing the things we wanted to, it seemed like Richard's life was full of misfortune. Well, a stroke of fortune landed on him. At the age of 32, a well-off uncle of his left him enough money to purchase a big farm in London. For the remaining years of his life, Richard devoted his time to writing fiction and growing produce.

Q. **Which of the following is correct according to the passage?**

(a) Richard majored in law at Oxford University.
(b) After living on the farm, Richard regained his health.
(c) Richard's poor health gave him trouble pursuing a career.
(d) Richard's uncle gave him an estate in London.

Section Switch

☐ **cleanliness** 청결
☐ **superfluous** 여분의
☐ **stink** 악취를 풍기다; 악취
☐ **condemn** 비난하다
☐ **prejudice** 편견
☐ **lyrical** 서정적인, 감상적인
☐ **childish** 유치한, 치기 어린
☐ **put emphasis on** ~에 중점을 두다
☐ **hindrance** 방해, 장애(물)
☐ **bully** 겁주다, 괴롭히다
☐ **prevent from -ing** ~하지 못하게 하다
☐ **a stroke of fortune[luck]** 뜻밖의 행운
☐ **extremely** 극단적으로, 매우
☐ **misfortune** 불행

Chapter 5
음악

STEP 1 Theme Best

출제 경향 파악

음악 분야는 바로크 음악에서부터 이어져 내려오는 각 사조의 특징 또는 그 사조에 해당하는 대표적인 음악가를 소개한다. 여기에서는 최근 TEPS에서 다음과 같은 내용들이 출제되었고, 또한 출제될 것이다.

1. 바로크 음악 - 바하, 헨델, 하이든
2. 고전파 음악 - 베토벤, 모짜르트
3. 낭만파 음악 - 슈만, 슈베르트, 리스트
4. 현대 음악 - 카라얀
5. 오페라 - 베르디, 푸치니

Sample

Among the peculiar artistic effects of musical tragedy we stressed an Apolline delusion which rescues us from immediate oneness with Dionysiac music, while allowing our musical emotion to be discharged in an Apolline sphere and in an interposed, visible middle world. At the same time we thought we had observed how that discharge made the middle world of the theatrical event, the drama itself, visible and intelligible from within to a degree unattainable in any other forms of Apolline art.

우리는 음악 비극의 고유한 효과 중에서 특히 아폴로적인 착각을 강조했다. 이 착각에 의하여 우리는 디오니소스적인 음악에 직접적으로 빨려드는 위험에서 구출될 수가 있다. 한편 우리의 음악적 흥분은 아폴로적 영역과 그리고 그 사이에 놓여진 가시적 중간 세계에 발산될 수가 있다. 동시에 우리는 발산에 의하여 무대 위의 사건이라는 중간 세계, 즉 일반적으로 연극이라고 하는 것이 아폴로적 예술 이외의 예술은 도달할 수 없는 정도로 가시적으로 그리고 명백하게 됨을 보았다고 생각한 바가 있었다.

Words

peculiar 독특한, 특유한
discharge 발산하다, 해방시키다

테마별 주요 표현 BEST

1. orchestra   ______________
2. accompaniment   ______________
3. romantic   ______________
4. overture   ______________
5. undertone   ______________
6. execution   ______________
7. performance   ______________
8. orchestra   ______________
9. percussion (the ~)   ______________
10. strings (the ~)   ______________

Answers

1. 오케스트라	2. 반주
3. 낭만적인	4. 서곡
5. 저음	6. 연주 솜씨
7. 공연	8. 관현악단
9. 타악기	10. 현악기

1.

Every attempt to describe Liszt's development during his childhood and early youth has met with difficulty from the lack of the available sources. Authors of a traditional line, such as Lina Ramann, Peter Raabe, and more recently Alan Walker, concentrated on the task depicting Liszt as already an artist of highest genius as a boy, and who, especially as a pianist, was surpassing everything that had existed previously in music history. But, taking this point of view, it is difficult to understand why he had to take further lessons.

Q. **What is the best title of the passage?**

    (a) The difficulty of explaining Liszt's early development

    (b) Liszt's early life

    (c) Liszt as the child prodigy

    (d) Liszt's artistic development

2.

A cappella music is vocal music or singing without instrumental accompaniment, or a piece intended to be performed in this way. A cappella was originally intended to differentiate between Renaissance polyphony and Baroque concertato style. In the 19th century a renewed interest in Renaissance polyphony coupled with an ignorance of the fact that vocal parts were often doubled by instrumentalists led to the term coming to mean unaccompanied vocal music. In modern usage, a cappella often refers to an all-vocal performance of any style, including barbershop, doo wop, and modern pop/rock.

Q. **What is the main idea of the passage?**

    (a) The characteristics of a cappella

    (b) The origin meaning of the term a cappella

    (c) The difference between a cappella and accompanied vocal music

    (d) The famous singers of a cappella

3. 고난이도

It was Schopenhauer who first said that all arts aspire to the condition of music; that remark has often been repeated, and has been the cause of a good deal of misunderstanding, but it does express an important truth. Schopenhauer was thinking of the abstract qualities of music; in music, and almost in music alone, it is possible for the artist to appeal to his audience directly, without a medium of communication in common use for other purpose. The architect must express himself in buildings which have some practical purposes. The poet must use words which are exchanged in the daily give-and-take of conversation. The painter usually expresses himself by the representation of the visible world. _______________.

Q. **Choose the option that best completes the passage.**

(a) All artists have this same intention, the desire to please

(b) Just as some people are color-blind, so they may be blinded to shape, surface and mass

(c) It is possible that some people are unable to perceive proportions in the physical aspects

(d) Only the composer of music is perfectly free to create a work of art out of his own consciousness, and with no other aim than to please

Section Switch

☐ **attempt** 시도

☐ **surpass** ~보다 낫다

☐ **accompaniment** 반주

☐ **polyphony** 다성부의

☐ **barbershop** 이발소; 남성 4부 합창

☐ **remark** 비평, 의견

☐ **architect** 건축가

☐ **consciousness** 의식

☐ **concentrate on** ~에 전념하다, 집중하다

☐ **exist** 존재하다, 있다

☐ **differentiate** 구별하다

☐ **concertato** 협주의

☐ **aspire** 열망하다, 갈망하다

☐ **abstract** 추상적인

☐ **color-blinded** 색맹의

Chapter 6

법률

STEP 1 Theme Best

출제 경향 파악

법률 분야는 법의 본질에서 출발해 구체적인 법의 영역, 즉 민법이나 형법의 영역까지를 다루며 최근 TEPS에서 다음과 같은 내용들이 출제되었고, 또한 출제될 것이다.

1. 법의 원리
2. 법의 종류 - 민법 / 형법
3. 형법에 따른 처벌 - 각 형법상의 죄의 적용(예: 절도죄, 사기죄)
4. 사법체계
5. 사형제의 찬반론 - 찬반의 이유

Sample

It is natural to ask, in the light of this discussion, why it is that countries have Constitutions, and why most of them make the Constitution superior to the ordinary law. If we investigate the origin of the modern Constitution, we find that, practically without exception, they were drawn up and adopted because people wished to make a fresh start, so far as the statement of their system of government was concerned.

Translation

이 논의에 비추어볼 때 나라마다 왜 헌법이 있으며 이들 나라 대부분은 어떻게 해서 헌법을 일반법보다 상위에 두고 있을까 하는 의문이 생기는 것은 당연하다. 현대 헌법의 기원을 조사해 보면 실제로 예외없이 이들 헌법은 국민이 그들의 정부 체제의 성명에 관한 한 새로운 출발을 하고 싶었기 때문에 제정되어 채택되었다는 사실을 알 수 있다.

Words

in the light of ~에 비추어볼 때
draw up (문서를) 작성하다
so far as ~ is concerned ~에 관한 한

테마별 주요 표현 BEST

1. civil law ___________________
2. embezzle ___________________
3. ex-convict ___________________
4. holdup ___________________
5. homicide ___________________
6. arson ___________________
7. blackmail ___________________
8. indict ___________________
9. swag ___________________
10. writ ___________________

Answers

1. 민법
2. 횡령하다
3. 전과자
4. 노상 강도
5. 살인
6. 방화
7. 협박하다
8. 기소하다, 나무라다
9. 장물
10. 영장, 공문서

1.

The days of legal professionals spending countless hours in law libraries conducting case research and going through stacks of documents may soon be over. Advances in computer technology have made life much easier and efficient for lawyers, paralegals, clerks and legal secretaries. Conducting legal research through traditional methods is extremely time-consuming process. Online databases such as LEXUS, NEXUS and Westlaw are available for lawyers and law clerks to conduct that research in a fraction of the time. By keeping the research time down, more work can be done in the same amount of time, and clients are charged less. Computers are also making life easier for legal support staff. For example, there are many software packages that help the legal secretary. There are programs that keep an automatic file for clients, perform docket tracking, store telephone numbers, print daily schedules, prepare monthly statements, etc. The use of such software allows the legal secretary to be much more organized and responsive to the attorney's needs.

Q. Which of the following is the main point of the passage?

(a) Legal professionals spend too much time on legal research.

(b) Traditional methods of research are inaccurate.

(c) Computer technology has substantially aided the legal profession.

(d) Law schools should teach computer skills to lawyers.

2.

Public international law concerns the structure and conduct of states and intergovernmental organizations. To a lesser degree, international law also may affect multinational corporations and individuals, with an impact that increasingly evolves beyond domestic legal interpretation and enforcement. Public international law has increased in use and importance vastly over the twentieth century, due to all the increase in global trade, armed conflict, environmental deterioration on a worldwide scale, awareness of human rights violations, rapid and vast increases in international transportation and a boom in global communications.

Q. What can be inferred from the passage?

(a) Public international law is about the organization of NGOs.

(b) Public international law has developed a lot because of the increase in global problems.

(c) Public international law only deals with human rights.

(d) Public international law does not pertain to individuals.

3. 〔고난이도〕

Capital punishment is often the subject of controversy. Opponents of the death penalty argue that it has led to the execution of innocent people, that life imprisonment is an effective and less expensive substitute, that it discriminates against minorities and the poor, and that it violates the criminal's right to life. Supporters believe that the penalty is justified for murderers by the principle of retribution, that life imprisonment is not an equally effective deterrent, and that the death penalty affirms the right to life by punishing those who violate it in the most strict form.

Q. **Which is correct according to the passage?**
(a) Both opponents and supporters of the death penalty agree with the fact that it violates human rights.
(b) Until recently, capital punishment has been executed more frequently than life imprisonment.
(c) Supporters argue that capital punishment has led to execution of the innocent.
(d) Death penalty has been a hot potato for both opponents and supporters.

Section Switch

- ☐ case research 사례 연구
- ☐ paralegal 변호사 보조원
- ☐ in a fraction of time 순식간에
- ☐ responsive to ~에 응하는, 대답하는
- ☐ substantially 실질적으로, 충분히
- ☐ conduct 행위
- ☐ a lesser degree 정도는 덜하지만
- ☐ vastly 광대하게
- ☐ capital punishment 사형
- ☐ substitute 대체
- ☐ deterrent 억제책, 억제력
- ☐ stack 쌓아 올린 더미
- ☐ legal secretary 법률 서기관
- ☐ docket 소송 사건 일람표
- ☐ attorney 법률가
- ☐ public international law 국제 공법
- ☐ intergovernmental 정부간의
- ☐ multinational 다국적의
- ☐ deterioration 악화
- ☐ life imprisonment 종신형
- ☐ retribution 응보, 징벌
- ☐ affirm 단언하다

STEP 1 Theme Best

출제 경향 파악

사회학/철학 분야, 그 중에서도 순수 철학 분야는 자연철학으로 시작되는 고전 철학부터 현대의 실존철학, 실용철학까지를 다룬다. 이 분야에서는 최근 TEPS에서 다음과 같은 내용들이 출제되었고, 또한 출제될 것이다.

1. 고전철학 - 자연철학 / 소피스트
2. 소크라테스 - "너 자신을 알라" / "악법도 법이다"
3. 플라톤 - 국가론 / 이데아
4. 아리스토텔레스 - 경험론의 선구자 / 공리주의
5. 스토아 철학과 에피쿠르소 철학 - 쾌락주의와 금욕주의
6. 칸트와 헤겔 - 칸트의 사생활 / 니체
7. 실증주의 철학 - 콩트
8. 실용주의 철학 - 듀이

Sample

The history of philosophy does not begin with Aristotle, but the historiography of philosophy does. Aristotle was the first philosopher who systematically studied, recorded, and criticized the work of previous philosophers. In the first book of metaphysics he summarizes the teachings of his predecessors, from his distant intellectual ancestors Pythagoras and Thales up to Plato, his teacher for twenty years. To this day he is one of the most copious and most reliable sources of our information about philosophy in its infancy.

Translation

철학의 역사는 아리스토텔레스로부터 시작되지 않는다. 그러나 철학의 역사 문헌은 그로부터 시작한다. 아리스토텔레스는 이전 철학자들의 저작물들을 체계적으로 연구하고, 기록하고, 비판한 최초의 철학자였다. 그의 첫 번째 형이상학 책에서 그는 선배들의 가르침을, 멀게는 탈레스와 피타고라스에서 그의 20년간 스승이었던 플라톤까지 요약하고 있다. 오늘날 아리스토텔레스는 초기 철학 시기의 가장 풍부하고, 신뢰할 수 있는 지식의 근원 중 하나이다.

Words

historiography 역사 문헌, 수사론
systematically 체계적으로
predecessor 선배
distant 먼

테마별 주요 표현 BEST

1. deduction　　　________________
2. utilitarianism　________________
3. hypothesis　　 ________________
4. sceptic　　　　________________
5. ontology　　　 ________________
6. inference　　　________________
7. metaphysics　 ________________
8. nihilism　　　　________________
9. positivism　　 ________________
10. pragmatism　 ________________

Answers

1. 연역　　　　　　　　2. 공리주의
3. 가설, 가정　　　　　4. 회의론자
5. 존재론　　　　　　　6. 추론
7. 형이상학　　　　　　8. 허무주의
9. 실증철학　　　　　　10. 실용주의

1.

The most fundamental assumption of any sociology is that human behavior is ______________. In language, as in other human phenomena, one searches for regular patterns and rules governing language structure. The formulation of such rules or norms constitutes much of the work of linguists. The fact that such rules are affected by social context is one of the postulates of sociolinguistics.

Q. **Choose the option that best completes the passage.**
   (a) entirely incidental and governed by chance
   (b) exclusively interconnected and reciprocal
   (c) not entirely random or erratic
   (d) not exclusively behavioristic or cognitive

2.

To a philosopher, wisdom is not the same as knowledge. Facts may be known in prodigious numbers without the knower of them loving wisdom. Indeed, the person who possesses encyclopedic information may actually have a genuine contempt for those who love and seek wisdom. For the philosopher is not content with the mere knowledge of facts. He ______________ and probe the things hidden beneath the facts.

Q. **Choose the option that best completes the passage.**
   (a) loves to study philosophy as a subject
   (b) tries to reject all known wisdom
   (c) desires to integrate and evaluate
   (d) seeks to analyze encyclopedic information

3. 고난이도

Over the last 50 years we have got better homes, more clothes, longer holidays, and, above all, better health. Yet surveys show clearly that happiness has not increased in either the U.S., Japan, or Europe. In contrast, in poor countries, happiness is formed to rise when people's income increases. If you are near the bread line, absolute income is a matter of life and death. We can now show scientifically that an extra pound is worth more in happiness to a poor person than to someone who is richer. So, therefore, total happiness increases ______________ provided the disincentive effect is not too great. This argues for redistribution at home and to developing countries.

Q. **Choose the option that best completes the passage.**
(a) when the level of absolute income decreases
(b) when a poor person leaves a poor country
(c) if the wealth moves from a richer person to a poorer person
(d) if your poverty is relative to those around you

Section Switch

- ☐ **sociology** 사회학, 군집 생태학
- ☐ **erratic** 일정하지 않은, 변하기 쉬운
- ☐ **postulate** 자명한 원리, 기초[선결] 조건
- ☐ **cognitive** 인식이 있는
- ☐ **behavioristic** 행동주의적인
- ☐ **prodigious** 거대한, 막대한
- ☐ **knower** 알고 있는 사람, 이해하는 사람
- ☐ **encyclopedic** 해박한
- ☐ **integrate** 통합하다, 조정하다
- ☐ **bread line** 최저 생활 수준
- ☐ **disincentive** 의욕을 꺾는, (특히) 경제 성장[생산성 향상]을 저해하는
- ☐ **in contrast** 대조적으로
- ☐ **redistribution** 재분배

STEP 1 Theme Best

출제 경향 파악

사회학/철학 분야, 그 중에서도 사회학과 사회 문제 분야는 사회학의 탄생 배경에서 시작해 사회학자들을 다룬다. 또한 이 사회학 대두의 배경이 된 여러 가지 사회 문제들, 즉 빈부 격차 문제, 인구 문제, 여성 문제 등의 각 분야를 취급한다. 이 분야에서는 최근 TEPS에서 다음과 같은 내용들이 출제되었고, 계속해서 출제될 것이다.

1. 사회학의 탄생과 발전 - 막스 베버
2. 전체주의 / 민주주의
3. 마르크스 / 뒤르켐
4. 빈부 격차 문제 - 남북 문제
5. 인구 문제 - 맬더스 / 인구 감소 문제
6. 시민운동 - 시민 불복종 / 시민단체
7. 다원화 - 사회적 다양성

Sample

When industrialization became part of the life of the towns, things changed somewhat. Boys and girls rarely worked in mills or mines until they were ten years old or so, which meant that the period of infancy for working class children was extended by several years. The middle class, whose work was of a different kind and who came into prominence during the Industrial Revolution, used their children as showpieces of their affluence, dressing and educating them. In the nineteenth century, public education and child-labor laws extended infancy into the teen years.

Translation

산업화가 도시 생활의 일부가 되었을 때, 다소 변화가 있었다. 소년들과 소녀들은 10살 정도 될 때까지 공장이나 탄광에서 일하는 경우가 드물었고 이것은 노동자 계급의 어린이들의 유년기가 몇 년 연장되었음을 의미한다. 산업 혁명기에 막강해진 중산층은 자신들의 자녀들을 자신의 부를 과시하는 전시품처럼 옷을 입히고 교육을 시켰다. 19세기에 공교육과 어린이 노동법은 유년기를 10대로 확장시켰다.

Words

industrialization 산업화
showpiece 진열품, 우수한 견본
affluence 풍요함
come into prominence 막강해지다

테마별 주요 표현 BEST

1. alienation ______________
2. panic ______________
3. realism ______________
4. racialism ______________
5. totalitarianism ______________
6. anomaly ______________
7. anomie ______________
8. collective behavior ______________
9. life expectancy ______________
10. objectivity ______________

Answers

1. 소외
2. 공포, 당황
3. 현실주의
4. 인종차별주의
5. 전체주의
6. 변칙, 이례
7. 무규제 상태, 사회적 무질서
8. 집합 행동
9. 평균 수명
10. 객관성

1.

Throughout my working life, I've been involved with the social sciences — economics, social policy, international relations, finance — and I've always aimed to engage with intellectual life and academia. This University is an exciting place, somewhere buzzing with new ideas, events, debates outside the core curriculum — at the same time that excitement is linked with a practical engagement with society. Its international reputation is second to none. I'm very much looking forward to working with staff and students, and it will be a privilege to lead the university through its next stage of development.

Q. **What is this passage mainly about?**
(a) The opinion of someone quitting his or her office
(b) An advertisement for a university
(c) A fund raising speech
(d) A speech of a new school head

2.

If we can find approaches that meet the needs of the poor in ways that generate profits for business and votes for politicians, we will have found a sustainable way to reduce inequity in the world. This task is open-ended. It can never be finished. But a conscious effort to answer this challenge will change the world. I am optimistic that we can do this, but I talk to skeptics who claim there is no hope. They say: "inequity has been with us since the beginning, and will be with us till the end — because people just... don't... care." I completely disagree. I believe that there is more caring in this world than we know what to do with.

Q. **What is the tone of this passage?**
(a) Ironic
(b) Critical
(c) Uneasy
(d) Hopeful

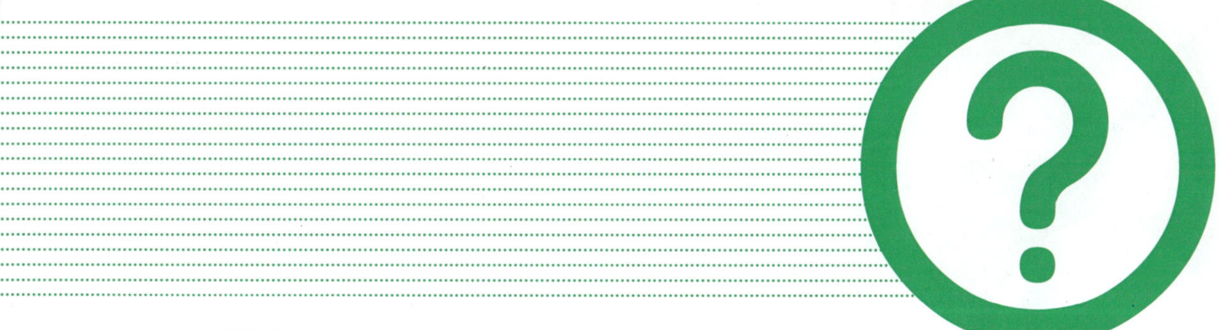

3. 〔고난이도〕

Do people tend to select romantic partners that are similar to them or opposite to them? And does spouse similarity lead to marital happiness? In one of the most comprehensive studies ever undertaken on these questions, researchers and polemists at the University of Iowa found that people tend to marry those who are similar in attitudes, religion and values. However, it is similarity in personality that appears to be more important in having a happy marriage. The findings appear in the February issue of the *Journal of Personality and Social Psychology*, published by the American Psychological Association.

Q. **What is the tone of this passage?**
(a) Inspiring
(b) Festive
(c) Decisive
(d) Objective

Section Switch

☐ **buzzing** 윙윙거리는
☐ **curriculum** 커리큘럼, 교육[교과] 과정
☐ **second to none** 첫째가는
☐ **reputation** 평판, 명성
☐ **privilege** 특권
☐ **inequity** 불공평
☐ **sustainable** 지속적인
☐ **open-ended** 끝이 없는, 제한이 없는
☐ **uneasy** 걱정되는
☐ **spouse** 배우자
☐ **marital** 혼인의
☐ **polemist** 논객(특히 신학상의)
☐ **comprehensive** 포괄적인, 이해력이 있는
☐ **personality** 성격, 개성, 인성
☐ **festive** 명랑한
☐ **decisive** 단호한

Chapter 9
일반 비즈니스

STEP 1 Theme Best

출제 경향 파악

비즈니스 분야, 그 중에서도 일반 비즈니스 분야는 회사 생활의 기본과 회사의 운영, 그리고 상거래 일반에 대해서 다룬다. 이 분야에서는 최근 TEPS에서 다음과 같은 내용들이 출제되었고, 또한 출제될 것이다.

1. 인사 조치의 내용 - 신입 / 전직 / 퇴사
2. 임금 인상의 조치
3. 휴가의 처리
4. 물건의 주문 및 배송 / 물류
5. 물건 구입의 불만 처리
6. 보험 - 보험의 가입 / 자동차 보험
7. 카드 - 대금의 지급 / 연체

Sample

Just as investors speculate on the future price of oil and other commodities, so do entrepreneurs, venture capitalists, and corporations speculate on the future of new designs. And just as oil prices can depend on a host of cultural and political factors well beyond the seemingly simple rules of supply and demand, so can the acceptance or rejection of a new or even a modified artifact depend on much more than how well or poorly its form suits, let alone follows, its function. Indeed, the investor in design is ill served by an adviser who looks too narrowly at technical indicators to prognosticate performance in the marketplace.

Translation

원유나 그 외 원자재의 선물가격에 투자가들이 투자하는 것처럼, 기업가들, 벤처기업 투자자들, 주식회사는 새로운 디자인의 미래에 투자한다. 그리고 원유 가격이 일견 단순해 보이는 수요와 공급의 법칙 이상으로 다수의 문화적 정치적 요인들에 좌우될 수 있는 것만큼이나, 새로운 가공물이나 심지어 수정된 가공물의 수용 또는 거부는 그것의 형태가 기능을 따르는 것은 물론, 기능에 얼마나 잘 맞는지 혹은 잘 안맞는지 이상으로 훨씬 더 많은 요소들에 의해 결정될 수 있다. 사실, 너무 편협하게 기술적 지표에만 집중하여 시장에서의 성적을 예측하지 못하는 조언가는 디자인에 투자하는 사람에게 별 도움이 되지 못한다.

Words

speculate 위험한 사업에 투자하다
venture capitalists 새로운 기술을 구사한 사업에 투자하는 사람들
a host of 다수의
artifact 가공물, 생산물
technical indicator 기술적인 지표

테마별 주요 표현 BEST

1. avocation ______________
2. barter ______________
3. budget ______________
4. covenant ______________
5. current price ______________
6. relegation ______________
7. index ______________
8. autarky ______________
9. interest ______________
10. inventory ______________

Answers

1. 취미, 부업
2. 물물 교환하다
3. 예산
4. 계약
5. 시가
6. 좌천
7. 지표
8. 자급 자족
9. 이자
10. 재고

1.

We regret to inform you that your order has been delayed due to a stock shortage. _______________, we would be happy to offer you item #35676 in a different color, or a full refund if that is not satisfactory.

Q. **Choose the option that best completes the passage.**
(a) For example
(b) By all means
(c) If you like
(d) In addition

2.

To Whom It May Concern :
It has been my pleasure for three and a half years to work with Cindy Kim. She has been a fantastic employee, and has excelled in her post as chief of the accounting department here at Universal Publishing Company. Mrs. Kim has been one of the most capable employees of the company during this time and we are very sorry that she is leaving us to move to Washington, D.C. Her creative planning and vision has helped our company to realize a growth rate of more than 10% in each of the last three years. While we will miss Cindy Kim, I strongly recommend her for an accounting or managerial position at your company or government office.

Sincerely, Laura Grinnell
Vice President of Operations

Q. **Which is true of this letter?**
(a) It was written by a government office manager.
(b) Ms. Kim used to work in the sales department at Universal.
(c) The writer is sorry that Ms. Kim is leaving.
(d) Cindy Kim is moving to Cleveland from Washington, D.C.

3. 고난이도

Owners of Toyota and Mutsubishi sport utility vehicles and Lexus luxury cars are paying more than other drivers for theft insurance because their cars are popular among thieves, a new report says. Eight of the 10 vehicles from model years 1995-1997 with the worst losses from theft were all sport utility vehicles or luxury cars, according to a Highway Loss Data Institute report released Tuesday. Owners of Toyotas are paying about $530 a year on average for theft protection under their comprehensive insurance coverage, the report said. Drivers of the Mitsubishi Montero ranked second, and owners of the Lexus GS 300 luxury car ranked third.

Q. **Which of the following best summarizes the above passage?**

(a) Owners of Lexuses pay more in insurance than owners of sport utility vehicles.

(b) Theft insurance is overpriced especially for the owners of Toyotas.

(c) Sport utility vehicles are becoming more and more popular in the U.S.

(d) Insurance rates for certain cars are high because they are popular among thieves.

Section Switch

☐ stock shortage 재고 부족

☐ refund 환불

☐ satisfactory 만족스러운

☐ excel in ~에서 뛰어나다, 탁월하다

☐ managerial 경영의, 관리의

☐ sincerely 진정으로

☐ theft insurance 도난 보험

☐ on average 평균적으로

☐ under their comprehensive insurance coverage 종합 보험으로 처리되는

☐ overpriced 비싼 값을 매긴

STEP 1 Theme Best

출제 경항 파악

비즈니스 분야, 그 중에서도 거래와 상업 그리고 새로운 전자 상거래 분야는 시장에서 일어나는 거래를 수요와 공급에서 출발해서 여러 가지 상거래의 형태, 특히 최근에 발달한 전자 상거래까지를 다룬다. 이 분야에서는 최근 TEPS에서 다음과 같은 내용들이 출제되었고, 또한 출제될 것이다.

1. 인터넷 상거래 - 전자 상거래 일반
2. 경매 - 이베이 / 옥션
3. 도매업과 소매업 - 마트
4. 수요와 공급
5. 재고 조사

Sample

Seed money literally means the money to seed for bearing fruits. In fact, financial institutions loan it to companies in distress to support their recovery. The seed money is necessary for the distressed company with a promising technology but temporarily having financial difficulties due to the frozen market. However, if the troubled company can not be revived through any means, the bank itself faces financial difficulty due to the loan. Hence, only after careful investigation should the banks make the decision to loan the seed money to the troubled company.

Translation

시드 머니(seed money)란 말 그대로 새로운 열매를 맺기 위해 씨앗으로 뿌리는 돈을 뜻한다. 실제로 부실 기업의 회생을 지원하기 위해 금융 기관에서 이 돈을 융자해준다. 좋은 기술력을 가지고 있지만 시장이 얼어붙어 자금 사정이 어려워 부실 기업이 된 경우에는 금융 기관의 이러한 시드 머니가 필요하다. 하지만 회생이 불가능할 것이 뻔히 보이는 부실 기업이라면 새로 자금을 빌려준다는 것은 금융 기관의 부실까지도 초래할 수 있다. 그러므로 금융 기관에서는 신중한 조사를 마친 후, 부실 기업에 시드 머니를 융자해 줄 지를 결정해야 할 것이다.

Words

literally 글자 그대로
temporarily 일시적으로
distress 곤궁하게 하다
recovery 회복

테마별 주요 표현 BEST

1. lucre   _______________
2. revenue   _______________
3. rush   _______________
4. slump   _______________
5. shut-down   _______________
6. glut   _______________
7. gratuitous   _______________
8. recession   _______________
9. stock-taking   _______________
10. remuneration _______________

Answers

1. 이익(부당한 수단에 의한 혹은 명예스럽지 못한)
2. 세입, 세수
3. 급수요, 주문 쇄도
4. 푹 떨어지다, 빠지다
5. 공장 폐쇄
6. 공급 과잉
7. 무상의
8. 퇴거, (경기) 후퇴, 불경기
9. 재고 조사, 현황 파악
10. 보수, 보상, 급료

1.

There is quality furniture in every price range, whether you have limited funds or lots to spend. However, it will be helpful to know which features best match ______________.
When selecting upholstery, a solid frame and resilient cushion construction are essential for pieces that will be used everyday. For a cover that will stand up to the rigors of an active family, choose a tightly woven fabric or leather.

Q. **Choose the option that best completes the passage.**

    (a) your need for toughness and durability

    (b) your preference for style and color

    (c) your taste for design and decoration

    (d) your concern for comfort and safety

2.

People are bidding on the Internet to buy a bucket of water on an auction website. The fabulous bucket of tap water has so far attracted a highest bid of $18, and nearly 600 people have read the auction details on the site. It reads; "Here's your chance to own a bucket of fresh water, poured straight from the finest water supply. This is a unique opportunity for all water collectors out there who want something cool and refreshing." The owner said that he put the bucket of water up for auction as a joke and that he was stunned by the response.

Q. **What is the best title for the passage?**

    (a) A Bizarre Salesman

    (b) A Joke Auction

    (c) A Most Expensive Auction

    (d) A Drink Tap Water Campaign

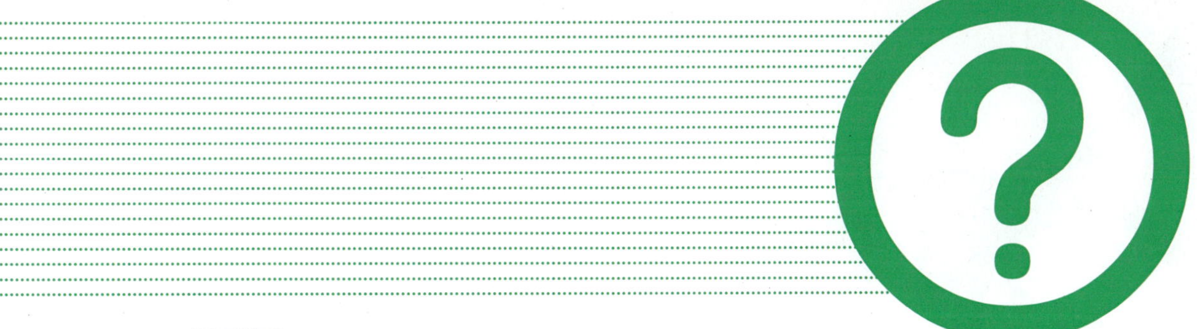

3. 고난이도

A customer came in once and demanded money back for an evening dress that had apparently been worn. She claimed it was a different color after dry cleaning and that the cleaner said the fabric was faulty. I quickly told her we'd happily return her money, even though I didn't think she was being honest. I decided it was more important to keep other customers from hearing her and maybe doubting our high-quality merchandise.

Q. **Which one of the following can not be inferred from the passage?**

(a) The customer tell other customers or her complaints if she was not reimbursed.

(b) The author was not reluctant to grant refunds certain purchases.

(c) A used dress can be returned whenever the customer wants.

(d) The color of the high-quality fabric doesn't change after dry cleaning.

Section Switch

☐ **upholstery** 가구(의자 · 융단 · 커튼 따위)

☐ **feature** 특색으로 삼다

☐ **resilient** 되튀는, 탄력 있는 (buoyant)

☐ **fabric** 직물

☐ **fabulous** 황당무계한, 믿을 수 없는

☐ **auction** 경매

☐ **refreshing** 상쾌한, 후련한

☐ **response** 반응, 응답

☐ **merchandise** 제품

☐ **apparently** 분명하게, 또렷하게

☐ **keep A from B -ing** A가 B하는 것을 방지하다

Chapter 11

제품 광고

STEP 1 Theme Best

출제 경향 파악

제품 광고 분야는 각 제품을 선전하는 광고를 다루는 분야이다. 특히 최근에 주변에서 자주 보는 휴대폰이나 컴퓨터 등의 선전 내용들이 많이 나온다. 이 분야에서는 최근 TEPS에서 다음과 같은 내용들이 출제되었고, 또한 출제될 것이다.

1. 전자제품 - 휴대폰 / 전화기
2. 컴퓨터 - 프린터 / 주변기기
3. 자동차 - RV카
4. 보험 광고 - 상해 보험 / 자동차 보험
5. 먹을 것 광고 - 아이스크림 / 과자류 / 음식점
6. 입을 것 광고 - 옷의 종류
7. 마실 것 광고 - 콜라 / 건강 음료 / 이온 음료 / 기능성 음료 / 포도주
8. 놀 것 광고 - 놀이공원 / 유원지
9. 관광 상품 광고

Sample

If you think that there are too many choices, complications, and not enough service in the cellular phone market today, you're not alone. We at Digital Technology are well aware of the problems and so we are proud to present our new line of cellular phones and paging equipment. Our products stand out in the vast crowd of portable communication technology because of our commitment to providing the best quality and service, at reasonable prices. Recently placed in the top 5 by "Technology Digest," we think you'll agree with the experts, "Digital Tech's products are superb in every way..."

Translation

이동 전화 시장이 난립되어 있고, 얼기설기 얽혀 있으며, 서비스는 불충분하다는 데 많은 사람들이 의견을 같이 하고 있습니다. 저희 디지털 테크놀러지는 고객 여러분의 고충을 십분 이해하고 있으며, 그래서 새로운 이동 전화기와 무선 호출기를 자랑스럽게 선보이는 바입니다. 저희는 최상의 품질과 서비스를 적당한 가격으로 공급하는 일을 사명으로 하고 있으며, 그렇기 때문에 저희 제품이 타사의 수많은 제품들과 비교할 때 단연 돋보이는 것입니다. 최근 〈테크놀러지 다이제스트〉가 상위 5개 제품을 선정 발표하면서 내놓은 '디지털 테크의 제품은 모든 면에서 단연 최고이다...' 라는 전문가들의 평가에 대해 여러분들도 의견을 같이하게 될 것입니다.

Words

paging equipment 호출 장비, 호출기
on the market 시판 중인
commitment to -ing ~한다는 약속[사명]

테마별 주요 표현 BEST

1. bargain   __________________
2. brochure   __________________
3. browse   __________________
4. vending machine __________________
5. voucher   __________________
6. emporium   __________________
7. extravagance   __________________
8. installment   __________________
9. list price   __________________
10. lump sum   __________________

Answers

1. 매매, 거래, 흥정
2. (제품이나 회사에 대한 정보를 제공하는) 소책자, 팸플릿
3. 구경하다
4. 자동 판매기
5. 보증서, 영수증, 상품권
6. 상업 중심지, 시장
7. 낭비
8. 할부금, (1회분어치) 할부금
9. 정가(regular price)
10. 총액 일시불

1.

Motorola Worldwide Com is the most versatile paging system in the world. This sophisticated system is designed to enable you, our valued customer, to go beyond spatial barriers. Not only will you be able to be in contact with all of your important associates, you can get the most recent business info and stock prices simply by reading your pager, anywhere in the world. Our state-of-the-art technology has made it possible to provide a revolutionary new way for busy business travelers to ______________, wherever they are, whenever they happen.

Q. **Choose the option that best completes the passage.**
    (a) avoid dangerous situations
    (b) travel efficiently
    (c) not rely on secretaries
    (d) stay abreast of all the latest events

2.

Numerous countries around the world make sparkling wine according to the method originally developed in Champagne, France. However, few of the imitators succeed in approaching the complexity of the original. True champagne only comes from the region of the same name. Grape varieties blended to make champagne are both red and white, with tastes that range from lemony and austere to rich and nutty.

Q. **Which of the following best describes the author's view of non-Champagne sparkling wine?**
    (a) The taste rivals that of champagne.
    (b) Its quality justifies its expense.
    (c) Blending grape varieties lower the quality.
    (d) It's not at the same level of true champagne.

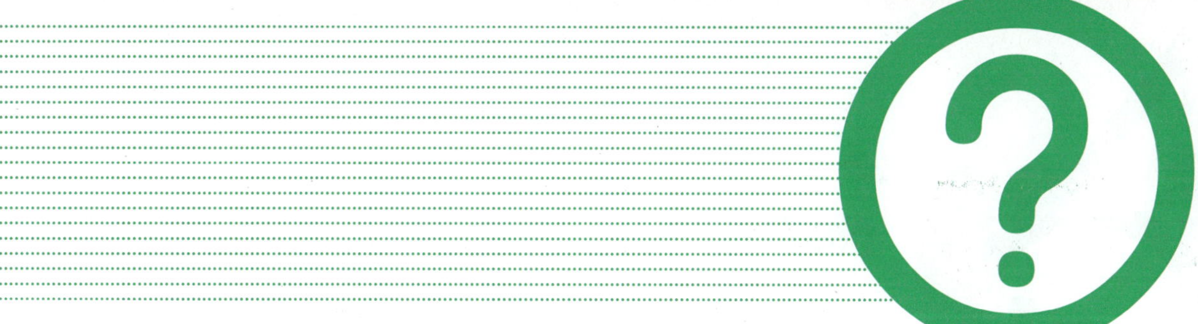

3. 고난이도

For the summer months only, The Seoul Bowl-a-rama Lanes is having half-price bowling from 10 a.m. to 2 p.m. every weekday. All you have to do is buy your lunch at our restaurant or snack bar to take advantage of our 50% rate. In addition, bowl just two games during the above times, and you'll automatically be entered into the raffle for one of many prizes including bowling balls, bowling shoes, T-shirts, hats, and more! So what are you waiting for? Come on in to Seoul Bowl-a-rama Lanes, and get in on the fun.

Q. **What do you have to do to qualify for the discount?**
(a) Bowl at least two games
(b) Buy lunch on the premises
(c) Enter the raffle
(d) Join in on the fun

Section Switch

- ☐ **versatile** 용도가 다양한, 다용도의
- ☐ **spatial barrier** 공간 장벽
- ☐ **not only will you be able to** ~을 할 수 있을 뿐만 아니라 (부정어 not only로 시작하는 도치 구문임)
- ☐ **associate** 동료, 친구
- ☐ **info** 정보 (information)
- ☐ **stock prices** 주식 가격
- ☐ **state-of-the-art** 첨단의
- ☐ **stay abreast of all latest events** 최근에 벌어지는 일에 대해 계속 정보를 얻다
- ☐ **sparkling wine** 발포 포도주
- ☐ **blend** 섞다, 혼합하다
- ☐ **lemony** 레몬 맛[향]이 나는
- ☐ **austere** 떫은 맛[향]이 나는
- ☐ **nutty** 견과 맛이 나는, 나무 열매 향기가 나는
- ☐ **weekday** 주중의 평일
- ☐ **raffle** 복권 판매[추첨]
- ☐ **get in on** (활동 따위에) 참여하다 (come in on)
- ☐ **qualify for** ~의 자격을 갖추다

Chapter 12
일반 정치

STEP 1 Theme Best

출제 경향 파악

정치 분야, 그 중에서도 일반 정치 분야는 정치 형태론에서 출발해 세계 역사상 유명 정치인에 대한 내용까지를 다룬다. 이 분야에서는 최근 TEPS에서 다음과 같은 내용들이 출제되었고, 또한 출제될 것이다.

1. 정치 형태론
2. 무정부론
3. 선거 - 선거제도 / 선거운동 / 선거 연설
4. 국회 - 국회의 운영 / 필리버스터
5. 정당론 - 다당제와 양당제
6. 정치인 - 링컨 / 처칠 / 케네디 / 루즈벨트

Sample

All ruler-ship has its original and its most legitimate source in man's wish to free himself from the trials of survival, and men achieved such liberation through violence, by forcing others to bear the burden of life for them. This was the essence of slavery, and it is only the rise of technology, and not the rise of modern political ideas, which has refused the old and terrible belief that only violence and rule over others could make some men free.

Translation

모든 통치권은 인간 자신이 생존의 시련에서 벗어나려는 욕구에 기원과 가장 정당한 근원을 두고 있다. 인간은 폭력에 의해 다른 사람으로 하여금 그들을 대신해서 삶의 짐을 떠맡게 강요함으로써 그와 같은 해방을 얻었다. 이것이 노예 제도의 핵심이었으며 오직 타인들에 대해 폭력을 행사하고 그들을 지배함으로써 일부 사람을 해방시킬 수 있다는 그 오래된 끔찍한 믿음이 논박된 것은 현대 정치 사상의 대두가 아닌 기술의 진보 덕택이다.

Words

legitimate 합법적인, 적법의
force others to bear 다른 사람들에게 ~을 강제로 떠맡기다

테마별 주요 표현 BEST

1. agenda ________________
2. anarchy ________________
3. aristocracy ________________
4. bicameral ________________
5. filibuster ________________
6. candidate ________________
7. delegate ________________
8. gerrymander ________________
9. referendum ________________
10. treason ________________

Answers

1. 의제, 의사 일정
2. 무정부 상태
3. 귀족 정치
4. 양원제의
5. 의사 진행 방해(자)
6. 후보자, 지원자
7. 대표자
8. 선거구를 유리하게 고치다
9. 국민 투표
10. 반역, 배신

1.

Anarchy is a political ideology that is opposed to all forms of government. Anarchists hold that the highest attainment of humanity is the freedom of individuals to express themselves, unhindered by any form of repression or control from without. Their fundamental belief is that the perfection of humanity will not be attained until all government is abolished and each individual is left absolutely free. Many people have believe, however, that it is out of the question to have individual freedom without governmental sovereignty. The assertion that _______________ is now being challenged in this era of information and technology which puts individual sovereignty before a national unity that demands individual sacrifices.

Q. **Choose the option that best completes the passage.**
(a) government should be abolished
(b) perfection of humanity is possible
(c) governmental sovereignty is oppressive
(d) anarchy is anachronistic

2.

I'm in. And I'm in to win. Today I am announcing that I will form an exploratory committee to run for president. And I want you to join me not just for the campaign but for a conversation about the future of our country — about the bold but practical changes we need to overcome six years of Bush administration failures. I am going to take this conversation directly to the people of America, and I'm starting by inviting all of you to join me in a series of web chats over the next few days. The stakes will be high when America chooses a new president in 2008.

Q. **What is the purpose of this passage?**
(a) To organize a committee
(b) To announce a presidential candidacy
(c) To have a conversation with Americans
(d) To invite people to the committee

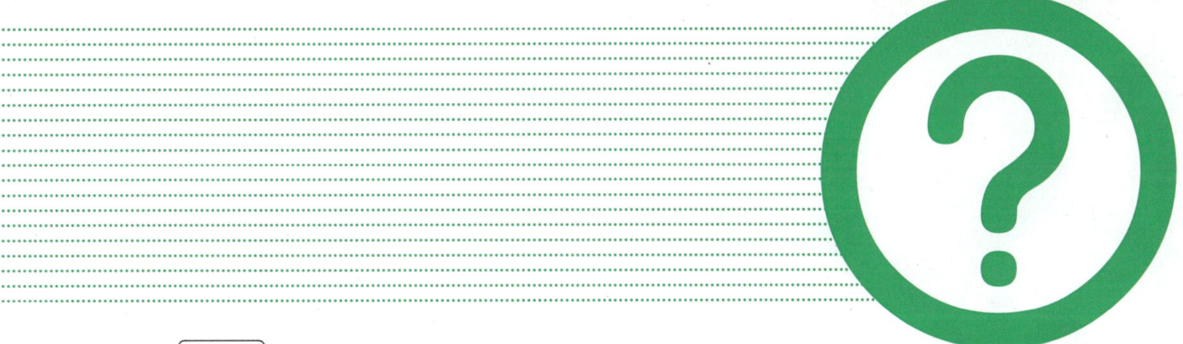

3. 〔고난이도〕

The basic issue of constitutional law is how to create a government strong enough to do what we want it to do, and yet limit the power of that government so that it doesn't do what we don't want it to do. One of the main things we don't want the government to do is to invade our "rights." What is meant by "right" changes over time but we have become used to the idea that there are certain things the government can't do to us. "Rights" can be divided into two groups. The first group of rights is process rights. These are about the procedures the government must follow. The second group of rights is substantive rights. These define the areas of individual freedom that the government cannot invade regardless of the procedures it must follow.

Q. **What can be inferred from the passage?**

(a) Governmental procedures have violated rights on occasion.

(b) "Right" means an individual freedom that will never change over time.

(c) Substantive rights are about the procedures the government must follow.

(d) The Constitution can't limit the power of the government.

Section Switch

- anarchy 무정부(론)
- sovereignty 주권
- put A before B B보다 A를 더 중시하다
- anachronistic 시대에 뒤떨어진
- announce 천명하다, 알리다
- constitution 헌법
- invade 침해하다
- illegal 불법적인
- from without 외부로부터
- assertion 주장
- oppressive 억압하는
- I'm in. 나는 뛰어들었다.
- Bush administration 부시 정부
- substantive 실체적인
- regardless of ~에 상관없이

Chapter 13
국제 정치

STEP 1 Theme Best

출제 경향 파악

국제 정치 분야는 각 나라의 실정에 따른 국제 정치상의 여러 가지 테마, 예를 들어서 이라크를 비롯한 중동 문제 등을 다루는 분야이다. 이 분야에서는 최근 TEPS에서 다음과 같은 내용들이 출제되었고, 또한 출제될 것이다.

1. 중동 - 이라크 / 이스라엘 / 오일 달러
2. 미국 - 오바마 대통령 / 부시의 이라크 개입
3. 중남미 문제 - 중남미의 정치 불안 / 베네주엘라
4. 유럽 - 신나치즘
5. 동남아시아 - 계발 / 이광요 수상과 싱가폴

Sample

International politics is anarchic in the sense that there is no higher government, but even in political philosophy there were two different views of how harsh a state of nature need be. Hobbes, who wrote in a seventeenth-century England wracked by civil war, emphasized insecurity, force, and survival. He summarized it as a state of war. A half century later, John Lock, writing in a more stable England, argued that although a state of nature lacked a common sovereign, people could develop ties and make contracts, and therefore anarchy was less threatening.

Translation

국제 정치는 상위에 정부가 없다는 점에서 무정부 상태이다. 그러나 정치 철학계에서는 자연 상태가 얼마나 가혹한 것인가에 대해 두 가지 견해가 갈린다. 내전으로 파괴된 17세기 영국에서 글을 쓴 홉스는 불안, 무력, 생존이라는 요소를 강조했다. 그는 자연 상태를 전쟁 상태라고 요약했다. 반 세기 후, 좀 더 안정된 영국에서 글을 쓴 존 로크는 자연 상태에 공동의 주권자가 없는 것은 사실이지만, 사람들이 관계를 발전시킬 수 있고 계약을 맺을 수 있다는 점에서 무정부 상태가 홉스의 생각만큼 위험하지 않다고 주장했다.

Words

sovereign 국가, 주권자
threatening 위협하는

테마별 주요 표현 BEST

1. accord　　　　　　　　　　＿＿＿＿＿＿＿＿＿
2. agreement　　　　　　　　＿＿＿＿＿＿＿＿＿
3. cease fire　　　　　　　　＿＿＿＿＿＿＿＿＿
4. consul　　　　　　　　　　＿＿＿＿＿＿＿＿＿
5. diplomatic immunity　　　＿＿＿＿＿＿＿＿＿
6. behind-the-scene　　　　＿＿＿＿＿＿＿＿＿
7. crackdown　　　　　　　　＿＿＿＿＿＿＿＿＿
8. delegate　　　　　　　　　＿＿＿＿＿＿＿＿＿
9. hostage　　　　　　　　　＿＿＿＿＿＿＿＿＿
10. intervention　　　　　　＿＿＿＿＿＿＿＿＿

Answers

1. 협정	2. 조약, 협약
3. 휴전	4. 영사
5. 외교적 면책 특권	6. 이면의, 막후의
7. 탄압, 강경 조치	8. 대표, 파견 의원
9. 인질	10. 간섭

1.

I have mixed feelings about Israel's celebration of its 50 years of statehood. The founding of the nation signified a birth to Jews but a burial to the Palestinians. Over time, Zionist terrorism was replaced by Palestinian terrorism, and war and grief were never far away. The perpetual threat of conflict forced increases in Israeli defense budgets — and made enormous economic support by the U.S. necessary. Against all odds, foreign and internal, the Israelis have managed to build and uphold the most democratic country in the Middle East. However, Israeli society is more torn than ever before, and the historic chance to achieve peace is fading. I wish Israel the best and hope its people recognize that the glittering prize, peace, could be theirs as this anniversary.

Q. **Which of the following statements agrees with the beliefs of the writer?**
(a) Enormous economic support by the U.S. made Israel's survival possible.
(b) Israel will achieve peace with Palestine in the near future.
(c) Faced with foreign aggressions, Israeli society shows a strong sense of unity.
(d) Israel's 50th anniversary is cause for celebration, but peace has yet to be achieved.

2.

The attacks on the U.S.A. on September 11, 2001 have intensified the debate about Islam and its role in the modern world. Some think that Islamic concepts are incompatible with modern aspirations. Islam seems to have ended up with a bad image. But in the past many Muslim scientists contributed a substantial amount to modern science. And today many Muslims are working in many technological and scientific fields. Obviously these Muslims, as an example, have found a way to reconcile their faith with modernity. It is ______________ that Islam is incompatible with modern society or any form of civilization.

Q. **Choose the option that best completes the passage.**
(a) a reasonable conclusion
(b) a well-known fact
(c) a groundless prejudice
(d) an understandable reaction

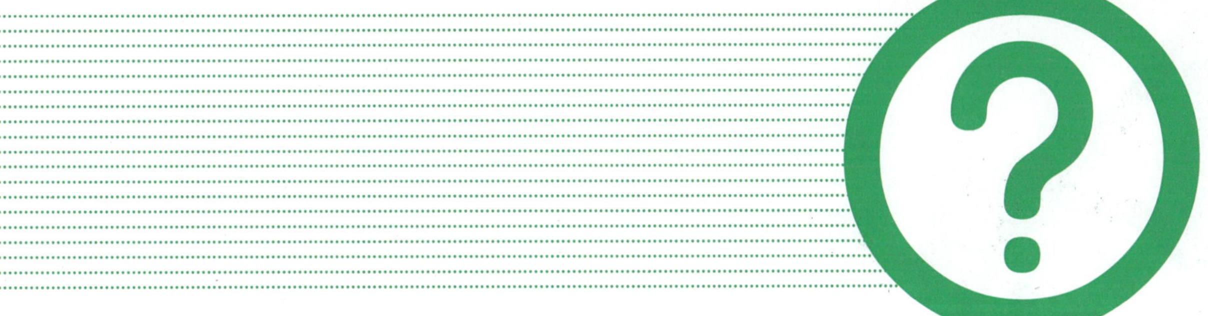

3. 〔고난이도〕

Though the United States borders Canada, there are lots of differences between the two nations. What differences are there between Canadians and Americans? This question often arouses strong emotions when citizens from these two nations get together. What ideas do you have about this? Which of these countries do you know better? Why? Huck Sawyer, one of the USA's leading writers and broadcasters (for both TV and radio), gives his thoughts on the subject in the following excerpts from his essay "My country."

Q. **What can be inferred from the passage?**

(a) The following section might deal with the subject of up-to-date broadcasting.
(b) Canadians express their emotions more openly than Americans do.
(c) Huck Sawyer deals with comparisons of the USA and Canada in his essay.
(d) Citizens from USA and Canada get emotional easily.

Section Switch

- ☐ statehood 국가, 국가로서의 위상
- ☐ founding of ~의 설립
- ☐ perpetual 영속적인
- ☐ against all odds 모든 승산을 거슬러서, 모든 어려움에 대항하여
- ☐ intensify 격렬하게 하다
- ☐ aspiration 열망; 포부
- ☐ incompatible 양립할 수 없는
- ☐ modernity 현대성
- ☐ reconcile 화해시키다, 조화하다
- ☐ groundless 근거 없는
- ☐ prejudice 편견
- ☐ arouse 깨우다, 자극하다, 불러일으키다
- ☐ excerpt 발췌문
- ☐ comparison 비교

STEP 1 Theme Best

출제 경향 파악

국제 분야, 그 중에서도 국제 기구와 협력 분야는 UN을 필두로 한 국제 협력 기구에 대해서 다루는 분야이다. 우리의 실생활과도 밀접한 관련이 있는 IMF 관련 독해 지문도 최근 빈번히 출제된다. 이 분야에서는 최근 TEPS에서 다음과 같은 내용들이 출제되었고, 또한 출제될 것이다.

1. 국제 기구
2. 국제 공통의 문제 - 식량 문제 등
3. IMF - 구제 금융
4. UN - 평화 유지군 / 반기문 사무총장
5. 경제 관련 조약과 조직체 - GATT / NAFTA / OECD
6. OPEC(석유 수출국 기구)

Sample

The U.N. designers also created a Security Council composed of five permanent members, and a rotating pool of non-permanent members. The Security Council can be seen as a nineteenth century balance of power concept integrated into the collective security framework of the U.N. The Security Council is able to pass binding resolution under Chapter VII of the Charter. If the five great power policemen do not agree, they each have a veto, which is like a fuse box in a house lighting system. Better a veto that makes the lights go out than letting a great power burn down the entire house.

Translation

유엔의 창설자들은 5개의 상임 이사국과 순환 방식으로 선출되는 비상임 이사국들로 구성된 안전보장이사회 또한 만들었다. 안전보장이사회는 19세기 세력 균형의 개념이 유엔이라는 집단 안보의 틀에 통합된 것이라고 볼 수 있다. 안전보장이사회는 유엔 헌장 7조에 따라 구속력 있는 결의안을 통과시킬 수 있다. 세계의 경찰격인 5대 강대국이 어떤 문제에 합의를 보지 못할 경우 각국은 거부권을 갖게 되는데, 그것은 집안 두꺼비집의 퓨즈 같은 것이다. 한 강대국이 집안 전체를 불태우도록 방치하느니 차라리 집안의 전기를 나가게 하는 거부권을 주는 것이 낫기 때문이다.

Words

integrated 통합된
collective 총체적, 집단적

테마별 주요 표현 BEST

1. embargo   _______________
2. envoy   _______________
3. espionage   _______________
4. ratify   _______________
5. summit talk   _______________
6. territorial waters   _______________
7. nuclear disarmament   _______________
8. repatriation   _______________
9. treaty   _______________
10. sanction   _______________

Answers

1. 통상 금지
2. 특명 전권 공사, 특사, 외교 사절
3. 스파이 행위, 첩보 활동
4. 비준하다
5. 수뇌[정상] 회담
6. 영해
7. 핵군축
8. 강제 송환
9. 조약, 협정
10. 재가, 허용; pl. (국제법을 어긴 국가에 대한) 제재 조치

1. Read the passage. Then identify the option that does NOT belong.

Most of the population of Hesse is in the southern part of Hesse in the Rhine Main Area. (a) The Rhine borders Hesse on the southwest without running through the state, only one old arm — the so-called Alt-Rhein — runs through Hesse. (b) The mountain range between the Main and the Neckar river is called the Odenwald. (c) Hesse has one of the best transportation infrastructures in Europe. (d) The plain in between the rivers Main, Rhine and Neckar, and the Odenwald mountains is called the Ried.

2. Read the passage. Then identify the option that does NOT belong.

Of the more than six billion people in the world today, over one billion have no access to improved drinking water and about 2.6 billion people, most of them living in underdeveloped countries, do not have access to improved sanitation. (a) According to the U.N. children's agency UNICEF, polluted water and lack of basic sanitation claim the lives of over 1.5 million children every year, mostly from waterborne diseases. (b) "Despite commendable progress," says UNICEF executive director Ann Veneman, "an estimated 425 million children under 18 still do not have access to an improved water supply." (c) She said those who die are by no means the only children affected but "many millions more have their health undermined by water-related diseases." (d) The UNICEF report gives a clean bill of health for the world's industrialized nations, which have reached nearly universal levels of coverage for both water and sanitation.

3. 고난이도

Mexico's drug war is bound to have a profound effect on the lives of Mexican immigrants in the United States. On the one hand, the image of Mexico's chaos as a spreading contagion most likely will strengthen the hand of anti-immigrant forces. On the other, as Mexican newcomers look back at their increasingly dangerous homeland, they will, consciously or unconsciously, ______________.

Q. Choose the option that best completes the passage.
(a) set down deeper roots in the United States
(b) make more money to send to their homeland
(c) break off relations with their family
(d) prevent contagion from spreading to Mexico

Section Switch 

☐ **border** 경계
☐ **run through** 가로지르다
☐ **infrastructure** 기반 시설
☐ **mountain range** 산맥
☐ **sanitation** 위생
☐ **commendable** 칭찬할 만한, 훌륭한
☐ **undermine** (건강 등을) 서서히 해치다
☐ **clean bill of health** (의사가 발부하는) 건강 증명서
☐ **bound to do** 꼭 ~하게 되어 있는
☐ **profound** 깊은
☐ **contagion** 세균, 전염병(infection)
☐ **consciously** 의식적으로
☐ **break off relations with** ~와의 관계를 끊다

Chapter 15

질병

STEP 1 Theme Best

출제 경향 파악

의료 분야에서는 우리 인간에게 자주 발병하는 감기 등의 단순 질병에서부터 심각한 치명적 질병인 암까지 여러 가지 질병을 다룬다. 이 분야에서는 최근 TEPS에서 다음과 같은 내용들이 출제되었고, 또한 출제될 것이다.

1. 간염 - 간경화 / 간암
2. 뇌졸중
3. 심장마비
4. 암 - 흡연과 폐암 / 유방암과 정기 검진
5. 백혈병 - 혈액암
6. 소아마비

Sample

The U.S. Food and Drug Administration (FDA) has approved rifapentine, a new drug for the treatment of pulmonary tuberculosis. The approval marks the first new medication for tuberculosis (TB) to be approved in 25 years, and makes the U.S. the first country to approve the new drug, according to an FDA statement. Studies show that the drug therapy including rifapentine requires fewer doses over the long term, making this regimen easier for patients to follow than current dosing schedules. This is expected to increase the number of patients that stick to taking the prescribed drugs. This increase in patient compliance with TB therapy should reduce both the risks of TB transmission to others and the emergence of more resistant strains of the bacteria.

Translation

미국 식품의약청은 새로운 폐결핵 치료약 리파펜틴을 승인했다. 식품의약청이 밝힌 바에 따르면, 이 약은 결핵 치료용 신약으로는 25년 만에 처음 승인을 받는 약이고 미국이 세계에서 처음으로 신약을 승인한 나라이다. 연구에 의하면 리파펜틴을 이용한 치료법은 장기간 소량을 복용하게 되어 있어 환자들이 현재 복용법보다 간편해 한다고 한다. 이로 인해 약을 꾸준히 복용하는 환자가 늘어날 것으로 보인다. 결핵 치료에 순응하는 환자가 늘어나면 결핵이 다른 사람에게 전염될 위험과, 내성을 키운 변종 박테리아가 출현할 위험이 줄 것이다.

Words

pulmonary 폐의
regimen 처방[투약] 계획
stick to ~을 준수하다.
prescribed drugs 처방된 약
compliance 규정을 지키는 것(여기서는 약을 규칙적으로 먹는 것을 말함)

테마별 주요 표현 BEST

1. astigmatism　　　________________
2. athlete's foot　　　________________
3. autism　　　________________
4. chronic　　　________________
5. diabetes　　　________________
6. dyspepsia　　　________________
7. fit　　　________________
8. fracture　　　________________
9. gastric ulcer　　　________________
10. stroke　　　________________

Answers

1. 난시	2. 무좀
3. 자폐증	4. 만성의
5. 당뇨병	6. 소화불량
7. 발작	8. 골절
9. 위궤양	10. 뇌졸중

1.

A few years ago, Timothy Smith, a young professional in his early thirties who had acute leukemia was referred to me for consultation. With medical treatment, Tim was given a 25 percent chance of survival ; without it, he would die in a few months. Tim was stunned. His reaction was a desperate, angry preoccupation with suicide and a request for support in carrying it out. He was worried about becoming dependent and feared both the symptoms of his disease and the side effects of treatment. Tim's request speaks directly to the question at the heart of assisted suicide. Does our need to care for people who are terminally ill and to ______________ require us to give physicians the right to end patients' lives? This controversial issue of euthanasia may tear our society apart.

Q. **Choose the option that best completes the passage.**
(a) sympathize with their death wish
(b) enhance their chance of survival
(c) make the ends meet
(d) reduce their suffering

2.

Are you tired of so-called "miracle pills" that promise weight loss, but the only thing that seems to get lighter is your wallet? Have you purchased hundreds of dollars' worth of exercise equipment that just sits in the corner collecting dust? If you answered "yes" to these questions, we have a product made just for you. Our new line of pre-prepared meals is made with Olestra, a fat substitute. Olestra contains no calories while retaining all of the flavor. So eat the foods you want, when you want, without worrying about gaining weight.

Q. **What is the main claim of the advertisement?**
(a) Olestra is not harmful to your health.
(b) Olestra makes food taste good without the calories.
(c) Miracle pills work only in conjunction with exercise.
(d) Eating whatever you want will lead to obesity.

3. 〔고난이도〕

In the latest proof of "road rage" on U.S. highways, a survey released Friday found that more than half of New Jersey's 5.4 million licensed motorists are angry while behind the wheel and nearly half ______________ other drivers on the road. "These findings are very troubling. The problem appears much greater than anyone realized," said John Tiene, executive director of the New Jersey Insurance News Service. Angry or aggressive drivers represent a real danger in New Jersey, the most densely populated state in the nation, the News Service said.

Q. **Choose the option that best completes the passage.**
   (a) unconsciously resent
   (b) are not considerate of
   (c) shoot at
   (d) try to punish

Section Switch

☐ **acute leukemia** 급성 백혈병
☐ **chronic** 만성의
☐ **be stunned** 깜짝 놀라다
☐ **preoccupation with** ~에 집착함
☐ **side effects** 부작용
☐ **assisted suicide** 조력 자살
☐ **be terminally ill** 불치병에 걸리다
☐ **tear ~ apart** ~를 분열시키다
☐ **line** 종류, 품종
☐ **substitute** 대용품, 대체물
☐ **in conjunction with** ~과 결합하여
☐ **obesity** 비만
☐ **licensed motorist** 면허 있는 운전자
☐ **behind the wheel** 운전대 뒤에 있는 (즉, 운전하는)
☐ **executive director** 전무이사
☐ **densely populated** 인구가 밀집한

Chapter 16
인간의 행동과 인체

STEP 1 Theme Best

출제 경향 파악

의학 분야, 그 중에서도 인간의 행동과 인체 분야는 인체의 여러 부분과 그 기능(예: 뇌의 기억 작용)을 다룬다. 이 분야에서는 최근 TEPS에서 다음과 같은 내용들이 출제되었고, 또한 출제될 것이다.

1. 수면 - 불면증 / 수면 장애
2. 운동
3. 호흡 - 천식
4. 영양과 식사 - 영양의 섭취
5. 기억과 뇌 - 알츠하이머 병 / 장기 기억과 단기 기억
6. 생식 - 수정 / 착상 / 생리

Sample

Endoscopy, as its etymology implies, is the study of the internal parts of the human body. Endoscopy is now so common that one tends to take it for granted, but in order to fully appreciate the present state-of-the art technology that permits visualization from inside the body, even within blood vessels, it is important to understand how the endoscope developed. It is also fascinating to look at the great variety of accessory equipment designed for a wide range of diagnostic and therapeutic procedures. Modern endoscopic techniques include simple biopsies, the use of lasers for diagnosis and treatment of cancer, and sophisticated endoscopic surgical procedures that avoid large incisions in the surface of the body.

Translation

내시경 검사법은 그 어원이 의미하는 것처럼 인체의 내부 영역에 대한 연구이다. 내시경 검사법은 지금은 너무 흔해 우리는 당연하게 받아들이지만, 인체 내부, 심지어 혈관 내부까지 투시하는 최첨단 기술 전체를 인식하려면 내시경 검사법이 어떻게 발전되어왔는가를 이해하는 것이 중요하다. 또한 광범위한 진찰 및 치료법을 위해 개발된 다양한 도구를 조망하는 것도 흥미로운 일이다. 현대의 내시경 기술은 단순한 생체검사, 암의 진단과 치유를 위한 레이저 사용, 그리고 신체 표면에 커다란 절개를 피할 수 있는 정교한 외과용 내시경을 이용한 수술법도 포함된다.

Words

etymology 어원

blood vessels 혈관

biopsies 생체검사, 생검

state-of-the-art 최신식의

endoscope 내시경

incisions 절개 수술

테마별 주요 표현 BEST

1. hiccup _______________
2. insomnia _______________
3. semination _______________
4. dimple _______________
5. disinfect _______________
6. hypnosis _______________
7. inoculate _______________
8. ointment _______________
9. olfactory _______________
10. symptom _______________

Answers

1. 딸꾹질

2. 불면증 (sleep disorder)

3. 생식

4. 보조개

5. 소독하다, (백신을) 접종하다

6. 최면

7. 예방하다

8. 연고

9. 후각의

10. 징후, 조짐

1.

Sunscreen lotions may not protect against skin cancer. Some British doctors insist that sunscreens do not provide total protection against skin cancer and that they are almost like a last line of defence. They advise that people should stick on a hat and stay in the shade. According to them, people shouldn't assume that just because they're wearing sunscreen they are completely protected. _______________, wearing sunscreen and being sensible in the sun is far better than doing nothing.

Q. **Choose the option that best completes the passage.**
(a) However
(b) Besides
(c) Consequently
(d) Similarly

2.

Scientists have done research on the relationship between sleep and cancer and found that sleep can alter the balance of hormones in the body. The hormone cortisol plays a role in determining whether someone develops a tumor. _______________, cortisol helps regulate the immune system such as the cells that help the body fight cancer and the levels of the hormone peak at dawn and decline during the day. Research demonstrated that women at high risk of breast cancer had a shifted cortisol cycle. A cortisol rhythm disrupted by sleeping problems could make a person more cancer-prone.

Q. **Choose the option that best completes the passage.**
(a) Consequently
(b) To be more specific
(c) Nevertheless
(d) Frankly speaking

3. 고난이도

Each child is born with a basic temperament that is shaped by life events. When a child fits nicely with her parents and her environment, she flourishes. When circumstances are adverse, the child suffers. Some circumstances are innocent; for example, I treated a young woman who, having autism, was an artist. Unfortunately for her, she was born into a family of accountants — nice people, but they had no idea what to do with her, and she suffered from feeling different and unvalued. In a more serious instance, a young man had been born with heart defects that required repeated surgeries until he was fifteen. His mother had already nursed her own parents through fatal illnesses and hated taking care of him. Whatever normal shyness he started with became distorted, and he was a withdrawn, ashamed, and angry young adult by the time I met him.

Q.   What can be inferred from the passage?
   (a) Childhood personality and past experiences shape the present.
   (b) Family environment is an important factor for shaping childrens' characters.
   (c) Parents' genes affects their children's biological and mental characters.
   (d) When parents understand their child, the child grows up healthily.

Section Switch

- [ ] **cancer** 암
- [ ] **sunscreen** 햇볕타기 방지제
- [ ] **assume** 가정하다
- [ ] **completely** 전적으로, 완전하게
- [ ] **cortisol** 코티솔(부신 피질에서 생기는 스테로이드 호르몬의 일종)
- [ ] **disrupt** 분열시키다, 혼란케 하다
- [ ] **demonstrate** 증명하다
- [ ] **nevertheless** 그럼에도 불구하고
- [ ] **temperament** 기질
- [ ] **flourish** 무성하게 자라다, 번창하다
- [ ] **instance** 사례
- [ ] **surgery** 수술
- [ ] **autism** 자폐증

Chapter 17

환경과 인간/대체의학

STEP 1 Theme Best

출제 경향 파악

의학 분야 중에서도 환경과 인간/대체의학 분야에서는 사회적 문제로서의 환경 문제가 아니라 개인의 건강에 영향을 미치는 환경 문제에 대해서 다룬다. 즉 오존층이나 황사 문제가 대표적일 것이다. 이 분야에서는 최근 TEPS에서 다음과 같은 내용들이 출제되었고, 또한 출제될 것이다.

1. 살충제 - 과다 사용 / 해충의 내성 증가
2. 오존층 - 오존층의 영향
3. 황사 - 중국
4. 중독 - 마약 / 알코올
5. 스트레스
6. 대체 의학 - 서양 의학의 한계 / 침술
7. 태양과 인간 - 흑점의 변화와 인간의 행동 변화

Sample

Ecology is the study of the complex interactions that make up our living planet. It is rapidly becoming one of the most important branches of biology, because only by understanding how plants and animals depend on each other and on their environment can we help them to survive in our changing world. This complex set of relationships, in which one organism is linked to another and then another, constitutes the main concern of ecology.

Translation

생태학이란 우리의 살아 있는 지구를 형성하는 복합적인 상호작용을 연구하는 학문이다. 생태학은 생물학의 가장 중요한 영역 중 하나로 빠르게 자리잡고 있다. 그 이유는 어떻게 식물과 동물들이 서로 그리고 환경에 의존하는지를 이해함으로써만, 우리는 이 변화하는 세상에서 그것들이 살아 남을 수 있도록 도와줄 수 있기 때문이다. 이 복합적인 일련의 관계, 즉 하나의 생물체가 다른 생물체 그리고 또 다른 생물체와 연결되어 있는 이러한 관계는 생태학의 주요 관심사를 구성한다.

Words

interaction 상호작용
organism 유기체, 생물체
constitute ~을 구성하다

테마별 주요 표현 BEST

1. addiction   ____________________
2. antidote   ____________________
3. insecticide   ____________________
4. damp   ____________________
5. dreary   ____________________
6. secrete   ____________________
7. sneeze   ____________________
8. sputum   ____________________
9. transfusion   ____________________
10. (human) vegetable   ____________________

Answers

1. 중독	2. 해독제
3. 살충제	4. 습기
5. 음산한	6. 분비하다
7. 재채기하다	8. 가래
9. 수혈	10. 식물인간

1.

Although modern medicine is making many new treatments possible, doctors are learning that some of the old ways are useful too. For example, doctors are now paying more attention to the connection between diet and health. Even the leeches have found a place in modern medicine. In certain kinds of surgery, cutting edge surgeons are using leeches to prevent a patient's arteries from getting plugged up.

Some people believe that nature has all of the cures for human problems. Others believe that technology is more helpful. It just might be that, together, tradition and technology will help people everywhere live better and healthier lives.

Q. **What is the main idea of the passage?**

(a) Leeches have been used in preventing patients' arteries from becoming clogged since early times.

(b) The harmony of tradition and technology will make people live more abundant life.

(c) We should learn more from traditional treatments.

(d) Doctors have been more interested in traditional oriental medicine recently.

2. Read the passage. Then identify the option that does NOT belong.

Doctor Who is a long-running, award-winning British science fiction television programme produced by the BBC. (a) The programme depicts the adventures of a mysterious alien time-traveller known as "the Doctor" who travels in his space and time-ship, the TARDIS, which appears from the exterior to be a blue police box. (b) It was intended to be educational and for family viewing on the early Saturday evening schedule. (c) With his companions, he explores time and space, solving problems and righting wrongs. (d) The programme is listed in Guinness World Records as the longest-running science fiction television show in the world and is also a significant part of British popular culture.

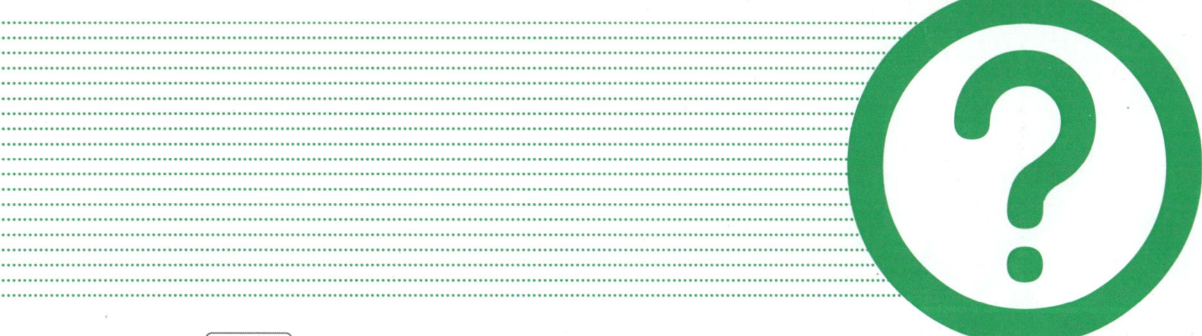

3. 고난이도

There have been many studies on the health effects of pesticide exposure to those who work on farms. Even when pesticides are used correctly, they still end up in the air and bodies of farm workers. Through these studies, organophosphate pesticides have become associated with acute health problems such as abdominal pain, dizziness, headaches, nausea, vomiting, as well as skin and eye problems. In addition, there have been many other studies that have found pesticide exposure is associated with more severe health problems such as respiratory problems, memory disorders, dermatologic conditions, cancer, depression, neurological deficits, miscarriages, and birth defects.

Q. **Which is correct according to the passage?**

(a) The use of pesticides may have deleterious effects on the health.

(b) When pesticides are used correctly, they disappear in the air immediately.

(c) Exposure to pesticides may induce coughing.

(d) Farm workers are using pesticides more and more these days.

Section Switch 

☐ **pay attention to** ~에 유의하다

☐ **surgery** 수술

☐ **leech** 거머리

☐ **artery** 동맥

☐ **long-running** 장기간 방영된

☐ **depict** 그리다, 묘사하다

☐ **significant** 뜻깊은, 중요한

☐ **exterior** 외관

☐ **pesticide** 살충제

☐ **organophosphate** 유기 인산 화합물의

☐ **abdominal** 복부의

☐ **dermatologic** 피부(병)의

☐ **miscarriage** 유산

Chapter 18

환경 문제

STEP 1 Theme Best

출제 경향 파악

환경 분야는 지구 환경의 변화와 공해를 다루는 분야이다. 특히 산성비나 오존층 파괴 등 시사적인 문제들이 많이 나온다. 이 분야에서는 최근 TEPS에서 다음과 같은 내용들이 출제되었고, 또한 출제될 것이다.

1. 지구
2. 기후
3. 수질 오염
4. 대기 오염
5. 토양 오염
6. 산성비

Sample

Today, the world's population grows by 76 million people every year. That is about 240,000 people every day. By the year 2050, researchers predict that the population of the world will be 9.1 billion. Does the Earth have the natural resources to support this many people? Unfortunately, the answer to this question depends on information we don't have. For example, we don't know how people will choose to live in the future. We don't know what their standard of living will be. We also don't know what new technologies will be available in the future.

Translation

오늘날 세계의 인구는 매년 7600만 명씩 증가하고 있다. 이 수치는 매일 거의 24만 명의 사람들이 증가한다는 이야기이다. 학자들은 2050년이면 세계의 인구가 91억 정도 될 것이라고 예상하고 있다. 이 지구에는 이렇게 많은 사람들을 부양할 수 있는 천연 자원이 있을까? 불행하게도, 이 물음에 대한 답은 우리가 가지고 있지 않은 정보에 달려 있다. 예를 들면, 우리는 미래에 사람들이 어떠한 삶의 방식을 택할 것인지 알지 못한다. 우리는 그들의 삶의 수준이 어떻게 될지 모른다. 또한, 미래에 어떠한 새로운 기술이 이용 가능하게 될 것인지도 모르고 있다.

Words

predict 예언하다, 예상하다
standard 기준, 수준
available 이용 가능한

테마별 주요 표현 BEST

1. acid rain　　　　　_______________
2. glacier　　　　　_______________
3. humidity　　　　　_______________
4. weather　　　　　_______________
5. weather-bureau　　_______________
6. precipitation　　　_______________
7. serene　　　　　_______________
8. meteorology　　　_______________
9. torrid　　　　　_______________
10. sultry　　　　　_______________

Answers

1. 산성비　　　　　　　2. 빙하
3. 습도　　　　　　　　4. 날씨; 풍화시키다
5. 기상청　　　　　　　6. 강수량
7. 고요한, 잠잠한　　　8. 기상학
9. 매우 더운　　　　　　10. 찌는 듯이 더운

1.

The earth's protective ozone layer will hit its all-time thinnest by 2000 or 2001, the World Meterological Organization said Monday. Despite forecasts that international measures to halt the decline will help the layer improve by the middle of the next century, the ozone layer is at its most _______________ stage now and things will get worse before they get any better, the WMO said. The ozone layer is a protective fragile shield of gas that absorbs the harmful ultraviolet rays of the sun but has been increasingly pierced by holes caused by man-made chemicals. The holes are blamed for causing skin cancer.

Q. **Choose the option that best completes the passage.**
   (a) inactive
   (b) sophisticated
   (c) strengthened
   (d) vulnerable

2. Read the passage. Then identify the option that does NOT belong.

People have always dumped wastes into lakes, rivers, and estuaries, because it is easier than land-based waste disposal. The large volumes of water dilute foul or dangerous substances, and in rivers, currents carry away garbage, chemicals, and sewage. (a) This was not really a problem when the number of people in the U.S. was small. (b) However, problems with water quality surfaced when the nation's population started to take off. (c) Many rivers and lakes are recovering, but in some ways, water quality has always been in control. (d) Water quality problems resulted from exceeding the capacity of lakes and rivers to absorb and dilute pollutants.

3. 고난이도

Wood is in great demand to fuel fires in developing countries. In many areas, people depend on wood to cook their food. As the population grows, the need for wood grows, too. But when too many trees are cut at once, forests are destroyed. Small farmers who are desperate for land also move in. They cut down the rest of the trees and burn them. In this way, many millions of acres of forests are destroyed every year. Unfortunately, forest soil is not good for growing food. Thus, these poor farmers ______________. In turn, this results in the lose of forest resources.

Q. **Choose the option that best completes the passage.**
   (a) are no longer so desperate for food
   (b) get richer while the land burns
   (c) remain as poor as they ever were
   (d) have to clear even more land

Section Switch

- [ ] **hit one's all-time+최상급** 전례 없이 가장 ~하다
- [ ] **meteorological** 기상학
- [ ] **measure to do** ~하는 조치
- [ ] **things will get worse** 상황이 더욱 악화될 것이다
- [ ] **pierce** 관통하다, 찌르다
- [ ] **sophisticated** 고도로 세련된
- [ ] **vulnerable** 상처를 입기 쉬운
- [ ] **estuary** (간만의 차가 있는) 큰 강의 어귀
- [ ] **foul** 더러운
- [ ] **dilute** 희석시키다
- [ ] **sewage** 하수 오물, 오수(汚水)
- [ ] **take off** 상승하다
- [ ] **desperate** 필사적인, 절박한
- [ ] **resource** 자원
- [ ] **destroy** 파괴하다

Chapter 19

재난

STEP 1 Theme Best

출제 경향 파악

재난 분야는 환경 문제 중에서도 계절적, 일시적으로 우리에게 피해를 가져다 주는 환경 재난을 다룬다. 지진이나 폭우, 태풍 등이 대표적인 예가 될 것이다. 이 분야에서는 최근 TEPS에서 다음과 같은 내용들이 출제되었고, 또한 출제될 것이다.

1. 지진
2. 산사태
3. 태풍 - 카트리나/태풍이 가져다 주는 피해(질병 감염 등)
4. 폭우
5. 강풍 - 허리케인/토네이도
6. 가뭄

Sample

As the death toll rose on Tuesday, Feb. 10, to 173 in Australia's worst wildfire disaster, suspicions that some of the 400 blazes were caused by arson led police to declare some of the incinerated towns as crime scenes. Whole forests were reduced to leafless, charred trunks. Farmland was in ashes. The scale of the disaster shocked a nation that endures deadly firestorms every few years. Officials said panic and the freight-train speed of the walls of flames probably accounted for the unusually high death toll.

Translation

2월 10일 화요일 호주 최악의 산불 재난의 총 사망자수가 173명으로 늘어나자 400곳의 화염 중 일부가 방화 때문이라는 의혹으로 인해 경찰이 잿더미가 된 몇몇 마을을 범죄 현장으로 선언하게 되었다. 숲 전체가 잎새 없이 불타버린 나무 줄기만 남았고 농지는 재가 되었다. 이번 화재의 규모는 몇 년마다 한 번씩 발생하는 치명적인 대화재를 견뎌내고 있는 전 국민에게 충격을 주었다. 관리들은 공포와 화차 속도로 밀려오는 화염벽이 예상 외로 많은 사망자 수의 원인일 것이라고 말했다.

Words

death toll 사망자 수

blaze 화염, 불꽃

arson 방화

incinerate 태우다, 태워서 재가 되게 하다

char (나무 등을) 숯으로 만들다

테마별 주요 표현 BEST

1. drought   _______________
2. landslide   _______________
3. inundation   _______________
4. earthquake   _______________
5. epicenter   _______________
6. avalanche   _______________
7. downfall   _______________
8. erupt   _______________
9. fallout   _______________
10. volcanic ashes   _______________

Answers

1. 가뭄	2. 산사태
3. 범람, 홍수	4. 지진
5. 진원지, 진앙, 중심	6. 눈사태
7. 폭우	8. 폭발하다, 분출하다
9. (핵폭발의) 낙진; 부산물, 여파	10. 화산재

1.

The fluid pressure in a vortex is lowest in the center where the speed is greatest, and rises progressively with distance from the center. This is in accordance with Bernoulli's Principle. The core of a vortex in air is sometimes visible because of a plume of water vapor caused by condensation in the low pressure of the core. The spout of a tornado is a classic and frightening example of the visible core of a vortex. A dust devil is _______________, made visible by the dust drawn upwards by the turbulent flow of air from ground level into the low pressure core.

Q. Choose the option that best completes the passage.
    (a) also the core of a vortex
    (b) a sheet of small vortices
    (c) considered to be circulating around the vortex line
    (d) at the boundary of the fluid

2.

Until the Aswan High Dam was built, Egypt received a yearly inundation — an annual flood — of the Nile. The ancient Egyptians did not realize this, but the flood came due to the heavy summer rains in the Ethiopian highlands, swelling the different tributaries and other rivers that joined and became the Nile. This happened yearly, between June and September, in a season the Egyptians called Akhet — the inundation. This was seen by the Egyptians as a yearly coming of the god Hapi, bringing fertility to the land.

Q. What can be inferred from the passage?
    (a) Egyptians regarded the inundation as an auspicious sign.
    (b) The Egyptians learned a method of measuring the height of the Nile known as the Nilometre.
    (c) The floods have decreased over the years.
    (d) If there was no flood, it would be a year of abundance.

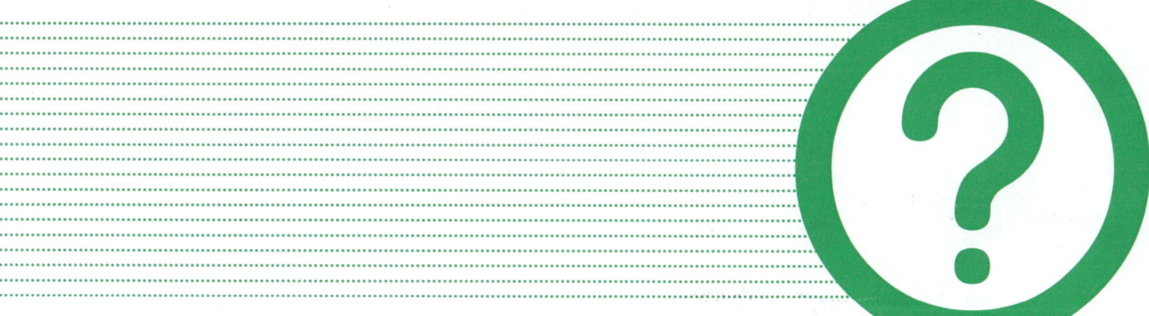

3. 고난이도

Read the passage. Then identify the option that does NOT belong.

Even small avalanches are a serious danger to life, even with companions properly trained and equipped to avoid avalanches. (a) Between 55 and 65% of victims buried in the open are killed, and only 80% of the victims remaining on the surface survive. (b) Historically, the chances of survival were estimated at 85% within 15 minutes, 50% within 30 minutes, 20% within one hour. (c) Consequently it is vital that everyone who escapes an avalanche participate in an immediate search and rescue operation for victims, rather than waiting for help to arrive. (d) If the person gets buried in an avalanche, the light cord stays on top of the snow and due to the color the cord is easily visible for rescue personnel.

Section Switch

- ☐ **fluid** 유동체[성]의, 불안정한
- ☐ **vortex** 회오리바람
- ☐ **dust devil** (열대 사막의) 회오리바람
- ☐ **turbulent** 몹시 거친, 사나운
- ☐ **inundation** 범람
- ☐ **tributary** (강의) 지류
- ☐ **fertility** 비옥함
- ☐ **avalanche** 눈사태
- ☐ **immediate** 즉시의
- ☐ **rescue personnel** 구조 요원

Chapter 20
컴퓨터/통신

STEP 1 Theme Best

출제 경향 파악

컴퓨터/통신 분야는 최첨단의 분야로서 컴퓨터와 휴대폰 등의 통신기기의 작동 원리와 구조 원리 등을 다룬다. 이 분야에서는 최근 TEPS에서 다음과 같은 내용들이 출제되었고, 또한 출제될 것이다.

1. 컴퓨터 - 마이크로소프트 / 빌 게이츠 / 윈도
2. 통신 - 휴대폰 / 광랜
3. 반도체
4. 소프트웨어 - 소프트웨어의 개발 / 불법 복제
5. 인공 지능 - AI / 로봇

Sample

Fuzzy logic has rapidly become one of the most successful of today's control systems technologies. With its aid complex tasks can be performed by amazingly simple, easily maintained, and inexpensive controllers. This logic is a method of easily representing analog processes on a digital computer. These processes are concerned with continuous phenomena that are not easily broken down into discrete segments, and where the concepts involved are difficult to model — sometimes extraordinarily so — along mathematical or strict lines.

Translation

퍼지 이론은 빠르게 오늘날 가장 성공적인 제어 시스템 기술의 하나가 되고 있다. 그 기술의 도움으로 놀랍도록 간단하고 쉽게 유지되며 저렴한 제어장치로 복잡한 과제를 수행할 수 있다. 퍼지 이론은 디지털 컴퓨터에서 아놀로그식 프로세스를 쉽게 구현하는 수단이다. 이런 프로세스는 별개의 세그먼트(크기가 가변적인 데이터 단위)로 쉽게 나뉘지 않는 연속적인 현상들과 관계가 있는데, 여기에 포함된 개념들은 수학적이거나 엄격한 방식을 따르기 어렵고 유난히 그런 경우가 있다.

Words

concepts involved 포함된 개념

테마별 주요 표현 BEST

1. android ________________
2. artificial intelligence ________________
3. flash memory ________________
4. space probe ________________
5. extension number ________________
6. junk mail ________________
7. virtual reality ________________
8. state-of-the-art ________________
9. toll-free call ________________
10. zip code ________________

Answers

1. 인조 인간 로봇
2. 인공 지능
3. 플래시 메모리
4. 우주 탐사선
5. 내선 번호
6. (광고물 · 선전 책자 등을 수취인의 명시도 없이 사서함 따위에 넣는) 광고 우편물
7. 가상 현실
8. 최첨단 기술을 이용한
9. (기업의 소비자 상담 · 공공 서비스 등을 위한) 무료 전화 서비스
10. 우편 번호

1.

Although supercomputers are dazzling in their power and engineering virtuosity, hardware alone will only partially achieve the eventual goal of computer scientists: the creation of systems that can mimic the decision-making power of ______________. This goal is called AI, artificial intelligence, and it has eluded computer programmers for decades.

Q. **Choose the option that best completes the passage.**

(a) a computer
(b) human beings
(c) supercomputers
(d) computer programmers

2.

The former Soviet Union laid claim to the world's largest magnet. The magnet, located at the Joint Institute for Nuclear Research at Dubna near Moscow, measures 60 meters in diameter, and weighs over 36,000 tons. However, this magnet cannot claim to have the strongest magnetic field strength in the world. This claim goes to a magnet made of superconducting niobium-titanium, located at the Francis Bitter National Magnet Laboratory at MIT. Needless to say, visitors are encouraged to remove all jewelry before going into the vicinity of these magnets.

Q. **Which is correct according to the passage?**

(a) The largest magnet in the world is located at MIT.
(b) The magnet with the strongest magnetic field is not the world's largest.
(c) Niobium-titanium is the densest material in the world.
(d) The former Soviet Union competed with MIT to build the largest magnet.

3. 고난이도

Installing spark plugs is one of the simplest do-it-yourself procedures for the burgeoning home mechanic. First, disconnect the ignition wires from the spark plugs. Be careful to tag each wire so that you reconnect them to the appropriate spark plug. Remove the old spark plugs using a spark plug socket and a 3/4-inch ratchet. Adjust the spark plug gap of the new plugs to the engine makers' specifications. Tighten the new spark plug with your fingers first, then with the ratchet, turn the spark plug about 1/2 to 3/4 of an additional rotation. Reconnect the ignition wires, and you're done.

Q. **Why should you tag each wire?**
(a) To replace them in the proper order
(b) To approximate the length of the wires
(c) To make sure the proper wire is reconnected
(d) To test the conduction of each wire before reconnecting

Section Switch

- virtuosity 묘기, 기교
- mimic 흉내내다
- lay claim to ~을 자칭하다, ~에 대한 소유[권리]를 주장하다
- magnetic field strength 자계력
- niobium-titanium 니오브-티타늄 합금
- spark plug (내연기관의) 점화전
- burgeon 갑자기 커지다, 빠르게 성장하다
- socket (전구 따위를 끼우는) 소켓
- specification 시방서, 설명서
- artificial intelligence 인공 지능
- elude 피하다, 알 수 없다
- diameter 직경, 지름
- superconducting 초전도의
- vicinity 근처
- do-it-yourself 손수 하는
- ignition 점화
- ratchet 래치트, 깔쭉 톱니바퀴를 이용한 도구
- conduction 전도

STEP 1 Theme Best

출제 경향 파악

수학, 물리학, 화학 분야의 독해에서는 0의 발명으로 시작되는 고대의 과학에서 아인슈타인의 상대성 이론까지 다양하게 다뤄진다.
이 분야의 독해에서는 최근 TEPS에서 다음과 같은 내용들이 출제되었고, 또한 출제될 것이다.

1. 고대의 과학 - 영의 발명 / 4대 발명품(활자, 화약, 나침반, 종이)
2. 고대 과학자 - 피타고라스 / 프톨레마이오스
3. 근대 과학자 - 코페르니쿠스 / 갈릴레이 / 뉴튼
4. 현대 과학자 - 아인슈타인 / 퀴리부인
5. 이슬람의 과학 발달

Sample

Friedmann made two very simple assumptions about the universe: that the universe looks identical in whichever direction we look, and that this would also be true if we were observing the universe from anywhere else. From these two ideas alone, Friedmann showed that we should not expect the universe to be static. In fact, in 1912, several years before Edwin Hubble's discovery, Friedmann predicted exactly what Hubble found!

프리드만은 우주에 대해 매우 단순한 두 가지 가설을 만들었다. 즉, 우주는 우리가 어느 방향에서 보든 동일하게 안다는 것과 또한 만약 우리가 또 다른 어디에서든지 우주를 관찰하더라도 그럴 것이라는 것이다. 오로지 이 두 개의 아이디어만으로, 프리드만은 우리가 우주는 정적일 것이라고 기대해선 안 된다는 것을 보여준다. 실제로, 1912년 에드윈 허블의 발견이 있기 몇 년 전에, 프리드만은 허블이 발견한 것을 정확하게 예측했다!

Words

assumption 가정, 가설
identical 동일한

테마별 주요 표현 BEST

1. buoyancy   ______________
2. centrifugal force   ______________
3. centripetal force   ______________
4. torsion   ______________
5. universal gravitation   ______________
6. vacuum   ______________
7. surface tension   ______________
8. theory of relativity (the ~) ______________
9. wave length   ______________
10. inertia   ______________

Answers

1. 부력
2. 원심력
3. 구심력
4. 비트는 힘, 염력
5. 만유인력
6. 진공의
7. 표면장력
8. 상대성 이론
9. 파장
10. 관성

1.

Water is contained in all kinds of food. It is possible to obtain water not only by drinking it but also by drinking milk and juices. Some water is produced when food is broken down within cells. Most fruit and vegetables are a good source of nutrients as well as water. They are also good sources of roughage, which is coarse, bulky food containing fiber that stimulates the muscles of the digestive tract.

Q. **Which of the following is true according to the above passage?**
(a) You can obtain water from milk and juice, but not from food.
(b) Vegetables and fruits usually provide much water and few nutrients.
(c) Fiber can be obtained from milk and juice rather than from fruits and vegetables.
(d) Fruits and vegetables are good for the muscles of the digestive tract.

2. Read the passage. Then identify the option that does NOT belong.

During the late Triassic period, about 210 million years ago, the continents as we know them today did not exist. (a) The continents had almost assumed the shape and the position they have today about 210 million years ago. (b) The surface of the earth included vast seas and one large landmass, Pangaea. (c) Almost imperceptibly, however, Pangaea split apart, and separate continents began drifting across the globe. (d) For millions of years, this drifting continued and, in a sense, it continues today.

3. 고난이도

Robots are machines that are programmed ______________. They have already been sent to the edges of outer space, telling us what they find there. They go into the deepest sea, gathering information useful for humans. They are also used in war and peace. Some of them are being used to explode mines, allowing battlefields to be transformed into farmlands.

Q. Choose the option that best completes the passage.
   (a) to do dangerous work for humans
   (b) to do boring household chores
   (c) to explore unknown lands
   (d) to analyze useful information

Section Switch

- ☐ **roughage** 조악한 음식물, 섬유소를 함유하는 음식
- ☐ **coarse** 조잡한, 조악한
- ☐ **digestive** 소화의
- ☐ **tract** 관(管), 도(道), 계통
- ☐ **Triassic** 트라이아스기(紀)의
- ☐ **landmass** 광대한 토지; 대륙
- ☐ **Pangaea** 판게아(트라이아스기(紀) 이전에 존재했다고 하는 대륙; 그 후 북의 *Laurasia*와 남의 *Gondwana*로 분리됨)
- ☐ **imperceptibly** 감지할 수 없게
- ☐ **in a sense** 어떤 점으로는, 어느 정도까지
- ☐ **explode** 폭발시키다
- ☐ **battlefield** 전쟁터
- ☐ **farmland** 농지

STEP 1 Theme Best

출제 경향 파악

일반 생물학 분야는 생물의 분류에서 출발해서 최근에 문제가 되는 생태학까지 포괄적인 내용을 다룬다. 이 분야에서는 최근 TEPS 에서 다음과 같은 내용들이 출제되었고, 또한 출제될 것이다.

1. 생물의 분류 - 동물의 분류 / 식물의 분류 / 린넨
2. 동물의 행동 - 도구 사용 능력 / 의사 소통 능력
3. 동물이 인간에게 주는 영향
4. 인간의 습성
5. 생태학의 유래

Sample

Garlic not only seems to keep vampires at bay, but it drives slugs and snails out of the garden. An experimental refined garlic spray called Ecoguard can effectively deter slugs. A large sum of money a year is spent to protect lettuce, potatoes and winter wheat from slugs and snails. Pesticides have been very helpful at preventing pests and increasing food availability. But amid growing awareness of their potential dangers, the number of pesticides available to gardeners and farmers has gone down in recent years. As more and more pesticides are withdrawn from sale, this common cooking ingredient might pose an inexpensive and eco-friendly alternative.

Translation

마늘은 흡혈 박쥐의 접근을 막아 줄 뿐 아니라 민달팽이와 달팽이들을 정원에서 몰아내준다. 에코가드라 불리는 실험적으로 만들어진 마늘 스프레이는 민달팽이들을 효과적으로 억제할 수 있다. 한 해에 많은 돈이 양상추, 감자 그리고 겨울 밀 등을 민달팽이와 달팽이들로부터 보호하기 위해 쓰이고 있다. 살충제는 벌레들을 막고 수확량을 증가시키는 데 매우 유용하다. 그러나 그것들의 잠재적인 위험에 대한 인식이 늘어가면서 정원사들과 농부들이 이용할 수 있는 살충제의 수는 최근 많이 줄었다. 더 많은 살충제들이 판매되지 않음에 따라 이 일반적인 요리 재료가 값이 싸고 환경 친화적인 대체제로 이용될 수 있다.

Words

keep ~ at bay ~을 가까이 못 오게 하다

slug 민달팽이, 괄태충

snail 달팽이

lettuce 상추, 양상추

pesticide 살충제

inexpensive 비용이 들지 않는, 값싼

테마별 주요 표현 BEST

1. amphibians ________________
2. carnivorous ________________
3. primates ________________
4. chromosome ________________
5. ecology ________________
6. metabolism ________________
7. metamorphosis ________________
8. mutation ________________
9. omnivorous ________________
10. ornithology ________________

Answers

1. 양서동물
2. 육식성의, 식충성의
3. 영장류
4. 염색체
5. 생태학
6. 신진대사
7. 변형, 변태
8. 돌연변이
9. 잡식성의
10. 조류학

1.

Aggression is a form of animal behavior characterized by an assault or attack by one animal on another. Aggression can take many forms derived from a variety of factors involved. One form of aggression is conflict between members of different species. It can include predatory aggression (food obtaining), defensive aggression, and aggression directed at competitors for resources such as food or water. Aggression of this sort typically does not involve emotions such as anger and can be perceived as a component of

________________.

Q. Choose the option that best completes the passage.
   (a) survival behavior
   (b) affective behavior
   (c) evolutionary processes
   (d) aggressive instincts

2. Read the passage. Then identify the option that does NOT belong.

The term ecology was coined a hundred years ago by the German biologist Ernst Haeckel. (a) The eco-, from the Greek oikos (house), is the same as the eco- in economics. (b) According to an old definition, what ecologists study is the economy of animals and plants. (c) Ecosystem means the community of living things and the physical environment in the area of nature an ecologist is studying. (d) In the now-standard definition, ecology is the science of the relations between organisms and their environment.

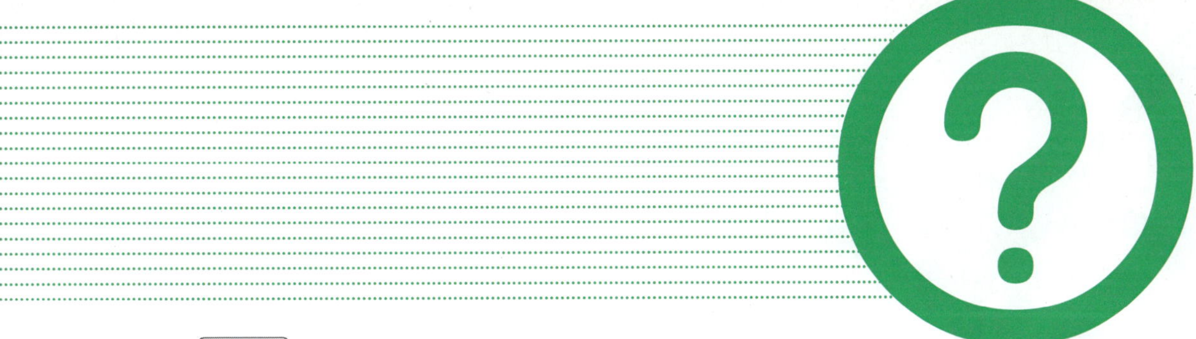

3. 고난이도

A white gorilla which is thought to be the world's only living one is dying of skin cancer. The white gorilla named Snowflake was captured by a hunter in Equatorial Guinea in 1966 and has been at the Barcelona zoo since then. Vets have known for quite a long time that the gorilla has the disease, but it has suddenly progressed. One of the zoo's vets said that though they had tried their best to protect him, the disease was incurable and that ______________.

Q. **Choose the option that best completes the passage.**

(a) his life would certainly be prolonged
(b) they would let it follow its natural course
(c) it would be unnecessary to make him suffer
(d) he should be kept in his cage anyway

Section Switch

☐ **be characterized by** ~이 특징이다
☐ **derived from** ~에서 유래된
☐ **predatory** 약탈하는, 육식의
☐ **be perceived as** ~로 인식되다
☐ **evolutionary process** 진화 과정
☐ **aggressive instinct** 호전적인 본능
☐ **ecology** 생태학
☐ **coin** (신어·신표현을) 만들어내다
☐ **definition** 정의
☐ **snowflake** 눈송이
☐ **equatorial** 적도의, 적도 부근의
☐ **vet** 수의(사)(veterinarian의 축약형)
☐ **incurable** 불치의

STEP 1 Theme Best

출제 경향 파악

진화 유전 분야는 다윈에서 출발하는 인간의 진화의 문제를 다루고, 유전은 멘델에서 출발해서 DNA의 발견으로 급격히 발전하게 된 첨단 생물학 분야를 주로 다룬다. 이 분야에서는 최근 TEPS에서 다음과 같은 내용들이 출제가 되었고, 또한 출제가 될 것이다.

1. 진화론 - 다윈
2. 유인원 - 오스트랄로 피테쿠스 / 호모 에렉투스 / 호모 사피언스
3. 초기의 유전 연구 - 멘델 / 드프리스 / 초파리 연구
4. DNA의 발견 - 왓슨과 크릭

Sample

One of the most dramatic controversies in the Victorian age concerned theories of evolution. This controversy exploded into prominence in 1859 when Charles Darwin's Origin of species was published, but it had been rumbling for many years previously. It was Darwin, however, with his monumental marshaling of evidence to establish his theory of natural selection, who finally brought the topic fully into the open, and the public as well as the experts took side.

Translation

빅토리아 시대에 가장 극적인 논쟁 중 하나는 진화론에 관한 것이다. 이 논쟁은 찰스 다윈의 종의 기원이 발표되었던 1859년에 폭발적으로 부각되었지만 그 이전부터 수년 간 계속되고 있었다. 그러나 마침내 이 문제를 완전히 공개의 장으로 드러내 놓은 사람은 바로 방대한 증거를 수집하여 자연도태설이라는 자기만의 이론을 수립한 다윈이었으며 전문가들은 물론 일반인들도 그의 편을 들었다.

Words

controversy 논쟁
rumble 나지막하고 굵직한 목소리로 말하다
monumental 기념비적인
marshal 정돈하다, 수집하다

테마별 주요 표현 BEST

1. photosynthesis ___________________
2. protoplasm ___________________
3. vestige ___________________
4. pigmentation ___________________
5. spore ___________________
6. survival of the fittest ___________________
7. ruminant ___________________
8. zoology ___________________
9. assimilation ___________________
10. atavism ___________________

Answers

1. 광합성 2. 원형질
3. 흔적 4. 색소 형성
5. 포자, 홀씨 6. 적자생존
7. 되새김하는, 반추 동물 8. 동물학
9. 동화 작용 10. 격세 유전

1.

Learning how to build a nest plays an important part in the breeding success of birds. For example, Dr. Snow has recorded the success of a number of blackbirds for several years. He finds that birds nesting for the first time are less successful in breeding than are older birds, and also less successful than they themselves are a year later. This cannot be a mere matter of size and strength, since blackbirds, like the great majority of birds, are fully grown when they leave the nest. It is difficult to avoid the conclusion that they benefit from their nesting experience.

Q. **What will be followed after this passage?**
(a) Blackbirds build better nests than other birds.
(b) The breeding success of birds nesting for the second time is not greater than that of birds nesting for the first time.
(c) Smaller and weaker blackbirds breed just as successfully as bigger and stronger blackbirds.
(d) Up to 30 percent of all birds are killed by predators before they start to nest.

2.

In ecosystems, causes and effects are often widely separated in both time and space. Accordingly, our interventions often yield unexpected consequences. After years of persistent of spraying pesticides to kill insects, we find that we have come close to wiping out the bald eagle: concentrated through food chains, pesticides accumulate in the tissues of eagles and certain other birds to the point of impairing reproduction. When we intervene in a complex system so as to produce a certain desired effect, we always get in addition some other effects, usually ones not desired.

Q. **What is the passage mainly about?**
(a) Interdependence in ecosystems
(b) Side effects of human interventions on ecosystems
(c) Complexity of ecosystems
(d) The great web of ecosystems

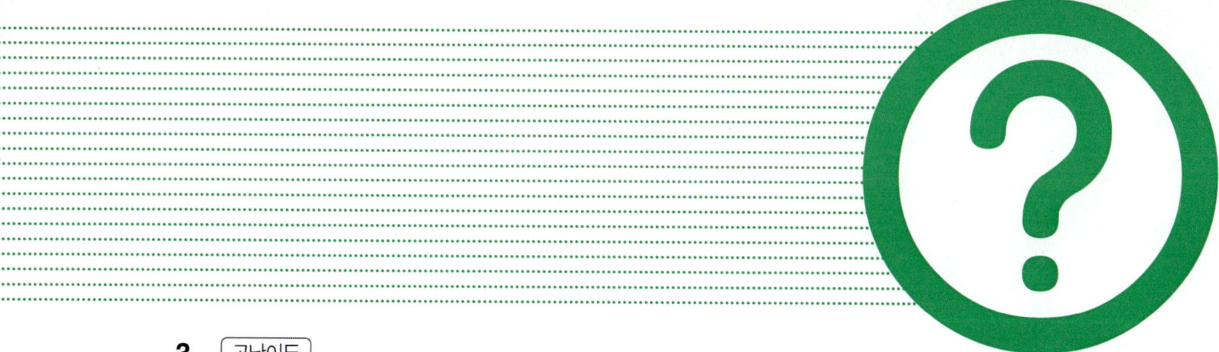

3. 고난이도

Turtles are reptiles of the order testudines most of whose body is shielded by a special bone or cartilaginous shell developed from their ribs. The order testudines includes both extant and extinct species. The earliest known turtles date from 215 million years ago, making turtles one of the oldest reptile groups and a more ancient group than lizards and snakes. About 300 species are alive today, and some are highly endangered. Turtles cannot breathe in water, but they can hold their breath for various periods of time. And although many species live in or around water they breathe air and don't lay eggs underwater.

Q. Which is correct according to the passage?

(a) Turtles usually breath in water.
(b) Turtles' bodies are covered with a special bone or shell evolved from its ribs.
(c) Turtles are the oldest reptile group.
(d) The order testudines includes only living species.

Section Switch

☐ **blackbird** 찌르레기
☐ **breed** 번식하다
☐ **predator** 약탈자, 포식자
☐ **consequence** 결과
☐ **persistent** (화학 약품) 분해하기 어려운
☐ **impair** 해치다 손상시키다
☐ **reproduction** 번식
☐ **reptile** 파충류
☐ **order testudines** 거북목 (order는 '질서, 명령' 의 의미로 쓰이지만 생물학적 분류로서 '목' 의 의미도 있다.)
☐ **cartilaginous** 연골성의
☐ **rib** 늑골
☐ **extant** 현존하는

Chapter 24

교육

STEP 1 Theme Best

출제 경향 파악

교육 분야는 주로 대학을 중심으로 한 교육 일선의 문제를 비롯해서, 시험과 개혁의 문제까지 폭넓게 다루고 있다. 이 분야에서는 최근 TEPS에서 다음과 같은 내용들이 출제되었고, 또한 출제될 것이다.

1. 대학 교육 일반
2. 시험 - 종류 / 준비 / 학점
3. 대학 교수 - 강의 / 테뉴어
4. 교육의 개혁 - 공교육의 개혁

Sample

The new direction in learning sharply contrasts with the way we still go about things today. For example, education now stresses process over measurement. The notion of collecting, storing, and exploiting blocks of isolated facts is being replaced by the idea of examining the flow of interconnected phenomena. Testing is being focused on conceptual abilities over empirical ones. Essays, oral discourse, and imaginative experiences will be the standard forms reflecting the need to think in terms of process. The external world will be examined not as a series of isolated casual relationships, but as a web of interrelated phenomena expressing many possibilities for movement and change.

Translation

학문에 있어 새로운 방향은 우리가 현재 나아가고 있는 방법과는 반대의 것이다. 예를 들면, 교육은 현재 평가보다 과정을 강조한다. 따로따로 분리된 사실을 수집해서 축적하고 개발해 간다는 생각은 서로 관련이 있는 현상의 흐름을 조사한다는 생각으로 바뀌고 있다. 시험에서는 실험적인 능력보다도 개념적인 능력을 보는 것에 초점이 맞춰지고 있다. 논문, 강의, 그리고 창의적인 체험은 과정이란 관점에서 생각해야 할 필요성을 반영하는 표준적인 형식일 것이다. 외부 세계는 우연히 발생하는 일련의 독립된 관계가 아니고, 이동하거나 변화하거나 하는 많은 가능성을 나타내는, 거미줄처럼 서로 얽혀 있는 여러 현상들로서 탐구될 것이다.

Words

exploit 이용하다
in terms of ~의 관점에서

테마별 주요 표현 BEST

1. alumnus _______________
2. academic standing _______________
3. assignment _______________
4. curve _______________
5. dean _______________
6. diploma _______________
7. enrollment _______________
8. lifelong education _______________
9. straight scale _______________
10. syllabus _______________

Answers

1. 졸업생, 동창생
2. 학업 성적
3. 과제
4. 상대 평가
5. 학장
6. 졸업장, 졸업 증서, 학위, 수여증
7. 등록, 입학
8. 평생 교육
9. 절대 평가
10. 강의 요강

1.

The highlight of each set of extension activities is a short video-based lesson centered on a stimulating, authentic clip from the CNN video archives. Each video lesson follows the same sequence of activities. Before You Watch encourages students to recall background knowledge based on their own experiences or from information presented in the readings. As You Watch asks students to watch for general information such as the topic of the clip. After You Watch gets the students to expand on the main points of the video by establishing further connections to the reading passages, their own experiences, and their ideas and opinions.

Q. **Which is correct according to the passage?**
(a) The students learn more open-ended contexts in After You Watch.
(b) Before You Watch reminds the students of background knowledge derived their own life.
(c) As You Watch enables the students to develop critical reading skills.
(d) All of the activities involve watching the CNN video clip.

2. Read the passage. Then identify the option that does NOT belong.

It is generally accepted that the experiences of a child in his first year largely determine his character and later personality. (a) Every experience teaches the child something and the effects are cumulative. "Upbringing" is normally used to refer to the treatment and training of the child within the home. (b) The ideals and practices of child rearing vary from culture to culture. (c) This is closely related to the treatment and training of the child in his school, which is usually distinguished by the term "education." (d) In a society such as ours, both parents and teachers are responsible for the opportunities provided for the development of the child, so that upbringing and education are interdependent.

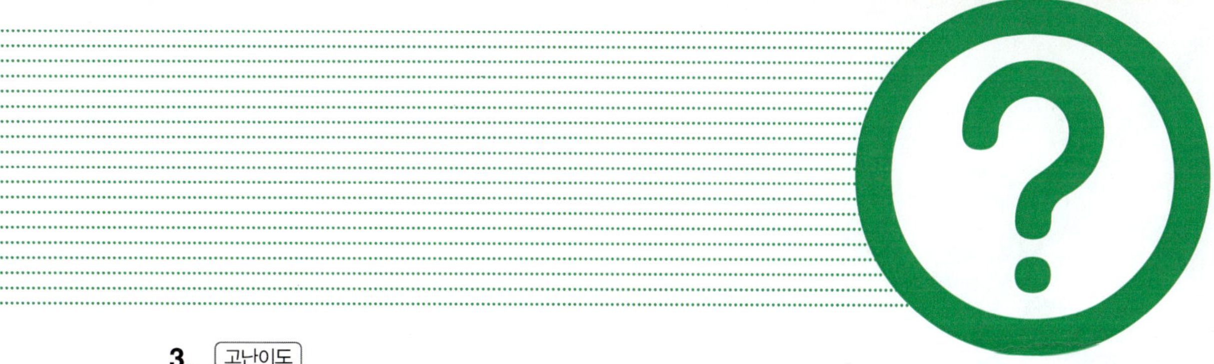

3. 〔고난이도〕

There are two main reasons why I have decided to attend Bingston University next year. First of all, there is the question of money: Bingston's tuition is reasonable, and I don't even have to pay it all at once. This is very important, since my father is not a rich man. With Bingston's "deferred payment plan," my father will be able to pay tuition without too much difficulty. The second reason is the fine education which I feel I will receive there in agriculture, my chosen field. It is a well-known fact that Bingston hires only the finest professors for its Agriculture Department. Moreover, the university requires all students of agriculture to gain practical experience by working on farms in the area while they are still going to school.

Q. **What is the main idea of the passage?**
(a) Better education in Bingston University
(b) Reasons for attending Bingston University
(c) Invaluable experience in Bingston University
(d) Bingston's deferred payment plan

Section Switch 

☐ **highlight** 중요한 부분
☐ **stimulating** 자극적인, 격려하는
☐ **authentic** 확실한, 진짜의
☐ **archive** 보관소
☐ **sequence** 절차, 순서
☐ **recall** 상기하다
☐ **determine** 결정하다
☐ **cumulative** 누적되는
☐ **upbringing** 양육
☐ **interdependent** 서로 의존하는
☐ **tuition** 수업료
☐ **reasonable** (가격이) 적당한, 비싸지 않은
☐ **deferred payment plan** 등록금 후불 제도
☐ **agriculture** 농업

STEP 1 Theme Best

출제 경향 파악

생활 문화 분야는 사는 곳, 먹는 것, 입는 것 등의 의식주 문제에서 출발해서 어떻게 하면 잘 사는 것인가를 고민하는 웰빙의 문제까지 출제가 된다. 이 분야에서는 최근 TEPS에서 다음과 같은 내용들이 출제되었고, 또한 출제될 것이다.

1. 웰빙 - 건강한 먹거리
2. 먹는 것(음식)
3. 입는 것(의복)
4. 사는 것(주거)
5. 여가 - 적당한 운동 / 명상 / 오락 / 휴식

Sample

Most human beings crave the warmth and security of belonging to a group. We usually join a group because we want the comfort of feeling "at home" among others whose life style, values, and interests are similar to our own. Some people have a strong need to define themselves as insiders, "we" as opposed to the outsiders, "they" whose life style, values, and interests are different. There are individuals who feel no need for identification with any group. They often discover, however, that society has made this identification for them. With or without their consent, they are classified as soldiers, taxpayers, Jews, the underprivileged, or whatever other category, benevolent or malevolent, their society or its government finds useful.

Translation

대부분의 인간은 집단에 속했을 때 느끼는 따스함과 안정감을 갈구한다. 대체로 우리는 생활 방식과 가치와 관심이 자신과 비슷한 타인들 속에서 느끼는 '평온함'이라고 하는 안락함을 원하기 때문에 집단에 참여한다. 생활 방식과 가치와 관심이 다른 외부인, 즉 '그들'에 대비하여, 자신들을 내부사람, 즉 "우리"로 규정하는 강력한 필요를 느끼는 사람들도 있다. 반면, 어떤 집단과도 동일화의 필요성을 느끼지 않는 사람들도 있다. 그러나 그들은 흔히 사회가 자신들을 대신해서 이 동일화를 이룩해버린 것을 발견한다. 그들의 동의 여부와 관계없이 그들은 군인, 납세자, 유태인, 빈곤층으로 분류되거나 아니면 호의든 악의든 그들의 사회나 정부가 유용하다고 판단하는 어떤 다른 범주로 분류된다.

Words

crave 간절히 바라다
as opposed to ~에 대립하는
identification 동일시, 동일화
the underprivileged 빈곤층, 최하층

테마별 주요 표현 BEST

1. amusement _______________
2. banquet _______________
3. cater _______________
4. entertain _______________
5. pastime _______________
6. recreation _______________
7. refresh _______________
8. relaxation _______________
9. stroll _______________
10. brunch _______________

Answers

1. 즐거움; 오락
2. 공적인 연회
3. 음식물을 제공하다, 충족시키다
4. 즐겁게 하다
5. 오락, 소일거리
6. 오락, 기분 전환
7. 원기를 회복시키다
8. 휴식, 기분 전환
9. 산책; 산책하다
10. 아침 겸 점심

1.

When we receive our wages, salaries or fees, we may feel content, for we are receiving what we have worked hard for. However, a windfall, money that ______________, puts a big smile on our faces.

Q. Choose the option that best completes the passage.

(a) is gained by hard work
(b) we deserve
(c) comes from overtime work
(d) we have not earned

2.

Organic foods are produced according to certain production standards, meaning that they were grown without the use of conventional pesticides, artificial fertilizers, human waste, or sewage sludge, and that they were processed without ionizing radiation or food additives. For animals, it means they were reared without the routine use of antibiotics and without the use of growth hormones. In most countries, organic produce must not be genetically modified. Organic food production is legally regulated. Currently, the United States, the European Union, Japan and many other countries require producers to obtain organic certification in order to market food as organic.

Q. What is the purpose of the passage?

(a) To warn
(b) To explain
(c) To advertise
(d) To suggest

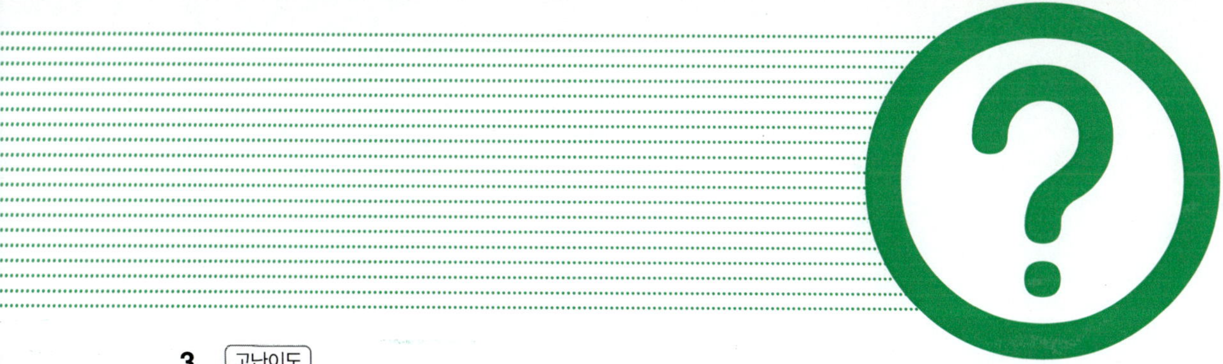

3. 고난이도

Although I never planned on a career as a writer or publisher, much of my job in marketing has depended on good writing and creative layout skills. My part-time college job with a newspaper taught me a lot about desktop publishing, how to position something on a page effectively, and how to write short sentences with maximum impact. In all of my marketing jobs, I've been able to explain my goals clearly to graphic designers, which has helped me avoid costly design revisions. These technical skills have now become my important assets.

Q. **What is the tone of this passage?**
(a) Positive
(b) Decisive
(c) Solemn
(d) Confident

Section Switch 

☐ **wage** 급료
☐ **content** 만족한
☐ **windfall** 뜻밖의 횡재
☐ **deserve** ~할 만하다
☐ **organic food** 유기농 식품
☐ **conventional** 전통적인, 재래식의
☐ **pesticides** 살충제
☐ **artificial** 인공적인
☐ **sewage** 하수
☐ **sludge** 침전물
☐ **ionizing radiation** 전리 방사선
☐ **antibiotics** 항생제
☐ **certification** 증명서
☐ **layout** (신문, 광고 등의) 지면 배치
☐ **maximum impact** 최대의 효과
☐ **costly design revisions** 돈이 많이 드는 디자인 수정
☐ **asset** 자산
☐ **solemn** 엄숙한

Final Test

파이널 테스트 1

파이널 테스트 2

Final Test 1

1-16. Read the passage. Then choose the option that best completes the passage.

1. In a time-honored practice in South Korea's corporate culture, the 38-year-old manager at an online game company took his 10-person team on twice-weekly after-work drinking bouts. He exhorted his subordinates to drink, including a 29-year-old graphic designer who protested that her limit was two glasses of beer. "Either you drink or ____________," the boss told her one evening. She drank, fearing that refusing to do so would hurt her career. But eventually, unable to take the drinking any longer, she quit and sued.

    (a) I will appreciate your fever
    (b) you would be punished
    (c) you will be raised
    (d) I can not lay you off

2. The Japanese researchers have backed their argument by inserting Einstein's equation, $E=mc^2$, into the DNA of the bacterium Bacillus subtilis(a kind of bacteria). Yoshiaki Ohashi, a molecular biologist at the Institute for Advanced Biosciences at Keio University, chose to work with the hardy Bacillus subtilis, a harmless soil bacterium that forms spores resistant to ultraviolet light, dehydration, oxygen and nutrient starvation, and organic solvents. He selected the relativity equation because it is "one of the most important legacies" of the 20th century, although, he adds, "we are not fanatic admirers of ____________.

    (a) Dr. Einstein
    (b) Bacillus subtilis
    (c) data-storage
    (d) genome

3. People are very paranoid these days about identify theft, and they have good reason. Tactics including computer hacking, paying off dishonest sales clerks, dumpster diving, and mail theft have turned up a gold mine for thieves of social security numbers and credit card applications. A good reason to buy a paper shredder or obtain a post office box! You have to be very careful to guard your privacy because identity theft can take months or even years to _____________!

(a) figure out
(b) straighten out
(c) phase out
(d) sweep out

4. UCLA psychologist Matthew Lieberman and his colleagues hooked 30 people up to functional magnetic resonance imaging (fMRI) machines, which scan the brain to reveal which parts are active and inactive at any given moment. They asked the subjects to look at pictures of male or female faces making emotional expressions. Below some of the photos was a choice of words describing the emotion — such as "angry" or "fearful" — or two possible names for the people in the pictures, one male name and one female name. Do you have a really bad memory, or past heartache, that you would prefer to forget? Researchers at Harvard and McGill University (in Montreal) are working on a(n) _____________ that blocks or deletes bad memories. The technique seems to allow psychiatrists to enlarge the biochemical pathways that allow a memory to be recalled.

(a) amnesia drug
(b) insomnia pill
(c) articular neuralgia drug
(d) headache drug

5. Too many people focus just on calories and not the _______________ of the food they eat. The nutrients in food have a direct effect on the endocrine system, which differently governs the human body. The endocrine system will respond regular consumption of healthy food or heavily processed food. The healthier the diet the faster results of exercise will be seen.

(a) ingredients
(b) weight
(c) dose
(d) source of the calories

6. In the old days humans had little power over nature. The only available devices for obtaining mechanical energy were clockwork, water-wheels and windmills. All transport was by foot or by horse, and all water transport by rowing or sailing. Men were constantly _______________ seasonal food shortages and were periodically decimated by epidemics, whose causes they did not understand and which they had no rational means of combating.

(a) driven to
(b) at the mercy of
(c) in the hand of
(d) on the lookout for

7. Man must be the most aggressive and cruel of all living creatures. If we say a violent man is behaving "like a beast," we are slandering animals, for no beast behaves as violently as man. When a territorial animal or bird encroaches upon the territory of another creature of the same species, the latter will only perform ritual gestures of hostility to warn off the intruder. Nevertheless neither creature will be badly hurt, for the loser will save himself by making a gesture of submission. Normally one animal will only kill another for food, and _______________ an animal kill a member of its own species.

(a) rarely does
(b) in the customary way
(c) otherwise
(d) no more aggressively

8. There is no other species on Earth that does science. Science is not perfect, and can certainly be misused. It is only a tool, but it is by far the best tool we have, self-correcting, and applicable to everything. It has two rules. First, there are no sacred truths: all assumptions must be critically examined; arguments from authority are worthless. Second, whatever is inconsistent with the facts must be discarded or revised. We must understand the cosmos as it is and not confuse how it is with how we wish it to be. _______________; the unexpected is sometimes true.

(a) The false is always expected
(b) What is done cannot be undone
(c) The obvious is sometimes false
(d) The truth is not always convincing

9. For a very long time dowsing has been looked upon by many people with skepticism and suspicion, or simply designated under the label of the supernatural defying logical explanation. Both these viewpoints _______________ what is now becoming appreciated as a skill, although a paranormal skill, but one which is not beyond the grasp of the common man.

(a) make allowances for
(b) take it for granted
(c) do little justice to
(d) keep track of

10. In 1847, Michael Moore, a poverty-stricken seventeen-year old farm worker, left Ireland for America. What the future held in store for him, he did not know. However, _______________. He had grown up during the Great Famine in Ireland and had known what it was to be very hungry. He had watched his mother die of typhus a month before; his father had died a year after Michael was born. There was nothing to keep him in Ireland, so, on a bright June morning, he stepped on board a ship bound for America.

(a) he did know that he was going to have a hard time
(b) he did know that it could not be worse than the past
(c) he did not know that it was to hold new hopes for him
(d) he did not know what he should do when he got there

11. Many people are worried about what TV has done to the generation of children who have grown up watching it. For one thing, recent studies tend to show that TV stifles creative imagination. Some teachers feel that TV has taken away the child's ability to form mental pictures in his own mind, resulting in children who can't understand a simple story without visual illustrations. Secondly, too much TV too early tends to cause children to withdraw from real-life experiences. Thus, they grow up to be passive spectators who ______________, but not initiate it.

(a) can only respond to action
(b) merely look on life
(c) are willing to participate in action
(d) act as they are told to

12. One of the spin-off effects of the constitutional settlement of the seventeenth century was that it gave increased prominence to the workings of parliament. Today, we think of statutes as creatures of parliament. The rhetorical formula we use when we speak of an enactment is that it was passed by the Queen in parliament, but for all intents and purposes, the Royal role is just a formal, rubber-stamping one. ______________, though, statutes were simply a decree, the term derived from the Latin statuere : to set up ; to command.

(a) Eventually
(b) Originally
(c) As a result
(d) Conveniently

13. Dennis Hope, self-proclaimed Head Cheese of the Lunar Embassy, will promise you the moon. Or at least a piece of it. Since 1980, Hope has raked in over $9 million selling acres of lunar real estate for $19.99 a pop. So far, 4.25 million people have purchased a piece of the moon, _______________ celebrities like Barbara Walters, George Lucas, Ronald Reagan, and even the first President Bush. Hope says he exploited a loophole in the 1967 United Nations Outer Space Treaty, which prohibits nations from owning the moon.

(a) containing
(b) embracing
(c) including
(d) excluding

14. The gulf region is about to enter a particularly delicate period, when the Arabian Peninsula creates huge sandstorms that blow southward. This year's storms could suck up soot from the oil fires and large amounts of dirt loosened by explosions. Intensified by heat from the fires, the storms could spread a mist of soot and oil across a belt of countries, ranging from Saudi Arabia to India. _______________ posing a health threat to the people closest to ground zero, the pollution is likely to harm wildlife, agriculture and fisheries. At worst, fallout from the oil fires may disrupt the region's annual monsoon rains.

(a) Apart from
(b) Since
(c) At first sight
(d) In the end

15. Anthropology must be concerned with the accuracy of its data. Anthropology is unique among the sciences ______________ a human being is the major research instrument, and other human beings are supplying most of the data. At least in the initial stages of research anthropologists have to rely to a great extent on informants as well as observation for their data. Informants are people who have a deep knowledge of their own culture and are willing and able to pass this knowledge on to the anthropologist.

(a) even if
(b) for which
(c) as to
(d) in that

16. One of the most serious complaints frequently made by elementary school teachers is that children exhibit a low tolerance for the frustration of learning. ______________ they have been conditioned to see all problems resolved in 30 or 60 minutes on TV, they are quickly discouraged by any activity that promises less than instant gratification. But perhaps the most serious result is the impact of television violence on children, who have come to regard it as an everyday thing. Most experts now concede that under certain conditions, some children will imitate antisocial acts that they witness on TV.

(a) For
(b) Because
(c) Although
(d) Moreover

17-37. Read the passage and the question. Then choose the option that best answers the question.

17. Obviously, the first meaning of money lies in its power to buy satisfaction of basic physiological needs — food, clothing and shelter. Closely allied to these basic needs are certain acquired needs with a physiological basis, such as the need for tobacco. It is only after these fundamental drives have been relatively well satisfied that any major amount of money will be diverted towards other goods.

Q. **What is the above passage mainly about?**
(a) What money can buy
(b) Basic human needs
(c) How to spend money effectively
(d) Money for basic needs

18. Like the millions of Americans who regularly follow a vigorous exercise program, I know that working out makes me feel good. But there is an added enticement you may not be aware of : keeping healthy may save you insurance dollars as well. How can you trade a pound of flesh for an ounce of cash? First of all, you must be a standard risk: those with dangerous professions or hobbies are automatically disqualified. Beyond that, no physical exertion is actually required for the most basic premium discount: the nonsmoker's life insurance discount.

Q. **What is this passage mainly about?**
(a) Dangers of smoking
(b) Rewarding dangerous activities
(c) Insurance policy concerning fitness
(d) Insurance companies' physical fitness programs

19. There are simply hundreds of wines out there. They may be products of a great vintage, or may represent an undervalued category, an unsung region, an unheralded variety, or may be closeouts or downturn deals, but they're out there, and you should stock them. My idea is to define a dozen slots for can't-miss values, with a few options for each slot: six red, six white, all of them under $15, all of them reliable — not overreaching, just satisfying and honest. Let's start with the whites. It's springtime, so these selections are heavily weighted toward light, fresh, herbaceous wines, mostly devoid of oak and ready to complement a light spring meal.

Q. **What is the purpose of this passage?**
(a) To advertise
(b) To recommend
(c) To appreciate
(d) To criticize

20. The Contra Costa Transportation Authority, a public agency overseeing a county-wide two billion dollar Transportation Improvement and Growth Management Program, is currently seeking candidates to serve as Chief Financial Officer. We are looking for a qualified individual with extensive finance and administration management experience, preferably in the public sector. Candidates must have at least a BA degree with emphasis on public administration, business, finance and/or accounting, and a minimum of 7+ years' experience in public administration and finance that includes budget development and analysis, preparation of financial statements, management of investments, general ledger reconciliation, and working with auditors. If you meet the requirements and are interested in a challenging work experience, please send a cover letter and résumé to headhunter@contracosta.com

Q. **What's the purpose of the passage?**
(a) A resume
(b) PR of a Transportation Authority
(c) An application for employment
(d) A job offer

21. It was the start of the fiercest scientific debate about medical ethics since the birth of the first test-tube baby 15 year ago. Ethicists called up nightmare visions of baby farming. Policymakers pointed to the vacuum in U.S. bioethical leadership. Critics decried the commercialization of fertility technology, and outraged protesters took to the streets, calling for an immediate ban on human-embryo cloning. Indeed, the results of a TIME/CNN poll taken suggest that Americans find the idea of human cloning deeply troubling: 3 out of 4 disapprove.

Q. **What is the main topic of the article?**
(a) Public opinion of cloning for cannibalization
(b) Ethical rationale for cloning animals
(c) Political leadership versus ethical leadership
(d) Ethical issues in human cloning

22. I guess it is true that big and strong things are much less dangerous than small soft and weak things. The ones that did not reproduce before they died, disappeared. But how about little faults, little pains, little worries? The ulcer comes not from great concerns, but from little irritations. A man is destroyed by nagging, small bills, telephones, athlete's foot, ragweed, the common cold, and boredom. All of these are negatives, tiny frustrations and no one is stronger for them.

Q. **What is the best title for this passage?**
(a) Negative Things
(b) The Cause of Cosmic Ulcers
(c) The Danger of Small Things
(d) The Strength of Small Things

23. Street preaching is a manifestation of personal commitment to the sect; fulfillment of this commitment confers status within the group. The impassioned style of street preachers is highly deliberate. They know that people usually will not stop to listen to them. Consequently their style is designed to "sow the seeds" in the hope that those who have heard them may at some future time "turn to the Lord."

Q. **Choose the sentence that best summarizes the above passage.**
(a) Street preachers are motivated by a desire to get status within the sect.
(b) Street preaching is a self-imposed activity designed to demonstrate how religious these preachers are.
(c) Street preaching is a highly committed activity aimed at future converts.
(d) Indifference to people's reaction is characteristic of street preachers.

24. Boys who play video games on school days spend 30 percent less time reading and girls spend 34 percent less time doing homework than those who do not play such games, U.S. researchers said on Monday. But they said video games do not appear to interfere significantly with time spent with family and friends. "Gamers did spend less time reading and doing homework. But they didn't spend less time interacting with their parents or their friends, nor did they spend less time in sports or active leisure activities," said Hope Cummings of the University of Michigan. The study comes as U.S. doctors voice growing concern about the long-term effects of video games.

Q. **Which of the following is most likely to follow this passage?**
(a) The positive effects video games
(b) The negative effect of video games
(c) The social function of video games
(d) The spare time of gamers

25. In recent times, it has been increasingly the custom for advertisers to borrow the prestige of science and medicine to enhance the reputation of their products. The alleged approval of such men carries great weight when it is a question of selling something, or inducing someone to believe something. Phrases such as "leading medical authorities say ..." or "independent laboratory tests show ..." are designed to transfer the prestige of science to a toothpaste or cereal. These mere phrases can have strong persuasion on the uncritical.

Q. **Why is the tactic of using alleged approval of scientists successful?**
(a) Because much of the public is uncritical and credulous
(b) Because products allegedly endorsed by scientists are better than products that are not
(c) Because scientists make more attractive models than politicians
(d) Because scientists are more trustworthy than priests

26. Many smokers may secretly welcome the corporate crusade against smoking. Many of them embrace the new corporate activism as an incentive to give up tobacco once and for all. More and more companies that have imposed restrictions on smoking are attempting to help their employees kick the habit. Abbott Laboratories hires smokers but urges them to sign a pledge to take a company-sponsored workshop that teaches people how to stop smoking. Despite the changes taking place, antismoking lobbyists continue to press for stricter limitations on smoking in the workplace.

Q. **Which of the following seems to be the case with smokers?**
(a) Most smokers are annoyed by their companies' interference with their freedom to smoke.
(b) Most smokers would like to stop smoking and appreciate the help they can get toward shaking the habit.
(c) Most smokers are worried they may lose their jobs on account of their smoking.
(d) More and more smokers are pretending to be non-smokers.

27. Rock samples from Mars show they contain a lighter form, or "isotope," of silicate that is identical to those found in a primitive class of meteorites called chondrites. Scientists think chondrites are shed remnants of the original building blocks of planets that have fallen to Earth. Silicates are compounds made of silicon and oxygen mixed with other elements. Unlike Mars, the Earth's silicon has been divided into two sorts — a portion that became a light element in the Earth's core dissolved in metal and the greater proportion which formed the silicon-oxygen bonded silicate of the Earth's mantle and crust.

Q. **What couldn't be found on Mars?**
(a) Chondrite
(b) Asteroids
(c) A lighter form of silicates
(d) A heavy form of silicates

28. A women's rights movement developed after 1820, and brought about some changes. In 1833, the Oberlin Collegiate Institute opened as the first coeducational college in the United States. Some men's colleges soon began admitting women, and new colleges for women were built. In 1848, Lucretia Mott and Elizabeth Cady Stanton organized a Women's Rights Convention in Seneca Falls, N.Y. The convention issued the first formal appeal for woman suffrage (the right to vote). But nationwide suffrage did not come about until 1920.

Q. **Which of the following generalizations could the passage support ?**
(a) The Oberlin Collegiate Institute was the first college for women in the United states.
(b) After 1848, every woman could possess personal property.
(c) The struggle for women's rights took many years.
(d) Women got the right to vote nationwide soon after the Seneca Falls Convention.

29. Villagers in central China dug up a ton of dinosaur bones and boiled them in soup or ground them into powder for traditional medicine, believing they were from flying dragons and had healing powers. The calcium-rich bones were sometimes boiled with other ingredients and fed to children as a treatment for dizziness and leg cramps. Other times the people in the village ground them up and made a paste that was applied directly to fractures and other injuries. The practice had been going on for at least two decades.

Q. **Which of the following is correct according to the passage?**
(a) People made the dinosaur bones into a paste for medical purposes.
(b) People found the dinosaur bones and donate 200kg of the bones to a research center.
(c) People mistook dragon bones for dinosaur bones.
(d) The dinosaur bones were used for the treatment of dizziness in adults.

30. In nature, one creature devours another, and this is an essential part of existence. The Buddhist who refuses to take life is really ridiculous, since if he eats only two grains of rice per day, it is two grains of life. We did not make creation, we are not the authors of the universe. And if we see that the whole of creation is established upon the fact that one life devours another life, one cycle of existence can only come into existence through the subjugating of another cycle of existence, then what is the good of trying to pretend that it is not so? The only thing to do is to realize what is higher and what is lower in the cycles of existence.

Q. **Which statement is not true of the passage?**
(a) The author seems to believe in survival of the fittest.
(b) In existence life-species is the highest which can devour, destroy, or subjugate all other life-species which it is pitted against.
(c) The Buddhist who refuses to take life is ridiculous, because he cannot destroy any form of life.
(d) Our existence and vitality is derived from absorbing energy from living creatures lower than ourselves.

31. There are distinct advantages that the electronic criminal has over the ordinary thief. For one, computer embezzlers make much more money per crime than do other embezzlers. And the computer thief takes fewer risks. Anyone with a home computer can use a telephone hookup to gain access to a system. Such a person can make millions without ever leaving his living room. Another advantage is that they do not have to count on other criminals to unload the stolen goods. Since these criminals work alone, there are no accomplices to share profits with. Still another advantage for this criminal is that law enforcement agencies have few experts in computer crime. Therefore this is the heyday of the computer criminal.

Q. **Which of the following is not listed as an advantage of computer theft over other forms of crime?**
(a) There is less probability of being caught.
(b) The thief can steal more at a time.
(c) The thief does not require the assistance of an accomplice.
(d) Rehabilitation is assured.

32. Why do I want to buy a Volkswagen? I have priced costs about $1700 and that price includes everything I want on it. Once I have a Volkswagen, the cost of running it is very low. It gets thirty-two miles to a gallon and uses no antifreeze because it is air-cooled. The cost of insuring it is less than half of that of an American car. Repairs are much cheaper and the tires will last the life of the car if one rotates them and keeps them properly inflated. License plates are one-third the cost of a big car. These figures are facts, not fiction.

Q. **Which of the following statements does not appear in the passage as a reason to buy a Volkswagen?**
(a) With proper care, the tires will not have to be replaced.
(b) Getting an American car repaired will be more convenient and less expensive than having a Volkswagen fixed.
(c) The insurance on a Volkswagen is less than on an American car.
(d) The license fee for a large car is much more than for a Volkswagen.

33. Imagine a world in the not too distant future that teems with 17 billion people. The last of the rain forests have been sacrificed for grazing land. Fresh water is so scarce that millions die of thirst. Wars are fought to control not oil but fields of wheat. It would not take much time to trigger such an apocalypse. The world's population reached 5.6 billion in 1994, with 93 million added each year. Demographers predict that at current growth rates, the total could easily double by the year 2050. No country could shield itself from the resulting devastation.

Q. **Which is NOT predicted for the future in the passage?**
(a) Rain forests will be used for raising crops.
(b) The population will triple in the waning years of the 20th century.
(c) Millions of people will die from lack of fresh water.
(d) Wars will erupt over the control of food supplies.

34. Human hopes are always of two kinds. A human being has hopes for himself — hopes that are individual and personal. At the same time, he has superpersonal hopes for the human race or for some fraction of it: his tribe, his family, perhaps, or his church. These two kinds of human hope are not always sharply distinguishable from each other. Self-centeredness is so powerful a force that it invades even our superpersonal hopes. On the other hand, our personal hopes may take the form of a moral reaction against self-centeredness and of an effort to transcend it.

Q. **What can be inferred from the passage?**
(a) Our superpersonal hopes are not different from our personal hopes.
(b) Our superpersonal hopes delude us into evil actions.
(c) A person who has superpersonal hopes can behave selfishly without a moral reaction against self-centeredness.
(d) Our superpersonal hopes are a collective counterpart of egotism.

35. Reagan's act of candor will raise public awareness of Alzheimer's in America and give support for research a powerful boost. In that way, he will walk in distinguished company once again. Dwight Eisenhower's frankness about his heart disease changed the way the world treated this affliction. The publicized bouts of Betty Ford and Nancy Reagan with breast cancer led thousands of women to undergo mammograms.

Q. **What can be inferred from the passage?**
(a) Reagan disclosed his disease because many other famous people are afflicted with it.
(b) Reagan's disclosure of his disease will benefit the public through the stimulating of research on the disease.
(c) The American public is indifferent to health threats unless some famous politician is afflicted with it.
(d) Americans regard Reagan as a weakling for disclosing his illness to win public sympathy.

36. A few years ago, the notion of an international Record Store Day might've felt more like a funeral than a celebration of the impact independent stores have had on music. As distribution of recorded music shifted into the Internet arena, Tower Records and hundreds of other music retailers nationwide went belly up. But when the second annual Record Store Day arrives Saturday, artists and labels will be out in force. Though the number of independent record stores has shrunk drastically in recent years, those that remain are hanging tough, and some are thriving despite a sluggish economy. A resurgence in interest in vinyl records has helped these independent operators stay in business.

Q. **Which is the following can be inferred from the report?**
(a) Until recently interest in Vinyl records had almost disappear.
(b) Artwork and artifacts have been reinvigorated by the Internet.
(c) Independent record stores are trying to run their business online.
(d) More and more of the Internet-generation is becoming interested in old-fashioned music.

37. Mythology confronts the student with a situation which at first sight could be looked upon as contradictory. On the one hand, it would seem that in the course of a myth anything is likely to happen. There is no logic, no continuity. With myth, everything become possible. But on the other hand, this apparent arbitrariness is belied by the astounding similarity between myths collected in widely different regions. Therefore the problem: if the content of a myth is contingent, how are we going to explain that throughout the world myths do resemble one another so much?

Q. **How does the writer view myths?**
(a) They are illogical.
(b) They have an inherent structure.
(c) They are not an integral part of culture.
(d) They are primitive.

38-40. Read the passage. Then identify the option that does NOT belong.

38. A prime example of the extravagance some ancient Chinese emperors enjoyed can be found in the outrageous lifestyle of Hu, the Tiger, who lived in the Age of Division. (a) He reminds us of Jabba the Hut in *Star Wars* who was extremely unattractive and grossly overweight. (b) He was so fat that it took twenty men to carry his litter to the royal hunt. (c) His main concern was the well-being of his people. (d) He had a revolving couch built so that men might spin it around to allow him to shoot in any direction.

39. By the middle of the 1700's, newspapers had grown in size and variety. (a) Previously all advertisements had been placed at the back of the newspaper. (b) But now some appeared toward the front. (c) Their publishers resisted advertising in their pages until the need for additional money became great. (d) In 1784, the first newspaper to become a daily became one largely because it had so much advertising.

40. It is perfectly clear that the extremists of the right and of the left share many of the same personality maladjustments commonly found among neurotics. (a) But what is missing in the whole concept of political personality is a soundly conceived theory of politics. (b) Neurotic personalities will be attracted to extremist political movements such as the fascists and the communists. (c) The factors which influence these specific political choices are the social and intellectual characteristics of the individual. (d) What is not explained, however, is why some neurotics turn to extremist political movements for a solution to their inner conflicts while others take to drink, sexual promiscuity, and the divorce circuit.

Final Test 2

1-16. Read the passage. Then choose the option that best completes the passage.

1. The publication of "very Thai," a unique guide to Thai pop and folk culture, coincides with the country's biggest debate about national identity in more than half a century. In the World War II era, the military Phibunsongkharm regime rallied under the slogan "Thailand for the Thais." Today, the country seems mesmerized again by _______________. Schools and colleges have been ordered by the Ministry of Education to display the flag more prominently and play the national anthem at a higher volume. "Thai-ness" is once again a useful political concept.

   (a) euphemism
   (b) liberalism
   (c) nationalism
   (d) republicanism

2. If you name your emotions, you can tame them, according to new research that suggests why meditation works. Brain scans show that putting negative emotions into words calms the brain's emotion center. That could explain meditation's purported emotional benefits, because people who meditate often label their negative emotions in an effort to "_______________". Psychologists have long believed that people who talk about their feelings have more control over them, but they don't know why it works.

   (a) let it be
   (b) let it go
   (c) let's do it
   (d) let me do it

3. Although the term blue oceans is new, ______________. They are a feature of business life, past and present. Look back one hundred years and ask yourself; how many of today's industries were then unknown? The answer: many industries as basic as automobiles, music recording, aviation, petro-chemicals, health care, and management consulting were unheard of or had just begun to emerge at that time. Now turn the clock back only thirty years. Again a plethora of multi-billion dollar industries jumps outs — mutual funds, cell phones, gas-fired electricity plants, biotechnology, discount retail, express package delivery, minivans, snowboards, coffee bars, and home videos, to name a few. Just three decades ago none of these industries existed in a meaningful way.

(a) their existence is not
(b) their true being turns red ones
(c) their "counter-examples" avail
(d) their origin is simple

4. Pepsi released two new cola products in the U.S. market ______________ instead of high-fructose corn syrup last week. Pepsi Natural comes in a 12-ounce glass bottle and features sparkling water, sugar, apple and kola extracts. Pepsi Throwbacks serves up the old, real-sugar formula of the Pepsi we knew in the '70s, before high-fructose corn syrup flooded the U.S. soft drink market. Ostensibly, Pepsi produced the new drinks to appeal to natural-food fans and those with nostalgia for the old Pepsi formula. They didn't do it because they think there's anything wrong with high-fructose corn syrup, Pepsi says. Of course not. But, whatever the reason, we're happy to see real sugar being used in some Pepsi again.

(a) using real sugar
(b) featuring natural soda
(c) hiding original recipe
(d) which were highly antcipated

5. People suffering from chronic low back pain who received acupuncture treatments fared better than those receiving only conventional care, according to a recent study. Interestingly, the study also showed that people receiving ______________ — toothpicks were inserted instead of needles — also fared better than those receiving conventional care. "This adds to the growing body of evidence that there is something meaningful taking place during acupuncture treatments outside of actual needling," said Dr. Josephine P. Briggs, director of the National Center for Alternative Medicine. "Future research is needed to delve deeper into what is evoking these responses."

(a) single prescription for acupuncture points
(b) standardized acupuncture
(c) standard medical care
(d) simulated acupuncture

6. Leisure is indeed an affair of mood and atmosphere rather than simply of the clock. It is not a chronological occurrence but a spiritual state. It is unhurried pleasurable living among one's native enthusiasms. Leisure consists of those pauses in our lives when experience is a fusion of stimulation and repose. Genuine leisure yields at once a feeling of vividness and a sense of peace. It consists of moments so clear and pleasant in themselves that one might wish they were ______________.

(a) real
(b) pleasurable
(c) spiritual
(d) eternal

7. Unless more of us become environmentally active, both as individuals and in organized groups, the Environmental Revolution will not succeed. Success depends on overcoming human inertia and some of the structural impediments of society. The behaviour of corporate leaders is shaped by the pressures of short-term profit-making. Politicians are influenced by short-term reelection concerns and by special interest groups. But environmental groups can take the long view, _______________.

(a) speaking for the majority
(b) patiently waiting for change to happen
(c) speaking for the future generations
(d) securing in the knowledge that they will win in the end

8. Competition can be a cause of unethical business practices. Some firms slip into questionable business practices as a way to _______________ competitors, who may in turn have established their dominant market position by using under-the-table practices to attract and retain large numbers of important customers. Companies on the edge of bankruptcy may employ dubious means to get or keep customers whose business can make the difference between survival and financial failure.

(a) keep pace with
(b) give rise to
(c) get along with
(d) keep tabs on

9. Because of the medical links between smoking and such major killers as heart disease and lung cancer, insurance companies have been rewarding nonsmokers with lower rates for twenty years. Today four out of five life insurance companies offer discounts averaging from 10 to 15 percent. Others — such as the Metroplitan Life Insurance Company, the country's second-largest insurer — reserve their best rate for those who ______________. Smokers are automatically disqualified.

(a) are blue-collar workers
(b) are involved in policy-making processes
(c) have long been their criteria
(d) meet certain health criteria

10. The amount of computer crime is increasing rapidly. Because losses to computer crime amount to billions of dollars yearly, industries are ______________ who used computers to commit theft. The big companies are eager to have the services of these experts, who are able to penetrate computer systems. The very people who know how to enter the system can better prevent others from doing so. Computer criminals, who are able to penetrate computer systems, can be rehabilitated and gainfully employed because their skills are so much in demand. Ironically, they become successful businessmen and consultants.

(a) contracting IT professionals
(b) hiring former thieves
(c) arresting hackers
(d) investigating former hackers

11. Researchers duplicate a human embryo, provoking cries that ______________. The news that human embryos had been cloned flew around the world with the speed of sound bites bouncing off satellites. That afternoon the switch-board at George Washington logged 250 calls from the press. By the next day more calls and faxes were flooding in from as far as Spain, South Africa and Australia. The Vatican's L'Osservators Romano warned on a front-page editorial that such procedures could lead humanity down "a tunnel of madness."

(a) politicians have passed the buck
(b) medical doctors have fallen behind
(c) science has come a long way
(d) technology has gone too far

12. Back in the 1970s, medical researchers were debating whether humanity's victory against infectious disease was ______________. The polio virus had been tamed by the Salk and Sabin vaccines; the smallpox virus was virtually gone; the parasite that causes malaria was in retreat; once deadly illnesses, including diphtheria, pertussis and tetanus, seemed like quaint reminders of a bygone era, like silent movies.

(a) a huge contribution to medical history
(b) a matter of time
(c) a mere inconvenience
(d) a coincidence

13. It is not certain yet that Prime Minister Andreotti has been involved in large embezzlement schemes, but there is overwhelming proof that he has systematically promoted the career of politicians whose ties with the mafia were notorious; he cannot escape the charges of abuse of public office. While his legal crimes are yet to be proved, what is beyond question at the moment is his ______________.

(a) connection with the mafia
(b) political ineptitude
(c) loss of public trust
(d) moral and political responsibility

14. Of the countries where English is primarily a second language, South Africa has the largest number of people who speak English as their first language-over 1,800,000. At the time of writing there are eleven official languages: English and Afrikaans, a language related to Dutch, and nine African languages. Dutch settlements began in the Cape in 1652 and were well established ______________ the British arrived in 1795 and then annexed the Cape in 1814. Many of the Dutch-speaking Boers soon moved away to establish their own republics, but after two wars won by the British the Boer republics were absorbed in the Union of South Africa in 1910 as a dominion of the British Empire.

(a) where
(b) when
(c) what
(d) who

15. Experience should also include knowledge of State and Federal funding regulations and practices, implementation of GASB financial statements, and analysis of public finance documents related to public debt issuance and investments. Proficiency with standard computer spreadsheet, word processing and Internet software, ______________ excellent organizational, communication (verbal and written) and presentation skills are a must. We offer a professional work environment and an excellent benefit package.

(a) so far as
(b) along with
(c) then
(d) as far as

16. In order to dare to venture out into the world an adolescent needs to feel that the home of his childhood is still unconditionally his, very much in the same way as the toddler needs to hold on to mother's apron strings or later on to a teddy bear in order to feel safe when venturing beyond his bed. ______________ the young child needs a physical object to hold on to, the adolescent needs the ready availability of the safety of home.

(a) Though
(b) When
(c) However
(d) So

17-37. Read the passage and the question. Then choose the option that best answers the question.

17. Studies have revealed that people react in different ways to different colors. For example, humans tend to become more excited when exposed to red light and more passive with blue light. Interestingly, pink, which is closer to red than to blue, seems to be the most soothing color of all. This finding has implications for interior decorators, particularly those charged with deciding which colors to paint the walls of hospitals and prisons.

Q. **What is this passage mainly about?**
(a) Different meanings of different colors
(b) The effects of colors on emotions
(c) The relationship between colors and ways of life
(d) The significance of color in hospitals and prisons

18. In understanding the relationship between what Americans believe and how they live, it is important to distinguish between idealism and reality. American values such as equality of opportunity and self-reliance are ideals that may not necessarily describe the facts of American life. Equality of opportunity, for example, is an ideal that is not always put into practice. In reality, some people have a better chance for success than others. Those who are born into rich families have more opportunities than those who are born into poorer families. Many black Americans have fewer opportunities than the average white American, in spite of laws designed to promote equality of opportunity for all races.

Q. **What is the passage mainly about?**
(a) The discrepancy between American idealism and reality
(b) American values
(c) The inequality of opportunity in American society
(d) The disadvantages of black Americans

19. As a global company, Nature Publishing Group (NPG) offers career opportunities around the world; in addition to our principal locations in London, New York and Tokyo, we have offices in cities around the world. As we continue to develop and expand our portfolio, job opportunities arise in all departments, including editorial, production and design, sales, marketing, advertising, IT, web publishing, business development, and administration. To view and apply for current vacancies, visit the web-site. NPG employees enjoy competitive compensation and benefits, and most importantly the satisfaction of working in a culture where talent is nurtured and achievements are recognized and rewarded.

Q. **What is the purpose of this passage?**
(a) To recommend
(b) To announce
(c) To advertise
(d) To recruit

20. For a long time parliament remained purely an advisory body, and the king was under no obligation to summon it on a regular basis. It was not until 1414, during the reign of King Henry V that the Crown formally acknowledged that no new statutes should be made without the assent of the commons. This incongruity of an increase in parliament's influence during the reign of a strong king was repeated during the time of Henry VIII. Henry's solution was to split with Church in Rome and establish a Church of England, with himself at the head. But in order to secure the cooperation of the important people of the realm in the Reformation — which to ordinary folk must have seemed a cataclysmic event — Henry had to involve parliament in his decision-making process a good deal more than his predecessors had done.

Q. **What's the most appropriate title of the passage?**
(a) Powerful monarchs in English history
(b) The changing roles of English parliament
(c) The history of Henry VIII
(d) The Reformation and parliament

21. Early results of wildlife testing on California's Central Coast have found that only a tiny fraction of the 866 animals sampled carried the virulent bacteria that contaminated spinach in a deadly 2006 outbreak. State wildlife officials are hoping the results will take the bull's-eye off deer and other wild animals. Central Coast growers declared war on wildlife in their fields after the outbreak, which was linked to cattle and wild pigs on a ranch east of Salinas. They shot deer, poisoned ponds to get rid of frogs and tore out trees and bushes. If wholesalers found evidence that deer had been in a field, they wouldn't buy the crop. But of the 311 samples collected from black-tailed deer, none came back positive for the bacterium. "Wildlife are not the Typhoid Marys some people think they are," said state wildlife biologist Terry Palmisano.

Q. **Which of the following is the best title of this passage?**
(a) The ranchers' methods of coping with wildlife
(b) The after-effect of the 2006 outbreak
(c) The problem of current wildlife testing
(d) The baseless blaming of wildlife

22. In order to make his survey, the philosopher must remain a spectator, taking no part in the action; he must, like the spectator at the games, watch them outside the arena. But the objective judgment which the philosopher's contemplation of the scene calls for is not to be induced by spatial distance alone. Temporal distance is equally essential; time in which to retreat from and consider the events, so that he may appreciate the passions which possess men in life, and perceive the motives.

Q. **What is the best title for this passage?**
(a) A survey of phenomena
(b) The philosopher's arena
(c) Spatial and temporal distance
(d) The philosopher's attitude

23. While initial fears that the fires might disrupt the global climate by causing a "nuclear winter" have vanished, some scientists are making new predictions that catastrophic effects could be felt hundreds, perhaps thousands, of kilometers beyond Kuwait's borders. Researchers still have little information about the size of the giant black cloud of oil, gases and smoke being pumped into the atmosphere day after day. But they now fear that what happens to this noxious mass during the next few weeks may affect the lives of hundreds of millions of people.

Q. **What kind of problems is the writer discussing?**
(a) Environmental
(b) Geographical
(c) Political
(d) Economical

24. The earth is overcrowded. Our technology is believed to be adequate to maintain comfortably a population significantly larger than 4.0 billion. The Earth is overcrowded in a psychological sense. For that ambition-driven fraction of mankind that has blazed new paths for our species, there are no new places to go. There are the ocean basins, but we are not yet committed to exploring them seriously. At just this time in our history comes the possibility of exploring our neighboring worlds in space.

Q. **Which of the following topics is most likely to follow the above passage?**
(a) Potential advantages of exploring ocean basins
(b) Serious effects of overcrowdedness on human beings
(c) Possible exploration of the Solar System
(d) Historical opportunities of colonizing neighboring countries

25. A great many of the computer crimes committed remain unreported, so there is no documentation of them. Those reported represent only fifteen percent of all computer crimes committed. Companies are concerned about causing an increase in the number of computer crimes by widely publicizing them. They fear aspiring thieves might learn from media accounts new techniques for entering computer systems.

Q. **Why are so many cases of computer crime concealed?**
(a) The criminals are too clever.
(b) There is no documentation of them.
(c) Victimized companies hesitate to publicize them.
(d) Law enforcement agencies have few experts in computer crime.

26. The most distant object visible to the unaided human eye is the Andromeda Galaxy. It's visible as a faint patch of light in the constellation Andromeda. If you have seen spectacular telescopic photos of the Andromeda Galaxy, with rich detail of spiral arms, dust lanes and glowing nebulae, don't be misled. Stars as bright as our Sun are far too faint to make any impression on the eye at this great distance. All you'll see of Andromeda with the naked eye is a small fuzzy glow representing only the very brightest stars in the central region of the galaxy.

Q. **What does the Andromeda Galaxy look like when viewed with the naked eye?**
(a) Like a blurred glow
(b) Like several dim stars
(c) Like a single bright star
(d) Like a spiral-shaped glow

27. Some people have attempted to solve puzzles concerning the evolution and social history of dogs. The enormous differences in appearance among modern dogs are not the result of different genetic origins but that of the intensive breeding by humans over the last 500 years. How or why humans domesticated dogs is not fully known, but the speed at which they seem to have multiplied and diversified show that dogs have played an important role in human history. One example is that dogs which helped humans to hunt well became an extremely successful breed, and so spread all over the world.

Q. **According to the passage, why do dogs look so different in appearance?**
(a) Because they are from enormously different origins
(b) Because they are originally from wolves from different parts of the world
(c) Because humans have bred them intensively for a long time
(d) Because dogs played an important part in human history

28. Your refund may be sent to you within eight weeks from the date of this notice unless you owe other taxes or other debts that we're required to collect. If you haven't received a refund or letter of explanation in eight weeks, you may call us at the telephone number shown above. We're sorry for any inconvenience this delay may cause you. We've enclosed publication 1, your rights as a taxpayer, for your information. Thanks you for your cooperation.

Q. **In what case does the taxpayer not receive a refund in eight weeks?**
(a) If he/she doesn't call the office.
(b) If the dependent's social security number is correct.
(c) If the review is not an audit.
(d) If the taxpayer has any kind of remaining balance.

29. Historians concur that Europe maintained a central position in the world during the 19th century. There were three factors that were primarily responsible. The first was the fact that there was, within the boundaries of Europe, an large portion of the world's farmland. As a result, European countries could feed their people without serious adversity and developed a thriving trade. The second factor was control of the seas. The Europeans could attack any other continent while defending themselves from annihilation at home. The third advantage that the Europeans enjoyed was their astounding development in science and technology.

Q. **Which of the following statements corresponds to the above passage?**
(a) Science helped European farmers enjoy prosperity in the 19th century.
(b) Historians contend that Europe was responsible for its own annihilation.
(c) European crops were exported to the rest of the world in the 19th century.
(d) Historians agree that control over seas helped free Europe from many problems.

30. In the sunniest version of South Africa's destiny, being the strongest economy in Africa, it will begin to lead the continent into the 21st century. But there is at the same time a dark vision of disintegration of economic disaster and tribal war. In the late 20th century, the world's people were engaged in a chaotic and often dangerous migration toward democracy. Race antagonism is surely the bitterest obstacle in the way of that procession. South Africa has now formally dismantled the barrier. But of course, the more formidable wall is the human heart.

Q. **Which of the following does NOT reflect the passage?**
(a) In the late 20th century many people have moved toward democracy, taking great risks.
(b) The move toward democracy in the late 20th century has been attended by a great deal of disruption.
(c) The move toward democracy in the late 20th century has often been obstructed by racial discords within the country.
(d) South Africa has overcome racial hatred, but there still remains the formal barrier between the races.

31. Critics of the Palestinian struggle for freedom sometimes lament the absence of a "Palestinian Mandela." I lament the absence of an Israeli F. W. de Klerk. Both will be needed because — through its withholding of equality from 1.2 million Palestinians citizens living inside Israel, its brutally violent repression of Palestinians in the occupied territories and its 60-year denial of the rights of ethnically cleansed Palestinian refugees to return to their homes — Israel increasingly represents an acute variant of apartheid.

Q. **Which of the following is correct according to the passage?**
(a) Israel represents intential ethnic discrimination.
(b) Some Palestinian refugees returned to their home.
(c) Palestinian refugees have been occupied by Israel for 60 years.
(d) Israel has given the right to return to their homes to the refugees.

32. There are really only three laws at the national level making it harder for dangerous people to get firearms. There are restrictions on access to machine guns and other fully automatic weapons that date back to the end of the Prohibition era; categories of "prohibited purchasers," such as felons and the dangerously mentally ill, as established in the Gun Control Act of 1968, passed after Robert F. Kennedy and Martin Luther King Jr. were assassinated; and the Brady Law which requires federally licensed gun dealers to check the records of "prohibited purchasers" supplied voluntarily by the states.

Q. **What is the main idea of the passage?**
(a) The history of restrictions on access to machine guns
(b) The acute situation of teen shooting incidents
(c) The need for more federal laws on purchasing weapons
(d) Psychiatric tests for prohibited purchasers by the states

33. Thank you for your interest in volunteering for the 2009 Los Angeles Times Festival of Books, to be held at UCLA. The fourteenth annual edition of the Festival of Books will be held on Saturday, April 25 and Sunday, April 26, and we would love to have you join us as a volunteer. Some details about volunteering:
- Volunteers will receive free parking, shuttle service from the parking lot, and lunch.
- We will provide T-shirts for volunteers to wear and keep after the event. (Please wear khaki, or beige pants or shorts.)
- The majority of volunteer activities require being on your feet for most of your shift. Please wear comfortable shoes.
- Volunteers must be 18 years of age or older. You cannot bring children under the age of 18 with you during your shift.

Q. **Which of the following is correct according to the passage?**
(a) Volunteers should provide their own T-shirts and pants.
(b) Even non-Californians can join the festival.
(c) The main volunteer activities are to keep an eye on the books.
(d) All books will be an discount for volunteers.

34. The fact that American ideals such as equality of opportunity and self-reliance are only partly carried out in real life does not diminish their importance. Most Americans still believe in them and are strongly affected by them in their everyday lives. It is easier to understand what Americans are thinking and feeling if we can understand what these basic American values are and how they influence almost every facet of life in the United States.

Q. **What can be inferred from the passage?**
(a) American values reflect the facts of American life.
(b) American values influence American life.
(c) American values describe American life.
(d) American values are accepted by all American.

35. Those who believe that political behavior is a function of deeper personality characteristics make no allowance for the accidental but nonetheless real factors of experience, learning, and social situations. Monistic psychological explanations by their very nature fail to bring out the complexity and variety of political phenomena. Furthermore, there is no type of personality that can exclusively be identified with a specific kind of politics. The same personality tendencies may be related to ideologies of the far left or the far right, and may also coexist with a moderate democratic ideology.

Q. **What can be inferred from the passage?**
(a) No relationship exists between a person's psychological make-up and his politics.
(b) There is a common psychological make-up among all people holding the same political views.
(c) There is no psychological explanation that can account for all of the complexities of politics.
(d) There is no normal person who is a political extremist.

36. There is another very popular argument against the introduction of scientific principles in literary analysis. We are told in this instance that science must be objective, whereas the interpretation of literature is always subjective. In my opinion this crude opposition is untenable. The critic's work can have varying degrees of subjectivity. This degree will be much lower if he tries to ascertain the properties of the work rather than seeking its significance for a given period of milieu. The degree of subjectivity will vary, moreover, when he is examining different strata of the same work.

Q. **Which of the following best describes the writer's tone?**
(a) Subjective
(b) Critical
(c) Analytical
(d) Objective

37. Individuals inherit a particular space within an interlocking set of social relationships. To know oneself as such a social person is not to, however, occupy a static and fixed position. It is to make progress goals; to move through life is to make progress toward a given end. Thus a completed life is an achievement and death is the point at which someone can be judged happy or unhappy. Hence the ancient Greek proverb "Call no man happy until he is dead."

Q. **What is the writer's view of happiness?**
(a) It is absolute.
(b) It is impossible to achieve in real life.
(c) It results from progress in life.
(d) It is a temporary emotional state.

38-40. Read the passage. Then identify the option that does NOT belong.

38. Risk tolerance is a mix of personality and practicality. (a) Your sunny disposition may convince you that what goes down will eventually go up and you shouldn't sweat short-term market moves. (b) Therefore, the market wants you to diversify your investment. (c) But if you've got a near-term goal that's likely to be derailed by a market upset, practical needs come first. (d) To evaluate your practical risk tolerance, look at how much you need to finance near-term needs — the goals that need to be paid for in the next three years. That could be next year's college tuition, a major repair for the junker in your driveway, or living expenses to handle a job loss or retirement.

39. Nothing is really new about employers preferring to hire younger candidates. Experiments have shown that even when credentials are absolutely identical, employers much prefer the younger candidates. There are no good reasons for this overall preference. (a) Study after study has shown that older workers take a much longer time than their younger counterparts to find a new job. (b) Older workers perform better across the range of relevant performance indicators — better skills, especially interpersonal skills, better attendance, more conscientious, and so on. (c) While one might assume that older workers cost more, in truth any premiums that older workers receive are related to experience, which affects performance. (d) And rather than simply assume that older workers will demand higher wages, the thing to do is present them with the offer and let them decide.

40. When clothes dryers account for at least 6% of the electricity used by U.S. households, is it any wonder that line-drying is coming back? (a) In places where the practice is banned as an unsightly nuisance to neighbors, right-to-dry activists and blogging eco-moms are forming an alliance. (b) Their cause is to reduce energy consumption, to call upon sunlight rather than bleach to get those whites even whiter. (c) And they want not to see poverty in the image of clean sheets blowing in the wind. (d) A 2001 Department of Energy report estimated that electric clothes dryers accounted for about 5.8% of total electricity usage in U.S. homes — a startling figure given that the same report said all indoor and outdoor lighting in American homes constitutes only 8.8% of electricity usage. Plus, the 5.8% attributed to dryers does not include electricity needed to power the motors of gas-heated dryers.

정답 및 해설

Chapter 1
고득점을 위한 빈칸 넣기

STEP 2 Actual Test

1.

해석_ 라디오와 텔레비전 산업에는 균형 잡힌 스케줄편성을 저해하고, 제공되는 프로그램의 질을 저하시키는 경향이 있는 몇 가지 요인이 있다. 이런 요인 중 하나는 방송국 간의 치열한 경쟁이다. 프로그램을 제작하는 사람들은 갈수록 더욱 많은 시청자를 끌어야 하는 끊임없는 압력하에 있다. 이런 목적을 달성하기 위해서 방송국은 현재 광범위한 대중의 인기를 얻고 있는 한 가지 형태의 프로그램을 더욱더 많이 제작하는 방법에 의존한다. 그 결과, 다양성이 무시되고 획일성이 지배적이 된다.

해설_ '방송국은 현재 광범위한 대중의 인기를 얻고 있는 한 형태의 프로그램을 더욱 더 많이 제작하는 방법에 의존한다'는 것은 다양성이 무시되고 획일적으로 된다는 뜻이다.

어휘_ resort to (어떤 수단, 방법에) 의존하다, ~을 쓰다, 호소하다
　　　 prevail 우세하다

정답_ (b)

2.

해석_ 미합중국 대부분 지역에서 날씨는 좋거나 나쁘거나 둘 중 하나이다. 맹렬한 기세로 비가 퍼붓거나 햇볕이 내리쬐곤 한다. 기후는 여러 측면에서 유럽과 다르다. 대륙을 가로질러 서풍이 불어오지만 대서양의 습기와 온난함이 없다. 겨울에는 북서풍이, 그리고 여름에는 남서풍이 주로 불어온다. 따라서 여름이면 전역이 영국보다 덥고 겨울이면 버지니아 주 북부는 영국보다 춥다. 또한 동일한 계절 내에서 최고 더위와 추위도 영국보다 심하다. 물론 동식물이 자라기엔 적당한 양이긴 하지만 강우량도 적다.

해설_ 빈칸 뒤의 내용은 미국과 유럽의 기후의 차이점에 대해 언급하고 있다. 따라서 빈칸에는 '(이 지역의) 기후는 여러 측면에서 유럽과 다르다'라는 내용이 들어가는 것이 적합하다.

어휘_ foul 몹시 나쁜
　　　 businesslike 실제적인
　　　 rainfall 강우량
　　　 perpetually 끊임없이

정답_ (b)

3.

해석_ 세계은행은 화요일 아시아가 불황의 골로 빠지고 있다고 발표했으며 일본에 이 지역을 경제적 추락의 위기에서 구해내는 데 지원을 요청했다. 세계은행의 한 지역 전문가는 아시아는 이제 깊고 긴 불황의 기로에 들어섰으며 전 세계적인 경제 슬럼프가 몇 달 안에 닥쳐올 수 있다고 경고했다. 그는 호주에서 열린 주요 무역 투자 회의에서 "우리는 짐작컨대 이 위기의 첫 번째 주기 끝에 있으며 깊은 경기 후퇴 단계로 접어들었고 심지어는 '공황'이라는 단어를 쓸 수도 있다"고 말했다.

해설_ 경기 침체를 다룬 기사문을 통해 대의 파악 능력을 측정하는 문제이다. 아시아의 경기 불황이 심각하여 공황에까지 이를 수 있다는 내용이므로 정답은 (a)이다.

어휘_ plunge into depression 경기 침체에 빠지다
　　　 call on Japan to 일본에 ~하도록 요구하다
　　　 nosedive 곤두박질, 폭락
　　　 be on the threshold of 이제 막 ~하려고 하다, ~이 임박해 오다
　　　 status quo 현재 상황, 현상 유지

정답_ (a)

STEP 2 Actual Test

1.

해석_ 미국 사회에서 사람들이 catch-22 상황에 대해 얘기하는 것을 흔히 들을 수 있다. 이 용어는 그것을 제목으로 한 인기 소설에서 유래되었고 다음과 같은 일련의 상황을 나타내고 있다. 즉 A는 B가 정정되지 않는 한 정정될 수 없고, B는 C가 정정되지 않는 한 정정될 수 없다. 그리고 C는 A가 정정 되지 않는 한 정정되지 못한다. 결과적으로 어떤 상황(A, B, C)도 실현되지 못한다. 미국에 오는 외국인 학생들은 자신들이 catch-22 상황에 처해 있다는 것을 매우 자주 깨닫는다. 예를 들면, 어느 외국인 남학생이 어느 미국인 여성과 결혼하고 싶은데, 여자 부모가 결혼 전에 직장을 갖기를 원한다는 것을 알게 될지 모른다. 그러나 미국 정부는 그를 취업시켜 주려 하질 않기 때문에 그는 직업을 가질 수 없다. 그래서 그는 결혼할 수 없다.

해설_ The term comes from a popular novel with that title ~ 에서 판단하건대, 이 용어는 원래 소설의 제목에서 나온 것이다.

어휘_ term 기간; 용어

　　　　for instance 예를 들어

　　　　vicious circle 악순환

정답_ (a)

2.

해석_ 꽤 오랫동안 "아메리칸 드림" 이란 말이 떠돌았다. 미국은 한때 많은 기회의 나라로 인식되기도 했었다. 실제로, 이것은 최근까지도 사실이었다. 매년 많은 한국인들이 더 나은 삶을 위해 성공적인 삶에 대한 열정과 희망을 품고 미국으로 이주했다. 하지만 열악한 고용 시장과 근무 조건의 나라라고 간주되던 한국은 이제 살기가 나아진 것처럼 보인다. 거의 모든 미국의 회사들이 감원을 함에 따라 미국으로부터 돌아오는 한국인의 수가 점점 늘어나고 있는 추세이다. 대부분의 사람들이 알고 있듯이 미국은 현재 세계 금융 위기의 진원지라고 간주되고 있기 때문에 우리는 "아메리칸 드림" 이라는 단어를 이제 잊어야 한다.

해설_ 평가절하되는 미국과는 달리, 한국의 상황이 비교적 나아지는 추세에 있는 이유로, 많은 한국인들이 역이민을 오고 있다는 내용의 글이다. 경제 위기에서 벗어나기 위해 미 정부나 기업들이 누구에게 어떤 일을 하는지는 지문을 통해 알 수 없다.

어휘_ downsize (인력, 규모를)축소하다.

　　　　epicenter (지진의) 발생지, (문제의) 핵심

　　　　financial crisis 금융 위기

정답_ (a)

3.

해석_ 목요일 영국 런던 O2 아레나에서 "This is It" 을 발표하기 위해 연단에 선 마이클 잭슨은 포즈를 잡고 손을 흔들며, 웃으면서 비명을 지르는 팬들에게 키스를 날렸다. 그리고 2001년 이후 처음 갖는 콘서트를 약간 머뭇거리면서 발표했다. 지난 10년간 그 가수는 건강 악화라는 소문에 시달렸고 음악보다는 말썽 많은 그의 사생활 때문에 많은 헤드라인을 장식했다. 그는 2003년에 아동 성추행 혐의로 체포되었고 캘리포니아에서 재판을 받은 후 2005년에 풀려났다. 재정적인 고통이 따랐고 작년에는 캘리포니아에 있는 2500에이커에 달하는 네버랜드 목장의 소유권을 포기했다. 그는 다음 달 네버랜드에서 가져온 2천 개 남짓한 개인 물건들을 경매할 예정이었지만 그의 부동산에서 가져온 기념물을 헐값에 팔 권리가 없다는 이유로 수요일에 줄리아나 경매 회사를 상대로 소송을 제기했다.

해설_ (a)는 성추행 혐의로 기소되었으므로 틀렸다. (b)는 소송을 제기 했으므로 틀렸다. 아직까지 모든 재산(부동산)이 팔린 것은 아니므로 (d) 역시 오답이 된다. 그러나 그는 아동 성추행으로 재판을 받도록 소환된 것은 사실이다. 따라서 정답은 (c)이다.

어휘_ podium 연단

　　　　haltingly 머뭇거리면서

　　　　buffet 사람을 괴롭히다, 못살게 굴다

　　　　acquit ~을 석방하다

　　　　ranch 농장

　　　　auction house 경매 회사

　　　　sell off 헐값에 팔아치우다

　　　　memorabilia 기념품, 기념할 만한 일

정답_ (c)

STEP 2 Actual Test

1.

해석_ 1960년대 동안 모든 선진 공업국의 사람들은 인간과 기술이 환경에 미치는 영향에 대해 더욱 걱정하게 되었다. 개인들, 조직들, 심지어 정부들도 걱정했다. 그 시대의 하나의 작은 징후는 영국 정부의 한 부처를 환경성이라 명명한 것이다. 경제가 쇠퇴하는 시대에, 환경보호에 대해 걱정한다는 것은 사치스러운 일로 보였을지도 모른다. 대다수 사람들은 주로 더 많은 재산, 더 많은 소비를 의미하는 생활수준의 향상에 관심을 나타냈다.

해설_ 본문에서 Department of the Environment(환경성)이라는 문구가 힌트가 된다. 즉, 큰 제목은 경제와 환경의 관계, 그것도 구체적으로는 영국에서의 관계가 문제가 된다.

어휘_ industrialized country 선진 공업국
　　　preserve 보존하다
　　　chiefly 주로
　　　consumption 소비

정답_ (c)

2.

해석_ 〈피넛츠〉라는 작품은 문자 그대로 마지막까지 슐츠 인생의 중심으로 남았다. 이 만화가는 그의 마지막 일요일자 연재 만화가 게재된 전날인 2000년 2월 12일에 암으로 죽었다. '슐츠와 피너츠'는 대부분의 독자들에게 알려지지 않은 의미를 가지고 있다. 작가인 마이클리스는 찰리 브라운과 루시의 관계를 다툼이 많았던 슐츠의 첫 번째 결혼과 비교한다. 그는 많은 캐릭터의 이름들이 — 셔미, 리누스, 심지어 찰리 브라운 — 실존 인물에 기원을 두고 있다는 것을 알았다. 그리고 그는 여행의 두려움에서부터 그의 어머니의 죽음에 이르기까지, 슐츠의 어두운 부분으로 들어가 관찰해 본다. "찰리 브라운은 세상에 대하여 슐츠의 창과 새총과 화살을 던진다"고 그는 말했다.

해설_ 찰리 브라운으로 유명한 작가인 찰스 슐츠와 그의 작품 〈피너츠〉에 대한 이야기로서 작가의 내면이 작품에 반영되었다는 내용이다.

어휘_ draw a parallel with/between A and B A와 B를 비교하다
　　　spear 창
　　　sling 새총
　　　arrow 화살

정답_ (d)

3.

해석_ 전갈잠자리는 붉은 머리와 꼬리, 검은색과 노란색의 몸체를 가지고 있다. 수컷은(짝짓기를 할 때 암컷을 잡기 위해서) 꼬리 끝에 한 쌍의 갈퀴를 가지고 있으며, 이것 때문에 비록 침을 가지고 있지는 않지만 전갈과 같은 외형을 띤다. 이것은 35mm의 날개폭을 가지고 있다. 머리는 돌출되어 아래로 향하고 있는 뾰족한 부리로 말려져 있으며, 끝에 입부분이 있다. 눈은 크다. 날개는 검은 반점과 얼룩이 많지만 대체로 깨끗하다.

해설_ 전갈잠자리의 생김새에 대해 묘사하고 있으므로 정답은 (d)이다.

어휘_ reddish 불그스름한
　　　clasper 걸쇠, 갈퀴
　　　prominent 돌출된
　　　beak 부리

정답_ (d)

Chapter 4
고득점을 위한 추론 문제

STEP 2 Actual Test

1.

해석_ 스타우드 호텔은 전 세계의 하버드 여행자들에게 할인을 제공합니다. 하버드 여행자들은 지금 해당 호텔의 최저 요금에서, 20% 할인된 가격에 예약할 수 있습니다. 스타우드 호텔 & 리조트 월드와이드 사는 9개의 브랜드(셰라톤, 포 포인츠 바이 셰라톤, 세인트 레지스, 럭셔리 콜렉션, 르 메르디앙, W 호텔, 웨스틴, 어로프트 그리고 엘리먼트 호텔)와 95개가 넘는 나라에 860개 이상의 호텔을 갖춘 세계적으로 손꼽히는 호텔 회사 중 하나입니다. 자격을 갖추려면, 귀하께서는 스타우드의 로열티 프로그램이나 스타우드 우량 고객 프로그램에 등록하셔야 합니다. 등록은 무료이며 쉽습니다.

해설_ 두 번째 문장에서 (a)의 내용을 쉽게 확인할 수 있다. (b)의 경우 860개 이상의 호텔을 전 세계에 보유하고 있다는 언급이 본문에 있으므로 틀리다. (c)는 확인할 수 없으며, 맨 마지막 문장에서 등록이 무료라고 했으므로 (d)도 옳지 않다.

어휘_ reserve 예약하다

　　　 eligible 자격이 있는

　　　 enrollment fee 등록비

정답_ (a)

2.

해석_ 나는 와인이나 맥주, 또 그외 다른 술들을 좋아한다. 많은 사람들이 술이 해롭다고 생각하지만 나는 정부가 나의 음주 권리를 규제하기를 바라지 않는다. 같은 이유로 나는 내가 술을 좋아한다고 해서 다른 사람의 물에 약간의 술을 탈 권리가 있다고는 주장하지 않을 것이다. 다행히도 내가 술을 마실 때 내 잔의 술이 흘러나와 다른 사람의 잔으로 들어가지는 않는다. 그러나 담배의 경우는 다르다. 흡연자들은 이 사실을 주지해야 하며 그들의 흡연권이 규제되어야 한다는 사실을 인정해야 한다.

해설_ 본문의 하단에 담배는 술과 달리 다른 사람이 있는 쪽으로 연기가 흘러가므로 흡연권이 규제되어야 한다고 했다. 즉 간접 흡연을 막아 비흡연자들이 맑은 공기를 마실 수 있어야 한다는 내용이다.

어휘_ restrict 제한하다, 규제하다

　　　 spirit 알코올, 독한 술

　　　 by the same token 같은 이유로

　　　 tobacco 담배

정답_ (a)

3.

해석_ 오스트리아 출신 화가인 구스타프 클림트는 비엔나 분리주의 회화파의 창시자였다. 세기의 전환기에 비엔나는 미적이고 에로틱한 것에 사로잡혀 있었다. 그때는 행복과 상실의 시대인 동시에 현혹적인 주지주의 시대이기도 하였다. 구스타프 클림트의 예술은 그의 시대의 깊은 심리적 진실을 대변했으며 흔히 있는 일이지만, 그것 때문에 격렬한 비난을 받기도 하였다. 클림트의 작품은 그의 시대의 모순을 반영했다. 그는 환희와 공포, 삶과 죽음, 금욕과 쾌락 같은 상반된 것들에 대한 육감적인 혼합물을 정교하게 결합시켰다. 비록 평면 위에 그려지긴 했지만 Kiss에 나타난 육감적인 모습들에서 2차원적 방식이 마치 영원성을 부여받은 것처럼, 마치 관능을 신성화하려는 듯이 금으로 장식되었다.

해설_ 윗글은 화가 구스타프 클림트와 그의 작품의 특징에 대해 알려주는(informative) 글이다.

어휘_ secession 분리파(1898년 비엔나에 일어난 예술 운동)

　　　 obsess (귀신·망상 따위가) 들리다, 붙다

　　　 dazzling 눈부신, 현혹적인

　　　 intellectualism 주지주의

　　　 ecstasy 무아경, 황홀

　　　 austerity 엄격, 준엄

　　　 jocose 우스꽝스런, 익살맞은(facetious)

정답_ (d)

STEP 2 Actual Test

1.

해석_ 마침내 생태계의 문제들은 더 이상 국경을 따지지 않게 되었다. 신체의 조직 속에 DDT가 대량 축적되어 있는 남극대륙의 전설적인 펭귄에 의하여 생생하게 나타났듯이, 대기와 바다의 오염은 국가를 초월하는 결과를 낳을 수 있다. 따라서 몇 가지 경우에서 이 문제를 이해하려면 세계적인 시각이 필요하다. 물론 수많은 나라들이 개입되므로 어떤 정책이든 행정적인 어려움은 증대된다. 그래서 특별 공해세 도입을 전 세계가 받아들이도록 하는 것은 매우 어려울 것이다.

해설_ (c)에 the administrative difficulties of any policy가 거론되었지만, 그 다음 곧바로 a particular pollution tax rate가 논의되는 것은 논리의 비약이므로 (d)는 부적절하다.

어휘_ ecological 생태학의
respecter (보통 부정문에서) 차별 대우하는 사람, 편파적인 사람 (e.g.: be no respecter of persons)
Antartica 남극대륙
D.D.T. 방역, 살충제의 일종
perspective 시각, 조망

정답_ (d)

2.

해석_ 라틴어와 고대 중국어, 즉 유럽과 동아시아라는 거대한 두 개의 지적 사회의 언어가 지금은 사용되지 않게 되었다. 이 두 지역에서 국제어로서 이 언어 대신 자리를 잡은 것이 있다면 그것은 영어다. 영어는 지구의 역사상 그 유래를 찾아볼 수 없을 정도로 과학의 언어로서 매우 보편적으로 자리 잡았다. 그 이유는 영어 본래의 장점과는 거의 관계가 없다. 영어의 오늘날의 지위는 주로 두 가지 사실에서 유래하는 것 같다. 영어는 다른 언어에 비해 배우기도 사용하기도 쉽지 않다. 사실 대부분의 언어보다 어려울지도 모른다. 그리고 다른 언어보다 더 논리적이거나 덜 애매한 것도 아니다.

해설_ 영어가 보편적인 국제어로서 기능하게 된 이유가 영어 그 자체에 있지 않다는 (b)의 내용 다음에는 그것을 뒷받침하는 구체적인 설명인 (d)가 와야 한다. (c)는 영어가 현재와 같은 지위를 누리게 된 두 가지 이유를 설명한다는 점에서 논리적인 흐름에 맞지 않다.

어휘_ gigantic 거대한, 방대한
disuse 쓰이지 않음
without a peer 비길 데 없는
inherent 본래의, 고유의

ambiguous 애매한, 모호한

정답_ (c)

3.

해석_ 상원은 소비자들이 신용카드 회사들과의 계약에 있어 새로운 보호를 받을 수 있는 획기적인 법안을 통과시켰다. 그 법안은 신용카드 업계에 전례가 없는 규제를 가하며 소급 이자율의 인상폭을 줄이고 이자율 인상 시 사전 통보를 하도록 강제하고 있다. 그리고 그 법안은 카드 소유자가 개별적인 채무의 변제에 늦었을 때 여신자가 이자율을 올리는 것을 금한다. 법안에 서명된 후 1년 뒤 효력이 발휘되는 그 상원의 조치는 또한 연방준비 이사회가 만든 신용카드 관례에 관한 일련의 규제보다 더 강하다. 그것은 또한 회사들이 대학생들에게 신용카드를 (만들도록) 졸라대는 것을 더 어렵게 만들고 청구서를 지불할 때 회사가 수수료를 부과하는 것을 막을 것이다.

해설_ 윗글은 상원이 통과시킨 신용카드 관련 규제 법안에 관한 것이다. (c)을 제외한 다른 것은 그 규제 법안 자체에 대한 내용을 담고 있다.

어휘_ unprecedented 전례가 없는
retroactive 효력이 소급하는
curtail 줄이다, 삭감하다

정답_ (c)

Mini Test

1.

해석_ 지금은 놀라운 디지털 신세계이다. 스티브 잡스는 맥월드에 모습을 보이지 않았고 빌 게이츠 역시 CES에서 기조연설을 맡지 않았다. 어젯밤 라스베이거스에서 치러진 CES 무대를 꿰찬 사람은 바로 마이크로소프트의 CEO인 스티브 발머였다. 그는 이 자리에서 Windows 7의 개발이 마무리 단계에 있고 일반 사용자들이 다운로드하여 사용할 수 있도록 내일부터 베타 테스트 버전을 배포하겠다고 밝혔다. Mac OS 10과 다소 비슷한 데가 있지만 발머는 애플을 별로 신경쓰고 있지 않다고 뜻을 비쳤다. "여러분들은 이 문제를 이렇게 봐야 합니다. 올 한해 Mac이 천만 대 판매를 기록하는 동안 PC는 무려 3억 대나 팔렸다는 것입니다. 이는 사람들이 개인용 컴퓨터 시장의 미래에 상당한 관심을 가지고 있다는 반증이라고 볼 수 있죠." 이 업데이트된 운영 체제는 1년 안에 새로운 PC에 장착될 예정이다.

해설_ 빈칸 뒤에서 '같은 기간 동안 Mac보다 PC는 30배나 더 팔렸다' 라고 언급한 것은 애플의 Mac에 대해서 별로 신경 쓸 필요가 없다는 뜻이다.

어휘_ obsess 끙끙거리며 걱정하다

　　　　operating system 운영 시스템

　　　　take the stage 무대를 차지하다

　　　　keynote 기조 연설을 하다

정답_ (d)

2.

해석_ 어린이 백신의 안전을 염려하는 부모들에게는 안심이 되어야 하지만, 모든 분들이 그럴 것 같지는 않다. 티메로살이 자폐증의 원인이라는 이론은 학계에서 꾸준히 부인되어 왔다. 이번 이탈리아에서 발표된 새로운 연구 논문도 많은 백신에 사용되어 온 이 수은 보존제가 어린이에게 유해하지 않다는 증거에 추가되고 있다. 백일해 백신에 관한 이번 연구에서 수천 명의 건강한 이탈리아 유아에게 두 가지 서로 다른 양의 티메로살을 투약하고 10년 후 1,400명의 아이들의 뇌 기능을 실험한 결과 단 한 명의 자폐증 사례만이 발견되었다. 이번 연구는 미(美) 질병 통제 예방 센터의 자금 지원으로 진행되었다.

해설_ '티메로살이 많은 백신에 사용되어 왔으며 이 수은 보존제가 어린이에게 유해하지 않다' 라는 내용이 힌트가 된다. preservative 를 (c)에서는 antiseptic으로 바꿔 표현했다.

어휘_ reassure 안심시키다, 장담하다

　　　　autism 자폐성(自閉性), 자폐증

　　　　discount 할인하다, 무시하다, 고려하지 않다

　　　　antiseptic 방부제

정답_ (c)

3.

해석_ 간 손상은 아마도 스테로이드 복용으로 생길 수 있는 모든 부작용 중에서 가장 선정적이다. 입을 통하여 복용한 대부분의 아나볼릭 스테로이드는 간을 통과한다. 어떤 것이 간을 통과할 때, 그것은 다양한 효소에 의해 분해되어 혈관으로 흘러간다. 입을 통하여 복용한 아나볼릭 스테로이드에 대한 대부분의 연구는 복용을 하면 간 효소가 상승한다는 사실에 초점을 맞춘다. 하지만 이것이 꼭 간이 손상되고 있다는 것을 뜻하는가? 간은 인체의 필터 역할을 한다. 어떤 것이 그것을 통과할 때마다 활동을 한다. 그것이 스테로이드가 간을 파괴한다는 것을 의미하는가?

해설_ 윗글은 스테로이드뿐 아니라 어느 것이 간을 통과하더라도 간은 필터로서 작용을 하므로 스테로이드가 꼭 간을 손상시킨다는 보장은 없다는 내용이다.

어휘_ sensationalize 감동적[선정적]으로 하다

　　　　orally 입을 통하여, 경구적(經口的)으로

　　　　enzyme 효소(酵素)

정답_ (c)

4.

해석_ 1998년 앤드류 로이드 웨버는 〈캐츠〉의 비디오 버전을 출시했다. 그 비디오 버전은 데이비드 말렛이 감독하였고 1981년 처음으로 공연을 한 도시인 런던에서 녹화되었다. 1981년에 초연된 오리지널 런던 공연의 출연진 중 다른 멤버에는 스티븐 웨인, 존 체스터, 셰론 리 힐, 제랄딘 가드너, 브라이언 블레스드, 그리고 피뇰라 휴즈 등이다. 오리지널 브로드웨이 작품의 출연진은 오리지널 런던 작품의 출연진보다 수가 더 적었지만 그 연극의 핵심적인 메시지는 동등한 효과를 발휘했다. 라이브 무대 공연을 잘 아는 어떤 사람이라도 한 번의 공연이 물리적으로 얼마나 힘든지 잘 안다. 〈캐츠〉가 성공적인 성과를 이루었다는 것은 아주 두드러진다. 전 세계 현지에서의 캐스팅은 〈캐츠〉를 연극 역사상 소중한 부분으로 만든다.

해설_ 런던과 뉴욕에서의 오리지널 캐스팅과 1998년 〈캐츠〉의 비디오 버전, 즉 새로운 필름에 대한 이야기가 주를 이루는 글이다.

어휘_ cast 배역, (the ~) 출연 배우들

　　　　nothing ~ of 아주 ~한

　　　　venue 개최지, 행위의 현장

정답_ (b)

5.

해석_ 지난 1980년대 후반에, 랜디 "더 램" 로빈슨은 프로레슬러 중 두각을 나타내고 있었다. 20년이 지난 지금 그는 뉴저지의 고등학교

체육관과 주민 센터 등에서 소수의 골수 레슬링 광팬들 앞에서 공연을 하며 근근이 살아가고 있다. 딸과의 관계가 소원해져 어떤 실질적인 관계를 유지할 수 없게 된 랜디는 쇼의 스릴과 그의 팬들의 찬사로 살아간다. 하지만, 심장마비가 그를 은퇴하도록 한다. 자기 정체성에 대한 의식이 희미해지자, 그는 그의 딸과 다시 연락을 시도하며 그의 인생 상황을 평가하기 시작한다. 그러나 이 모든 것은 링에 대한 매력과 랜디 "더 램" 을 프로레슬링 세계로 되돌아가게 하는 그의 공연에 대한 열정과 비교할 수 없다.

해설 빈칸의 앞과 뒤가 역접 또는 전환적인 내용이므로 빈칸에는 역접의 접속사가 들어가야 한다.

어휘 eke out 근근이 (생활을) 해나가다
　　　　handful 소량, 소수
　　　　diehard 완강히 저항하는, 끝까지 버티는
　　　　estranged (심정으로) 멀어진, 소원해진
　　　　adoration 예배, 동경

정답 (b)

6.

해석 여성이 그들의 전통적 가사일로부터 어느 정도 해방되지 않고, 그들이 사회에서, 특히 노동 시장에서, 중요한 역할을 하도록 허용되지 않으면, 경제가 장기간에 걸쳐서 급속히 발전한다는 것은 불가능하다. 이러한 관점에서 볼 때, 여성의 교육과 그들의 사회, 경제, 법률 및 정치적 지위의 향상은 감정적 인권 운동의 초점 이상의 것이 된다. 그것들은 국가 발전의 필수 조건으로 인식되어야 하며 엄밀히 실제적인 이유 때문에 높은 우선권이 주어져야 한다.

해설 '여성의 교육과 그들의 사회, 경제, 법률 및 정치적 지위의 향상은 감정적 인권 운동의 초점 이상의 것이 된다' 고 언급한 것은 여성 인권 등의 향상은 국가 발전에 직접적인 영향이 있다는 내용과 상통한다.

어휘 domestic 가정의
　　　　crusade 십자군, 개혁 운동
　　　　prerequisite 필수 조건
　　　　submission 복종, 순종

정답 (a)

7.

해설 1923년 12월 15일에 태어난 프리맨 존 다이슨은 양자 이론, 물리학 그리고 핵공학 분야의 업적으로 유명한 영국 출신의 이론 물리학자이며 수학자이다. 그는 물리학에서 말하는 환원주의는 '물리학 현상의 세계를 일련의 한정된 기초 방정식으로 단순화하려는 노력'으로 설명하고 양자 역학에서 슈레딩거와 디랙의 연구 결과를 인용하였는데, 여기에서 그들은 화학과 물리학의 어렵고 복잡한 문제들을 환원주의의 승리를 나타내는 사례로서 '두 줄의 대수학의 상징' 으로 단순화하였다.

해설 윗글에서 물리적 현상의 세계를 단순화하는 것이 환원주의라고 하였으며, 마지막 부분에서 화학과 물리학의 어렵고 복잡한 문제들을 '두 줄의 대수학의 상징' 으로 단순화하였다면 거기서 환원주의가 이용되었을 것을 추정할 수 있다.

어휘 reductionism 환원(還元)주의(생명 현상은 물리학적 · 화학적
　　　　으로 다 설명할 수 있다고 함)
　　　　algebraic 대수학의

정답 (b)

8.

해석 가치가 있는 어떠한 시도 소중하다는 것은 다른 모든 것에 앞서 개인적인 것이며 결과적으로 우리가 이용하는 그 문학적 용어는 적절한 설명이 아니다. 하지만 그것들은 쓸모가 있다. 형이상학파들은 그들이 형이상학파라는 것을 알지 못했고 낭만주의자들도 그들이 낭만주의자라는 것을 몰랐다. 하지만 우리는 그들이 그들의 선배들과 무엇이 같고 어디가 다른지 알고 있다. 마찬가지로 '모더니스트' 라는 용어는 시간을 거슬러서 적용되고 있다. 그것이 기술적으로 매우 유용한지는 거의 문제가 되지 않는다. 확실히 해둘 필요가 있는 것은 한편으로 어떤 것이 예이츠와 하디를 다른 한편으로는 엘리엇과 파운드를 구분하는지에 관한 것이다. 물론 예이츠와 하디는 서로 매우 다르며 파운드와 엘리엇도 그러하다. 하지만 시적 형식에 대한 그들의 자세는 그들이 어떻게 맺어져야 하는지를 결정한다.

해설 윗글은 문학적 용어의 사용에 관해 예이츠와 하디 등의 예를 들어 설명하고 있다.

어휘 metaphysical 형이상학의, (종종 M-) (시인이) 형이상학파
　　　　(派)의
　　　　retrospective 회고의, 배후의, 소급적인
　　　　descriptively 기술적으로, 묘사적으로

정답 (b)

9.

해석 한 사람이 5번가를 걸을 때, 그는 슈트라우스의 왈츠를 연주하는 현악 4중주의 음악을 들을 거라 기대하지 않는다. 그가 5번가를 걸을 때 들을 것으로 기대하는 것은 차 소리이다. 어떤 사람이 5번가를 걷는 동안에 정말 슈트라우스의 왈츠를 연주하는 현악 4중주의 음악을 들으면, 그는 5번가를 걷는 것이 아닌 올드 비엔나에 와있는 듯한 착각에 빠지기 쉽다. 만약 올드 비엔나에 와있는 듯한 상상을 하는 사람이 올드 비엔나에는 찰스 쥬르당의 세일을 하지 않는다는

것을 알게 될 때 매우 화 날 것이다. 그리고 그것이 내가 5번가를 지날 때 차 소리를 듣고 싶어하는 이유이다.

해설_ 필자는 5번가를 걸을 때 현악 음악보다는 차 소리를 듣는 것이 차라리 낫다는 것을 비꼬듯 언급하고 있다.

어휘_ quartet 4중주

fatuous 얼빠진, 어리석은

preposterous 앞뒤가 뒤바뀐, 상식을 벗어난

perilous 위험한, 위험이 많은

정답_ (a)

10.

해석_ NAFTA는 미국, 캐나다 그리고 멕시코 사이에서 거래되는 상품에 대해 관세의 대부분을 폐지했다. 나프타는 점차적으로 15년에 걸쳐 다른 관세들을 단계적으로 폐지하였다. 자동차, 컴퓨터, 직물 그리고 농업을 포함하여 많은 범주에서 규제가 없어졌다. NAFTA는 처음에 자유 무역을 지지하는 미국과 캐나다 정치인들에 의해 추진되었다. 이 조약은 또한 지적재산권(특허권, 저작권 그리고 상표)을 보호하며, 이 세 국가 사이의 투자 규제의 철폐를 개략적으로 규정해 놓고 있다.

해설_ NAFTA가 관세를 폐지하며 무역에서의 각종 규제를 없애는 조약임을 설명하고 있다. (c)는 NAFTA의 특징이라기보다 기원(origin) 또는 탄생에 관한 설명이므로 본문의 흐름에 적합하지 않다.

어휘_ eliminate 제거하다

tariff 관세

intellectual property right 지적재산권

patent 특허

trademark 상표

정답_ (c)

Chapter 1
예술

STEP 2 Actual Test

1.

해석_ '예술' 이라는 단어는 '맞추다' 를 뜻하는 라틴어 어원에서 유래하였으며 물건, 장인, 공예품 등의 단어들에서 나타난다. 그 단어의 역사는 옛날에는 예술과 실생활 사이에 구분이 없었다는 것을 명확히 보여준다. 그리하여 공예품은 미적·실용적 감각 모두에 맞게 만들어진 것이다. 그러나 오늘날 예술 작품은 일반적으로 오로지 미적 감각에만 '맞는' 데에만 적용되며 이것은 예술이 실생활의 다른 영역과 단절돼 있는 현재의 상태를 나타낸다.

해설_ 주제가 art의 어원에 대한 내용으로, 원래 to fit라는 뜻을 갖고 있다고 한다. 그 다음에 셋째 줄을 보면 옛날에는 예술에 있어서 art와 생활과의 차이가 없었다고 나오면서 미적인 면과 실생활적인 면 두 가지를 동시에 맞추었다고 되어 있다.

어휘_ artisan 장인

artifact 공예품

aesthetic 미적인

fragmentation 분열, 파쇄

정답_ (b)

2.

해석_ 다른 상들 중에서도 토니상의 최우수 뮤지컬 부문과 퓰리처상을 수상한 〈렌트〉는 동성애, 양성애의 인물들을 그린 첫 번째 브로드웨이 뮤지컬 중 하나였습니다. 게다가, 이 뮤지컬의 출연진은 이례적이라 할 만큼 인종적으로 다양했습니다. 〈렌트〉는 전통적으로 보수적인 이 예술 수단의 작품 치고는 논란의 여지가 많은 주제였으며, 보다 젊은 세대들 사이에서 뮤지컬 연극의 인기를 높이는 데 일조했습니다. "뮤지컬 〈헤어〉가 베이비 붐 시대에 태어난 사람들이나 1960년대에 자란 사람들에게 호소하는 것처럼 〈렌트〉는 X세대에게 감동을 주고 있으며, '우리 시대의 락 오페라, 90년대의 〈헤어〉' 라고 할 수 있겠습니다."

해설_ 뮤지컬 〈렌트〉가 보수적인 연극무대에 올리기에는 논란이 되는 주제이면서도 젊은 세대들 사이에서 인기가 많았다는 전체적인 내용을 요약한 (c)가 정답으로 적절하다.

어휘_ homosexual 동성애의

bisexual 양성애의

ethnically 인종적으로

conservative 보수적인

controversial 논란의 여지가 많은

정답_ (c)

3.

해석_ 이탈리아의 문화예술부 장관인 산드로 본디는 이미 무티나 주빈 메타를 비롯한 주도적인 음악가들에게 강하게 비판을 받은 바 있는 개념, 즉 라 스칼라 극장, 산타 세실리아 아카데미 등을 축구로 치면 1부 리그로 보고, 나머지 극장들을 군소집단으로 분류하는 등, 우수성에 따라 예술자금을 지원하는 논란 많은 제안으로 돌아갈 수도 있다고 암시했다. 그래서 많은 예술가들이 이 제안에 반대하고 있으며 지지자는 거의 없다.

해설_ 논쟁의 쟁점이 무엇인지, 또 그것이 어떤 이유로 몇몇 음악가들에게 강하게 비판을 받는지 파악해야 한다. 무엇을 근거로 하는 예술 지원인지는 a kind of premier league and other venues being relegated와 같은 단어들을 통해 유추할 수 있다.

어휘_ minister 장관, 수상, 성직자

venue 재판지, 범행지, 사건 발생지, 개최 예정지

relegate 분류하다, 격하시키다

정답_ (d)

Chapter 2
미술

STEP 2 Actual Test

1.

해석_ 파블로 피카소가 20세기 서양 미술을 지배했다는 사실은 이제는 상식이다. 50번째 생일을 맞이하기 전에 말라가 태생의 이 작은 사람은 공인으로서의 현대 미술가 전형이 되었다. 이전의 어떤 화가도 피카소만큼 생전에 대중적 추종을 받은 적이 없었다. 피카소의 추종자들, 다시 말해 그에 관한 얘기를 들어 보고 그의 작품을 복제품으로라도 보았던 사람들은 수천만 아니 수억에 달했던 것이다. 그와 그의 작품은 끊임없는 분석과 화젯거리, 미움, 찬미, 소문의 대상이었다.

해설_ 피카소의 예술 세계에 대한 설명문을 통해 대의 파악 능력을 측정하는 문제이다. 현대 미술의 원형으로서 많은 추종자가 있었던 화가 피카소에 대해 평을 하는 글이다. 빈칸 다음의 문장 That is ~ 의 내용으로 볼 때, 문맥에 적합한 내용은 '많은 사람들이 그를 따랐다' 는 (a)이다.

어휘_ by now 이제는

prototype 원형, 전형

tens, possibly hundreds, of millions 수천 만의, 아니 아마도 수억의

adoration 찬미, 아주 좋아함

have a mass following 대단히 많은 추종자를 거느리다

정답_ (a)

2.

해석_ 구스타프 클림트에 대해 들어본 적이 있나요? 당신은 그에 대해 정확히는 알지 못하더라도 그의 그림을 한 번쯤은 보셨을 겁니다. 구스타프 클림트(1862년 7월 14일~1918년 2월 6일)는 오스트리아의 상징주의 화가였으며 비엔나 아르 누보(비엔나 분리) 운동의 가장 저명한 인사 중 하나였습니다. 그의 주요 작품으로는 회화, 벽화, 스케치 그리고 기타 예술작품들이 있으며 많은 작품들이 비엔나 분리주의 미술관에 전시되었습니다. 클림트의 주된 주제는 여성의 육체였으며 그의 작품은 솔직한 에로티시즘으로 특징지어지는데, 이것은 연필로 그린 그의 수많은 그림들에서보다 더 분명하게 나타나는 작품은 없습니다.

해설_ 본문의 전체적인 내용을 볼 때, 클림트는 비엔나 분리 운동의 가장 저명한 멤버였고 따라서 (b)가 정답임을 알 수 있다. 클림트의 주된 주제는 여성의 육체였으므로 (a)는 틀리고, 클림트의 작품들은 솔직한 에로티시즘을 보여준다고 했으므로 (c)도 틀렸고, 클림트의 작품은 회화, 벽화, 스케치와 다른 예술 작품들이 있으므로 (d)도 틀렸다.

어휘_ symbolist 상징주의자

prominent 저명한

secession 탈퇴, 분리

mural 벽화

numerous 수많은

정답_ (b)

3.

해석_ 모자이크는 개별적인 재료의 조각들을 함께 배치하여 통합된 전체를 창조해내는 고대와 현대의 예술 양식입니다. 대개 사용되는 재료는 유리, 도자기, 대리석, 조약돌, 거울, 조개 그리고 사기 그릇 등입니다. 재료의 각각의 조각들에 붙여지는 이름은 테세라입니다. 풀이 개어지는 사이의 공간을 이르는 용어는 틈입니다. 안다멘토는 테세라의 움직임과 흐름을 묘사하기 위해 사용되는 단어입니다. 라틴어로 '작품' 이라는 뜻을 지닌 오푸스는 조각들이 잘라지고 배치되는 방식입니다.

해설_ 테세라는 재료의 조각들에 붙여지는 이름이므로 (a)와 (d)는 옳지 않으며, 첫 번째 문장에서 알 수 있듯이 모자이크는 고대와 현대의 예술 양식이므로 (b)도 틀리다. gravel이 pebble과 동의어임을 알면 정답인 (c)를 쉽게 고를 수 있다.

어휘_ ancient 고대의

contemporary 현대의

unified 통합된

pebble 조약돌

grout 시멘트 풀

정답_ (c)

Chapter 3
문학

STEP 2 Actual Test

1.

해석_ 미스테리물을 읽을 때, 사랑을 할 때, 그리고 스포츠 게임을 볼 때에는 결과를 모르는 것이 더 재미있고 대부분의 경우 모르는 것이 더 낫다. 예상하지 못한 놀라운 반전이 있어야 정신을 바짝 차리고 전개되는 이야기나 인물들 간의 관계, 혹은 게임에 관심을 가지고 몰두하게 된다. 셜록 홈즈 이야기를 읽을 때 누가, 어떻게, 언제, 왜, 사람을 죽였는가를 정확하게 알고 있다면 무슨 재미가 있겠는가? 아무런 재미도 없을 것이다. 이야기 속에 탐정이 등장할 필요도 없다. 결말이 어떻게 날 것인지 미리 알고 있다면 끝까지 읽지도 않을 것이다.

해설_ 결말을 알지 못하고 읽는 글의 흥미와 관심에 관한 내용으로 대의 파악 능력을 측정하는 문제이다. 추리 소설이나 탐정 소설 등에서 독자의 흥미를 계속 잡아둘 수 있는 것은 예측할 수 없는 결과, 즉 결말을 알지 못하고 책을 읽어 나가기 때문에 재미있게 읽을 수 있다는 점을 설명하는 글이다. 특정한 글쓰기에 관한 내용은 아니므로 (a)는 정답이 될 수 없으며, 셜록 홈즈 같은 특정 탐정 소설에 관한 얘기도 아니므로 (c)도 아니다. (d)의 '예상치 못한 결과의 충격'은 흥미를 끄는 소재는 되어도 전체 내용의 제목으로는 부적합하다.

어휘_ keep ~ alert 계속 정신을 집중하게 만들다
　　　　detective 탐정, 형사
　　　　unexpected outcomes 예상 밖의 결과

정답_ (b)

2.

해석_ 문학 비평가의 의무는 어떤 예술 작품의 영향을 그 모든 복잡 속에서 느낄 수 있어야 하는데, 그렇게 할 수 있는 비평가들은 별로 없다. 저급하고 건방진 성품을 가진 사람은 저급하고 건방진 비평밖에 쓸 수 없다. 감성적으로 교육받은 사람은 대천재와 같이 드물다. 현학적으로 교육을 받을수록 감성적으로 더욱 빈약하다는 것이 일반적인 경향이다.

해설_ 앞에 있는 It ~ to가 주제문이다.(일반적으로 '가주어 ~ 진주어' 구문이 주제문이 된다. 주어가 길어진 문장은 주어의 중요한 메시지가 깔려 있게 되기 때문이다.) 문학 비평가의 의무는 모든 것을 포괄하여 예술 작품의 영향을 느낄 수 있어야 한다고 말을 했다. 그 뒤의 which에 중요한 내용이 나왔다. 바로 그런 비평가들이 거의 없다는 것이다. 즉, 비평가를 비판하는 내용이다.

어휘_ paltry 하찮은, 보잘것 없는
　　　　impudent 뻔뻔스러운, 철면피의

phoenix 불사조, 대천재
scholastically 현학적으로

정답_ (a)

3.

해석_ 미국의 신문 칼럼니스트 프랭클린 P. 애덤스가 만든 것으로 알려진 신조어 앱트러님이라는 말은 그 이름을 갖는 사람에게 딱 들어맞는 이름을 말한다. 소설 속에 나오는 앱트러님의 예로는 존 번연의 〈천로역정〉에 나오는 수다쟁이 씨와 세속 현자 씨가 있다. 또한 대장장이(금속 세공인)는 금속으로 물체를 만드는 일에 종사하는 사람이다. 산업화 이전 시대에 대장장이는 높은 혹은 특별한 사회적 지위를 누렸다. 농업에 필요한 금속 도구(특히 쟁기)와 전쟁에 필요한 금속 도구를 제공하였기 때문이다. smith란 단어의 어원은 '때리다', '치다'를 의미하는 약간 고어풍의 영어 단어 smite와 동일하다. 원래 대장장이들은 쇠망치로 강타하여 금속에 모양을 내는 기능을 업으로 하는 사람이다. 영어의 접미사 -smith는 '전문 장인'의 의미를 내포하고 있다. 예를 들자면 wordsmith와 tunesmith는 각각 문필가나 작곡가의 능숙함을 말하는 데 사용되는 단어다.

해설_ 본문에서 '영어의 접미사 -smith는 '전문 장인'의 의미를 내포하고 있으며 wordsmith는 문필가의 능숙함을 말하는 데 사용되는 단어라고 하였으므로 이름과 그 이름을 가진 사람 사이에 연관이 있음을 설명한 것이다. (d)의 Mr. Talkative는 말이 많은 사람이지 현명한 것과는 관련이 없다.

어휘_ coin 신어나 표현을 만들어내다
　　　　cognate 같은 어원의
　　　　connote 내포하다

정답_ (d)

Chapter 4
문학가

STEP 2 Actual Test

1.

해석_ 톨스토이는 지나치게 청결한 것은 사회적 신분의 상징이라는 이유로 지나친 청결을 반대했다. 몸을 씻거나 내복을 자주 갈아입는 시간과 돈의 여유가 있는 것은 오직 부자들뿐이다. 생계를 위해 땀을 흘리거나 집에 목욕탕이 없거나 장롱에 여분의 옷이 없는 그런 노동자들은 악취를 풍기기 마련이다. 그가 악취를 풍긴다는 것은 당연하고, 또한 그것은 옳고 적절한 것이다. 노동은 기도요, 노동은 또한 악취가 난다. 그러므로 악취는 기도다. 대게 톨스토이는 이렇게 주장하고 있고, 그는 계속해서 부자들이 악취를 풍기지 않은 것에 대해, 그리고 자기 아이들이 모든 인간의 냄새에 대해서 그것들이 아무리 당연하고 명예로운 것이라고 해도 편견을 갖도록 양육하는 것을 비난하고 있다.

해설_ 마지막 문장에서 '부자들이 악취를 풍기지 않은 것에 대해, 그리고 자기 아이들이 모든 악취에 대해서 그것들이 아무리 당연하고 명예로운 것이라고 해도 편견을 갖도록' 하면 안 된다고 한 내용이 힌트가 된다.

어휘_ cleanliness 청결
　　　 superfluous 여분의
　　　 stink 악취를 풍기다; 악취
　　　 condemn 비난하다
　　　 prejudice 편견

정답_ (d)

2.

해석_ 상 파울로 대학의 번역가 바클리 셀스 씨는 몇몇 한국의 문학 작품들은 너무 감상적이고 번역되었을 때 약간 치기에 차있는 듯한 경향이 있다고 언급한다. 영국 컬럼비아 대학의 브루스 풀튼 교수는 해외에서 한국 문학의 번역 작품을 가르치는 데 있어 문제 중의 하나는 "한국의 문학적 전통은 장편 소설보다는 단편 소설의 중요성에 초점을 두는 데 있다"고 말한다. 그리고 미국에서 단편 소설 작품집만을 출판하는 출판사는 드물다고 한다. 하지만 한국 문학 번역 연구소의 윤지관 소장은 이러한 문제점들 중 한국의 문학 번역의 현장에서 가장 큰 걸림돌이 된 것은 아무 것도 없었다고 한다.

해설_ 앞서 제기된 한국 문학 번역에 있어서의 몇 가지 문제점들이 사실 별 문제가 되지 않았다고 말하는 것으로 미루어 보아 이에 대한 반론이 이어져야 문맥이 자연스럽다. (b) 다양한 한국의 문학적 전통에 대한 거론도 있을 법하나, 지나치게 넓은 주제여서 적합하지 않다.

어휘_ lyrical 서정적인, 감상적인
　　　 childish 유치한, 치기어린
　　　 put emphasis on ~에 중점을 두다
　　　 hindrance 방해, 장애(물)

정답_ (a)

3.

해석_ 리처드 도드릿지 블랙모어는 1825년 영국의 한 작은 마을에서 태어났다. 다른 위대한 작가들과 마찬가지로, 어린 리처드는 혹독한 유년기를 겪었다. 그의 어머니는 리처드가 태어난 지 몇 달 되지 않아 죽었다. 그 후 그는 그의 이모와 함께 생활했다. 몸도 허약하고 학교에서 따돌림도 받았지만 명문 옥스퍼드 대학에서 고전 문학 공부를 시작하고부터는 매우 우수한 성적을 보여주었다. 그의 나이 22살 때, 그는 학교를 우등으로 졸업하였다. 처음에 그는 법조계에서 경력을 쌓고자 했다. 그러나 그의 좋지 않은 건강 때문에 그 분야에 진입하지 못했다. 건강상의 문제가 그가 하고자 하는 일을 계속 방해했기 때문에, 그의 삶은 어쩌면 매우 불행해 보일 수도 있을 것이다. 하지만 행운이 우연히 찾아왔다. 부유한 그의 삼촌이 런던의 큰 농장을 구입할 수 있는 돈을 그의 나이 32살 때 그에게 남겨준 것이었다. 삶의 남은 기간 동안 리처드는 소설을 쓰고 농작물을 키우며 시간을 보냈다.

해설_ (a) 리처드의 전공이 법학인지, 문학인지는 지문을 통해서는 알 수 없다. (b) 농장에서 일을 한 뒤, 건강을 회복했는지 나와 있지 않고 다른 일을 할 수 없었다고 나와 있다. (d) 그의 삼촌이 남긴 것은 농장을 살 수 있는 충분한 돈이지 농장이 아니다.

어휘_ bully 겁주다, 괴롭히다
　　　 prevent from -ing ~하지 못하게 하다
　　　 a stroke of fortune[luck] 뜻밖의 행운
　　　 extremely 극단적으로, 매우
　　　 misfortune 불행

정답_ (c)

STEP 2 Actual Test

1.

해석_ 리스트의 유년 시절과 젊었을 때에 리스트의 발전을 설명하기 위한 모든 시도에서 이용할 수 있는 정보가 매우 취약하다는 어려움을 겪었다. 리나 라만, 피터 라브 그리고 더 최근에 들어서는 알란 워커와 같은 전통적인 라인의 작가들은 리스트가 이미 소년으로서 최상의 천재적 기질을 지닌 예술가였으며, 특히 모든 음악사에 존재했을 법한 모든 것을 능가하는 피아니스트였음을 묘사하는 작업에 집중했다. 하지만 이러한 관점에서는 그가 심화 수업을 받아야만 했다는 것에 대한 이유를 설명해 주지 못한다.

해설_ 본문의 내용은 많은 작가들이 리스트의 어린 시절에 대해 설명하려고 시도했지만, 어려움에 부딪치고는 한다는 내용이다. 따라서 가장 적절한 답은 (a)이다.

어휘_ attempt 시도

concentrate on ~에 전념하다, 집중하다

surpass ~보다 낫다

exist 존재하다, 있다

정답_ (a)

2.

해석_ 아카펠라 음악은 성악이며, 악기의 반주 없이 노래하는 것이나, 이러한 방식으로 공연되는 작품을 의미한다. 아카펠라는 원래 르네상스의 다성부 음악과 바로크의 협주곡 양식을 구별하기 위한 목적이었다. 19세기에 르네상스 다성부 음악에 대해 다시 시작된 흥미와, 성악부가 종종 기악 연주자들에 의해 겹쳐진다는 사실에 대한 무지가 결합된 것이 무반주 성악을 의미하는 용어로 연결되었다. 현대적인 사용법으로, 아카펠라는 종종 남성 4부 합창, 드왑 그리고 현대의 대중음악, 락을 포함한 어느 양식의 모든 노래를 언급하기도 한다.

해설_ 아카펠라의 의의에 대해 설명하고 있으며, 용어의 기원과 현대적인 쓰임새까지 아울러 설명하고 있다. 따라서 답은 (b)가 적절하다.

어휘_ accompaniment 반주

differentiate 구별하다

polyphony 다성부의

concertato 협주의

barbershop 이발소; 남성 4부 합창

정답_ (b)

3.

해석_ 모든 예술은 음악의 상태를 갈망한다고 맨 처음 말한 것은 쇼펜하우어였다. 그 말은 자주 되풀이되어 왔으며 많은 오해의 원인이 되었다. 그러나 그것은 중요한 진실을 나타내고 있다. 쇼펜하우어는 음악의 추상성에 대해 생각하고 있었다. 즉, 음악에서 거의 음악에서만이, 예술가는 다른 목적에 일반적으로 사용되는 전달 수단을 이용하지 않고 청중에게 직접 호소할 수가 있다. 건축가는 실용적인 목적이 있는 건축물로 자신을 표현하지 않으면 안 된다. 시인은 일상적으로 주고받는 말을 사용하지 않으면 안 된다. 화가는 눈에 보이는 세계를 묘사하여 자기 자신을 표현한다. 작곡가만이 자기 자신의 의식으로 오직 사람을 즐겁게 해줄 목적만으로 더할 나위 없이 자유롭게 예술 작품을 창작할 수 있다.

해설_ 쇼펜하우어가 말한 첫 번째 문장에서 음악이 가장 순수한 형태의 예술임을 밝히고 있다.

어휘_ aspire 열망하다, 갈망하다

remark 비평, 의견

abstract 추상적인

architect 건축가

color-blinded 색맹의

consciousness 의식

정답_ (d)

Chapter 6
법률

STEP 2 Actual Test

1.

해석_ 법률가들이 사례 연구를 하고 산더미처럼 쌓인 서류를 조사하면서 법률 도서관에서 무수한 시간을 보내야 하는 날들이 이제 곧 마감될 듯 싶다. 컴퓨터 기술의 발달은 변호사와 법률가 보조원, 법률사무소 사무원, 법률 서기관들의 삶을 훨씬 쉽고 효율적으로 만들어 주었다. 전통적인 방법으로 법률상 조사를 하는 것은 많은 시간을 필요로 하는 과정이다. LEXUS, NEXUS, 그리고 Westlaw와 같은 온라인 정보 서비스를 통해 변호사와 법률사무소 사무원들은 눈 깜짝할 사이에 법률상 조사를 수행할 수 있다. 조사 시간을 줄임으로써 같은 시간 내에 더 많은 일을 할 수 있게 되었고 사건 의뢰인에 청구되는 비용도 줄어들었다. 컴퓨터는 또한 법률 지원단의 삶도 편하게 만들어주고 있다. 실례로, 법률 서기관을 도와줄 많은 소프트웨어가 있다. 이러한 프로그램을 사용하여 자동으로 소송 의뢰인의 파일을 작성 보관하고, 소송사건 일람표를 열람하며, 전화번호의 저장, 일일 일정표의 인쇄, 그리고 월별 보고서 준비 등을 할 수 있다. 그러한 소프트웨어의 사용은 법률 서기관들로 하여금 훨씬 더 체계적으로 일을 하고 변호사들의 요구에 더 잘 부응할 수 있도록 만들어 준다.

해설_ 글의 요지는 문단 서두에 기술된 바와 같이 컴퓨터 기술의 발달로 법률가들이 더 편안하고 쉽게 업무를 처리할 수 있게 되었다는 것이다.

어휘_ case research 사례 연구
stack 쌓아 올린 더미
paralegal 법률가 보조원
legal secretary 법률 서기관
in a fraction of time 순식간에
docket 소송 사건 일람표
responsive to ~에 응하는, 대답하는
attorney 법률가, 변호사
substantially 실질상, 충분히

정답_ (c)

2.

해석_ 국제 공법은 국가의 구조와 행위 그리고 정부 간의 조직에 관한 법이다. 국제법은 또 정도는 덜하지만 다국적 기업과 개인에게 영향을 미치기도 하며, 그 영향은 또한 점점 국내의 법 해석과 집행을 초월하여 발휘되고 있다. 국제 공법은 국제 무역, 무력 충돌, 전 세계적인 규모의 환경 악화, 인권 침해의 인식, 국제 교통수단의 빠르고 거대한 증가와 국제적인 의사소통이 증대됨에 따라 지난 20세기 동안 유용성과 중요성에 있어서 크게 증가해 왔다.

해설_ (a)에서 국제 공법은 시민단체의 조직이 아니라 국가의 구조와 행위, 정부 간의 조직에 관한 것이므로 틀리다. (c) 국제 공법은 인권뿐만 아니라 국제 무역 등 여러 문제에 대해 다루며, (d)는 둘째 줄, 셋째 줄에서 다국적 기업과 개인에게도 영향을 미친다고 하였으므로 옳지 않다. (b)의 경우 본문의 마지막 문장에서 답을 찾을 수 있다.

어휘_ public international law 국제 공법
conduct 행위
intergovernmental 정부간의
a lesser degree 다소
multinational 다국적의
vastly 광대하게
deterioration 악화

정답_ (b)

3.

해석_ 사형은 종종 논란이 되는 주제이다. 사형을 반대하는 사람들은 이것이 무고한 사람들의 사형 집행으로 이어져 왔으며, 종신형이 효과적이고 희생이 적은 대안이 될 수 있다고 주장한다. 사형은 소수 집단과 가난한 사람들에 대해 차별하고 있으며, 범죄자의 살 권리를 파괴한다고 주장한다. 사형 제도를 지지하는 사람들은 사형 제도가 응보의 원리에 의해 살인자들에게 정당화될 수 있으며, 종신형은 동등하게 효과적인 억제책이 못되고, 사형이 생명권을 침해하는 자를 가장 엄격한 형태로 처벌함으로써 생명권을 지켜 준다고 주장하고 있다.

해설_ (a), (b)는 본문에 언급되지 않은 내용이며, (c)는 찬성하는 사람들이 아니라 반대하는 사람들에 대한 서술이다. 본문을 미루어보아 사형 제도에 대한 찬성과 반대가 첨예하게 대립함을 알 수 있으므로 답은 (d)이다.

어휘_ capital punishment 사형
life imprisonment 종신형
substitute 대체
retribution 응보, 징벌
deterrent 억제물, 억제력
affirm 단언하다

정답_ (d)

Chapter 7
순수 철학

STEP 2 Actual Test

1.

해석_ 어떤 사회학이라도 가장 기본적인 가정은 인간의 행태가 전적으로 임의적이거나 불규칙적이지는 않다는 것이다. 다른 인간 현상처럼, 언어에서 연구자들은 언어 구조를 지배하는 규칙적인 패턴과 규칙들을 찾는다. 그러한 규칙이나 규범의 체계화는 언어학자들의 대부분의 연구 작업을 구성한다. 그러한 규칙들이 사회적 맥락의 영향을 받는다는 사실은 사회언어학자들의 기초 조건 중 하나이다.

해설_ 빈칸 뒤에서 인간의 행태가 규칙적이라는 것을 언어의 예를 들어 설명하고 있다.

어휘_ sociology 사회학, 군집 생태학

　　　erratic 일정하지 않은, 변하기 쉬운

　　　postulate 자명한 원리, 기초[선결] 조건

　　　behavioristic 행동주의적인

　　　cognitive 인식이 있는

정답_ (c)

2.

해석_ 한 철학자에게 지혜란 지식과 같은 것이 아니다. 사실들은 그것을 아는 지혜를 사랑하는 사람들 없이 거대한 수로 알려질 수도 있다. 사실 해박한 정보를 가지고 있는 사람이 지혜를 사랑하고 추구하는 사람들에게 상당한 경멸을 느낄 수 있다. 철학자가 단순히 사실을 아는 것에 만족하지 않기 때문이다. 그는 사실 뒤에 가려져 있는 것들을 통합하고 재평가하고 탐구하기를 원한다.

해설_ 철학자가 단순히 사실을 아는 것에 만족하지 않기에 사실 뒤에 숨은 의미를 해석하길 원할 것이다.

어휘_ prodigious 거대한, 막대한

　　　knower 알고 있는 사람, 이해하는 사람

　　　encyclopedic 해박한

　　　integrate 통합하다, 조정하다

정답_ (c)

3.

해석_ 지난 50년 동안 우리는 더 나은 집과, 더 많은 옷들, 더 긴 휴가 그리고 무엇보다 더 건강한 삶을 살아왔다. 그러나 미국, 일본 또는 유럽에서 행복 지수가 증가되지 않았다는 사실이 조사를 통해 명확하게 나타났다. 대조적으로 가난한 나라에서 사람들이 수입이 늘어날 때 행복지수가 올라갔다. 만약 당신이 최저 생활 수준에 있다면 절대 수입은 삶과 죽음의 문제이다. 여분의 돈이 부자보다 가난한 사람의 행복에 더 큰 가치가 있다는 것을 우리는 이제 과학적으로 보여줄 수 있다. 따라서 의욕을 꺾는 효과가 크지 않다면 부가 부자에서 가난한 사람에게 옮겨질 때 전체 행복이 증가한다. 이것은 가정에서의 그리고 개발도상국으로의 재분배를 말해 준다.

해설_ 빈칸 앞의 '여분의 돈이 부자보다 가난한 사람들의 행복에 더 큰 가치가 있다' 는 내용이 힌트가 된다.

어휘_ in contrast 대조적으로

　　　breadline 최저 생활 수준

　　　disincentive 의욕을 꺾는, (특히) 경제 성장[생산성 향상]을 저해하는

　　　redistribution 재분배

정답_ (c)

STEP 2 Actual Test

1.

해석_ 나는 일생을 통틀어 사회과학-경제학, 사회 정책, 국제 관계, 재무-에 관여해 왔으며 나는 항상 지적인 생활과 학구적 생활에 전념하는 것을 목표로 삼아왔다. 이 대학은 흥미 있는 곳이며 새로운 아이디어, 사건, 주요 커리큘럼 외의 논쟁들이 윙윙거리는 곳이며 그 흥미는 실제적인 참여로 사회와 연관되어 있다. 그 국제적인 평판은 누구에게도 뒤지지 않는다. 나는 직원들 그리고 학생들과 함께 일하는 것이 매우 기대되며 대학을 다음 발전 단계로 이끌어가는 것은 큰 특권이 될 것이다.

해설_ 윗글은 사회과학자인 필자가 새로운 아이디어 등이 샘솟는 그 대학에서의 새로운 일, 즉 학장으로서의 일에 대해 흥미를 갖는다는 내용이다.

어휘_ buzzing 윙윙거리는

curriculum 커리큘럼, 교육[교과] 과정

second to none 첫째 가는

reputation 평판, 명성

privilege 특권

정답_ (d)

2.

해석_ 기업인에게는 이익을 가져다주고 정치인에게는 표를 가져다주는 방법으로 가난한 사람들의 필요에 접근하는 방법을 찾을 수 있다면, 우리는 이 세계에서 불평등을 줄여나갈 수 있는 지속적인 방법을 찾을 수 있을 것입니다. 이 과제는 끝이 없습니다. 그것은 결코 끝날 수 있는 것이 아닙니다. 하지만 이러한 도전을 해결하려는 의식적인 노력이 세상을 변화시킬 것입니다. 나는 우리가 할 수 있을 것이라고 낙관하면서, 희망이 없다고 주장하는 회의적인 사람들에게 말합니다. 그들은 "불평등은 태초부터 우리와 함께 했다. 그리고 끝까지 우리와 함께 할 것이다. 사람들은… 전혀 관심이 없기 때문이다." 라고 말합니다. 나는 이 말에 전적으로 동의하지 않습니다. 나는 우리가 무엇을 할지 아는 것 이상으로 관심을 가지고 있다고 믿습니다.

해설_ 낙관하면서 희망이 없다고 주장하는 회의적인 사람들의 말에 전적으로 동의하지 않는 것으로 봐서 저자는 희망적으로 보고 있다.

어휘_ inequity 불공평

sustainable 지속적인

open-ended 끝이 없는, 제한이 없는

uneasy 걱정되는

정답_ (d)

3.

해석_ 사람들은 자기와 유사한 사람을 자기의 연애 상대로 고를까 아니면 반대의 사람을 고려하려고 할까? 배우자와의 유사성이 행복한 결혼으로 이어질까? 이 질문에 대한 지금까지 수행된 것 중 가장 포괄적인 한 연구에서 아이오와 대학교 연구원과 논객들은 사람들은 태도, 종교, 가치관이 서로 유사한 사람과 결혼하는 경향이 있다는 사실을 발견했다. 그러나 행복한 결혼 생활에서 더 중요한 것처럼 보이는 것은 성격의 유사성이다. 이러한 연구 결과는 미국 심리학회가 출간한 〈인성, 사회심리학 저널〉 2월호에 나와 있다.

해설_ 연구 결과를 바탕으로 한 객관적인 어조로 말하고 있다.

어휘_ spouse 배우자

marital 혼인의

polemist 논객(특히 신학상의)

comprehensive 포괄적인, 이해력이 있는

personality 성격, 개성, 인성

festive 명랑한

decisive 단호한

정답_ (d)

STEP 2 Actual Test

1.

해석_ 귀하의 주문이 재고 부족으로 발송이 지연되고 있음을 알려드리게 되어 유감스럽습니다. 괜찮으시다면, 다른 색깔의 35676번 상품을 보내드리겠습니다. 만일 그렇게 하는 것이 만족스럽지 않으시다면 전액 환불해 드리겠습니다.

해설_ '~를 보내지 못하지만 …는 가능하다' 는 내용에서 빈칸에 들어갈 것은 '괜찮다면' 또는 '가능하다면' 이라는 표현이 적절하다.

어휘_ stock shortage 재고 부족
  refund 환불
  satisfactory 만족스러운

정답_ (c)

2.

해석_ 관계자에게:

신디 김과 3년 반 동안 일한 것은 즐거운 경험이었습니다. 신디는 훌륭한 직원이었고 이곳 유니버설 출판사의 회계부장으로서의 직위에서 탁월한 능력을 보였습니다. 신디 김은 이 기간 동안 저희 회사의 가장 유능한 직원 중 한 사람이었으며, 우리 회사를 떠나 워싱턴 DC로 가게 되어 매우 유감으로 생각합니다. 신디의 독창적인 계획 수립과 통찰력은 우리 회사가 최근 3년 동안 매년 10% 이상의 성장을 이루는 데 많은 도움을 주었습니다. 신디 김이 더 이상 우리와 함께 일하지 않게 되어 아쉽게 생각하지만, 귀사나 정부 기관에서 회계직 또는 관리직에 적합한 사람으로서 적극 추천합니다.

오퍼레이션지 부회장

로라 그린넬

해설_ 두 번째 문장과 마지막 서명을 통해 이 추천장을 쓴 이가 유니버설 출판사의 중역임을 알 수 있고, 이 추천인은 회계부장이었던 신디 김이 자사를 떠나게 된 것에 대해 아쉬움을 표현하고 있다.

어휘_ excel in ~에서 뛰어나다, 탁월하다
  managerial 경영의, 관리의
  sincerely 진정으로

정답_ (c)

3.

해석_ 어느 새로운 보고서에 의하면, 도요타와 미쓰비시의 레저용 다용도 차나 고급 렉서스를 소유한 사람들은 다른 사람들보다 차량 도난에 대비한 보험료를 더 많이 내고 있는 것으로 조사됐다. 그 이유는 이 차량들이 차량 절도범에게 인기가 있기 때문이다. 고속도로 도난 사고 집계국이 화요일에 발표한 보고서에 따르면 1995년에서 1997년 모델 가운데 가장 도난을 많이 당한 차량은 10대 중 8대가 레저용 다용도 차이거나 고급 승용차였다고 한다. 이 보고서에 따르면 도요타 차를 소유한 사람은 종합 보험료로 절도에 대비해 매년 평균 530달러 가량을 내는 것으로 되어 있다. 미쓰비시 몬테로를 모는 사람이 두 번째로 도난 대비 보험료를 많이 내고, 렉서스 GS 300을 모는 사람이 3위에 올라 있다.

해설_ 자동차 보험료에 관한 글을 통해 대의 파악 능력을 묻는 문제이다. '보험료가 비싼 이유는 도둑들이 선호하기 때문' 이라는 내용이므로 이를 잘 요약한 선택지를 고르면 된다. (a)는 사실과 일치하지 않으며, (b)와 (c)는 본문의 내용만으로는 알 수 없으므로 모두 정답이 될 수 없다.

어휘_ theft insurance 도난 보험
  on average 평균적으로
  under their comprehensive insurance coverage 종합 보험으로 처리되는
  overpriced 비싼 값을 매긴

정답_ (d)

Chapter 10

STEP 2 Actual Test

1.

해석_ 당신의 예산이 제한이 있든 쓸 돈이 많든 간에 품질이 좋은 가구는 모든 가격대에 존재한다. 그러나 당신에게 필요한 강도와 내구성에 대한 특징을 아는 것은 도움이 될 것이다. 가구를 선택할 때 단단한 골격과 탄력이 있는 쿠션 구성은 그것이 매일 사용된다면 중요하다. 활동적인 가족의 정열을 감당할 만한 외피를 위해서는 타이트하게 짜여진 직물 또는 가죽을 선택하라.

해설_ 빈칸 뒤에 가구를 구매할 때 활동적인 가족을 위해서는 내구력이 있는 가구를 골라야 한다는 내용이 있는 것으로 보아 빈칸에는 '강도와 내구성에 대한 당신의 필요' 가 적합하다.

어휘_ upholstery 가구(의자 · 융단 · 커튼 따위)

　　　　feature 특색으로 삼다

　　　　resilient 되튀는, 탄력 있는(buoyant)

　　　　fabric 직물

정답_ (a)

2.

해석_ 사람들은 경매 웹사이트에서 한 양동이의 물을 사기 위해 인터넷으로 입찰을 하고 있다. 그 황당무계한 양동이 수돗물은 지금까지 최고 18달러의 입찰을 받았으며 거의 600명이 그 사이트에서 경매 내역을 읽었다. 거기에는 이렇게 쓰여 있다. "여기에 훌륭한 수원에서 직접 공급받은 한 양동이의 신선한 물을 얻을 수 있는 기회가 당신에게 있습니다. 이것은 무언가 시원하고 상쾌한 것을 원하는 모든 물 수집가들에게는 독특한 기회입니다." 그 주인은 장난삼아 그 물을 경매에 붙였으며 그 반응에 놀랐다고 말했다.

해설_ '황당무계한 양동이 수돗물' 을 장난삼아서 경매 웹사이트에 올렸는데 그 반응에 대해 언급하는 등 장난 같은 경매 현황에 관한 글이다.

어휘_ fabulous 황당무계한, 믿을 수 없는

　　　　auction 경매

　　　　refreshing 상쾌한, 후련한

　　　　response 반응, 응답

정답_ (b)

3.

해석_ 어떤 고객이 입어서 낡아진 것이 분명한 이브닝 드레스를 갖고 와서 환불해줄 것을 요구한 일이 있었다. 그 손님은 드라이크리닝을 한 뒤 옷이 다른 색상으로 변했으며, 세탁소 종업원이 옷감이 잘 못되었다고 말했다고 주장했다. 나는 그 손님이 정직하다고 생각하지는 않았지만 즉각 환불해줄 것이라고 말했다. 그런 결정을 내린 이유는 다른 고객이 그 손님의 이야기를 듣지 못하게 해서 우리 회사에서 만든 좋은 품질의 제품을 의심하지 않도록 하는 것이 더 중요하다고 판단했기 때문이다.

해설_ 환불을 받지 못한 것을 불평하여 또 다른 문제가 야기되는 것을 원하지 않아 환불해주었다고 해서 낡은 옷도 손님이 원하면 언제든지 환불해주는 것은 아닐 것이다.

어휘_ merchandise 제품

　　　　apparently 분명하게, 또렷하게

　　　　keep A from B -ing A가 B하는 것을 방지하다

정답_ (c)

Chapter 11
제품 광고

STEP 2 Actual Test

1.

해석_ 모토롤라 월드와이드 콤은 세상에서 가장 다양한 기능을 지닌 호출기입니다. 이 정교한 통신기기는 저희의 소중한 고객 여러분이 공간 장벽을 뛰어넘을 수 있도록 고안된 것입니다. 당신은 중요한 동료들과 연락할 수 있을 뿐 아니라, 지구촌 어느 곳에서건 호출기를 읽음으로써 최신의 경제 정보와 증권 가격을 알 수 있습니다. 저희 첨단 기술은 최근에 벌어지는 일들이 언제 어디서 일어나든 관계없이, 바쁜 출장객들에게 획기적이고 새로운 방식으로 정보를 제공할 수 있게 하였습니다.

해설_ 제품 광고문을 통해 대의파악 능력을 측정하는 문제이다. 개인 호출기를 광고하는 내용으로서, 전체 문맥을 볼 때에 호출기를 통해 여행자가 최신 정보를 계속 얻을 수 있다는 내용이다.

어휘_ versatile 용도가 다양한, 다용도의

spatial barrier 공간 장벽

not only will you be able to ~을 할 수 있을 뿐만 아니라

(부정어 not only로 시작하는 도치 구문임)

associate 동료, 친구

info 정보 (information)

stock prices 주식 가격

state-of-the-art 첨단의

stay abreast of all latest events 최근에 벌어지는 일에 대해 계속 정보를 얻다

정답_ (d)

2.

해석_ 전 세계의 수많은 나라에서 프랑스 샹파뉴 지방에서 최초로 개발된 방법에 따라 스파클링 와인을 생산하고 있다. 그러나 그 어떤 제품도 원조 포도주의 정교한 맛을 따라잡지 못하고 있다. 진정한 샴페인은 오직 같은 이름을 가진 지역에서만 생산된다. 샴페인을 만드는 데 쓰이는 포도 종류는 적포도와 백포도인데, 레몬 향내와 씁쓸한 맛을 가진 샴페인에서부터 감칠맛과 나무 열매 향기가 나는 샴페인에 이르기까지 샴페인의 맛은 실로 다양하다.

해설_ 본문의 두 번째 문장을 보면, 저자가 샹파뉴 이외의 지역에서 생산되는 포도주에 관해 어떻게 생각하는지 알 수 있다. 한마디로, 정교한 맛에 관한 한 샹파뉴 지방산의 포도주에 필적할 만한 포도주는 다른 지역에서는 찾아볼 수 없다고 했으므로 답은 (d)이다.

어휘_ sparkling wine 발포 포도주

blend 섞다, 혼합하다

lemony 레몬 맛[향]이 나는

austere 떫은 맛[향]이 나는

nutty 견과 맛이 나는, 나무 열매 향기가 나는

정답_ (d)

3.

해석_ 여름 몇 달 동안에 한해 서울 볼러라마 레인스에서는 평일 오전 10시부터 오후 2시까지 볼링 시설 이용비를 절반 가격으로 할인해 드립니다. 저희 레스토랑이나 스낵바에서 점심을 드시기만 하면 50% 할인 혜택을 누리실 수 있습니다. 추가로, 상기 시간대에 두 게임을 치신다면 볼링공과 볼링화, 티셔츠, 모자 등 많은 상품 중 하나를 타실 수 있는 복권 추첨에 자동으로 등록됩니다. 뭘 주저하십니까? 어서 저희 서울 볼러라마 레인스에 오셔서 즐거움을 누리시기 바랍니다.

해설_ 두 번째 문장에 할인 가격으로 볼링을 칠 수 있는 방법이 명시되어 있다. 그것은 볼링장의 레스토랑이나 스낵바, 즉 구내에서 점심을 사먹는 것이므로 답은 (b)이다. (a)와 (c)는 경품 추첨에 관한 것이기 때문에 게임비 할인과는 무관하다.

어휘_ weekday 주중의 평일

raffle 복권 판매[추첨]

get in on (활동 따위에) 참여하다(come in on)

qualify for ~의 자격을 갖추다

정답_ (b)

Chapter 12
일반 정치

1.

해석_ 무정부론은 모든 형태의 정부에 반대하는 정치적 이데올로기이다. 무정부주의자들은 인류의 최고 성취는 외부로부터 어떤 형태의 억압이나 조정에 방해받지 않고 개개인이 자신의 의사를 표현할 수 있는 자유라고 주장한다. 이들이 근본적으로 믿는 바는 모든 정부가 철폐되고 각 개인이 절대 자유가 되기 전에는 인간성의 완성이 이루어지지 않을 거라는 점이다. 그러나 많은 사람들이 정부의 주권 없이 개인이 자유를 갖는 것은 불가능하다고 믿는다. 개인의 희생을 요구하는 국가적 통합보다 개인의 주권을 더 중요시하는 오늘날의 정보와 기술의 시대에 와서는 무정부론이 시대에 뒤떨어진다는 주장이 도전을 받고 있다.

해설_ 무정부론에 관한 글을 통해 문맥상 어울리는 절을 고르는 문제이다. '정부의 주권 없이는 개인의 자유도 있을 수 없다' 는 무정부론에 반대하는 주장이 있지만, 국가적 통합보다 개인의 자유를 중시하는 정보와 기술의 시대에서는 그런 주장이 도전을 받고 있다는 내용이다. 무정부론이 시대착오적이라는 선택지가 전체 문맥에 가장 적합하므로 정답은 (d)이다.

어휘_ anarchy 무정부(론)

　from without 외부로부터

　sovereignty 주권

　assertion 주장

　put A before B B보다 A를 더 중시하다

　oppressive 억압하는

　anachronistic 시대에 뒤떨어진

정답_ (d)

2.

해석_ 나는 뛰어들었습니다. 나는 이기기 위해 뛰어들었습니다. 나는 오늘 대통령 입후보를 위한 준비 위원회를 구성하겠다는 것을 천명하는 바입니다. 나는 여러분이 단지 선거운동에 동참하시길 바라는 것이 아니라 국가의 장래에 대한 대화를, 지난 6년간의 부시 행정부의 실책을 극복하기 위해 필요한 대담하고도 실질적인 변화에 관한 대화를 함께 하는 데 동참해 주실 것을 바랍니다. 나는 이번에 미국 국민과 직접 대화하고자 합니다. 며칠간 계속될 온라인 채팅에 여러분을 모두 초대함으로써 시작하고자 합니다. 2008년 새로운 대통령을 뽑는 일은 큰 도박이 될 것입니다.

해설_ 본문 중간에 '나는 이번에 미국 국민과 직접 대화하고자 합니다. 며칠간 계속될 온라인 채팅에 여러분을 모두 초대함으로써 시작하고자 합니다.' 라며 국민과 대화를 하고 싶다는 내용을 직접 밝히고 있다.

어휘_ I'm in. 나는 뛰어들었다.

　announce 천명하다, 알리다

　Bush administration 부시 행정부

정답_ (c)

3.

해석_ 헌법의 기본적인 쟁점은 정부가 국민이 원하는 일을 할 수 있을 만큼 강력한 정부를 만드는 방법과 국민이 원하지 않는 일은 하지 못하도록 정부의 권한을 제한하는 방법이다. 국민들이 정부가 하지 않았으면 하는 가장 중요한 것 중의 하나는 국민의 '권리' 를 침해하는 것이다. '권리' 가 무엇을 의미하는지는 시대에 따라 변하지만, 우리들은 정부가 우리들에게 할 수 없는 일정한 것들이 있다는 것에 대한 개념에 익숙해져있다. '권리' 는 두 개의 그룹으로 분류될 수 있다. 첫 번째 그룹은 절차적 권리다. 이것은 정부가 반드시 준수해야 하는 절차에 관한 것이다. 두 번째 그룹은 실체적 권리다. 이것은 절차에 관계없이 정부가 침해할 수 없는 개인의 자유 영역으로 정의된다.

해설_ 본문의 마지막 내용은 절차적 권리를 충족하였더라도 실체적 권리를 충족하지 못할 수도 있다는, 즉 정부가 절차를 따랐더라도 불법적인 경우가 있을 수 있었다는 내용이다.

어휘_ constitution 헌법

　substantive 실체적인

　invade 침해하다

　regardless of ~에 상관없이

　illegal 불법적인

정답_ (a)

Chapter 13
국제 정치

STEP 2 Actual Test

1.

해석 이스라엘 건국 50주년 행사를 바라보며 저는 착잡한 느낌을 금할 길이 없습니다. 이스라엘의 건국은 유태인들에게는 탄생을 의미했지만 팔레스타인 사람들에게는 죽음을 의미했습니다. 시간이 흐르면서 유대 민족주의자들에 의해 자행되던 테러는 거꾸로 팔레스타인 사람에 의해 자행되게 되었고, 전쟁과 슬픔이 그칠 날이 없었습니다. 분쟁의 끝없는 위협 속에서 이스라엘은 방위 예산을 늘릴 수밖에 없었고, 미국은 이스라엘에 경제적으로 막대한 지원을 하지 않을 수 없었습니다. 국내외적인 모든 고난을 딛고, 이스라엘 국민들은 중동에서 가장 민주적인 국가를 이룩해 왔습니다. 그러나 현재 이스라엘 사회는 그 어느 때보다도 분열되어 있으며, 따라서 평화를 이룩할 수 있는 기회는 점점 멀어져만 갑니다. 이스라엘에 영광이 있기를 기원합니다. 그리고 이스라엘 국민들이 건국 50주년에 걸맞게 반짝이는 평화의 상을 획득할 수 있다는 것을 깨닫기를 희망합니다.

해설 mixed feelings란 표현으로 볼 때에 저자는 이스라엘의 독립 국가로서 축하할 면과, 이스라엘과 팔레스타인 간의 평화 문제에 대한 회의적인 면을 동시에 보고 있음을 알 수 있다. 이런 두 가지 측면을 나타낸 (d)가 정답이다.

어휘 statehood 국가, 국가로서의 위상

founding of ~의 설립

perpetual 영속적인

against all odds 모든 승산을 거슬러서, 모든 어려움에 대항하여

정답 (d)

2.

해석 2001년 9월 11일에 발생했던 미국에 대한 공격들은 이슬람과 현대 세계에 있어 이슬람의 역할에 대한 논쟁을 더욱 증폭시켰다. 어떤 사람들은 이슬람의 사상이 현대 열망과 양립할 수 없다고 생각한다. 이슬람은 결과적으로 나쁜 이미지로 점철된 것처럼 보인다. 그러나 과거에는 많은 이슬람 과학자들이 현대 과학에 상당한 기여를 하였다. 그리고 현재 많은 무슬림들이 많은 기술과학 분야에서 종사하고 있다. 예를 들면 확실히 이러한 무슬림들은 그들의 믿음과 현대성을 조화하는 방법을 알아왔다. 이슬람이 현대 사회 또는 어떠한 유형의 문명과 양립할 수 없다는 것은 근거 없는 편견이다.

해설 빈칸 앞의 내용은 무슬림들이 현대 사회에 많은 기여를 하며 조화를 이루는 방법을 알고 있다고 하였으므로 무슬림이 현대 사회와 양립할 수 없다는 것은 '근거 없는 편견' 에 불과하다는 것을 알

수 있다.

어휘 intensify 격렬하게 하다

aspiration 열망; 포부

incompatible 양립할 수 없는

modernity 현대성

reconcile 화해시키다, 조화하다

groundless 근거 없는

prejudice 편견

정답 (c)

3.

해석 비록 미국과 캐나다가 경계를 접하고 있더라도 두 나라 사이에는 많은 차이점이 존재한다. 캐나다인과 미국인의 차이점에는 무엇이 있을까? 이러한 의문은 종종 두 나라 사람들이 함께 모여 있을 때 강한 감정을 불러일으킨다. 당신은 이것에 대해 어떻게 생각하는가? 두 나라 중에 어느 나라에 대해 더 잘 알고 있는가? 왜 그런가? 미국의 뛰어난 작가이자 방송인(텔레비전과 라디오 모두) 중 한 사람인 후크 소이어의 에세이 '나의 조국' 에서 발췌한 다음 글에 이 주제에 대한 그의 생각이 잘 나타나 있다.

해설 Huck Sawyer, one of USA's leading writers and broadcasters (for both TV and radio), gives his thoughts on the subject in the following excerpts from his essay "My country."에서 the subject가 캐나다인과 미국인의 차이점이므로 (c)로 답을 고를 수 있다. (b)와 (d)는 본문에서 알 수 없다.

어휘 arouse 깨우다, 자극하다, 불러일으키다

excerpt 발췌문

comparison 비교

정답 (c)

Chapter 14
국제 기구와 협력

STEP 2 Actual Test

1.

해석_ 헤센 주 인구의 대부분은 라인 강 본토 지역에 있는 헤센 주 남부에 있다. 라인 강은 주를 가로지르지 않고 남서쪽으로 헤센 주와 경계를 이루고 있으며, 알트 라인이라고 불리는 오직 하나의 오래된 지류가 헤센 주를 가로지른다. 마인과 네카 강 사이에 분포한 산맥은 오덴발트라고 불린다. 헤센 주는 유럽에서 최상의 교통기반 시설을 가지고 있다. 마인, 라인 그리고 네카 강과 오덴발트 산맥에 둘러싸인 평원은 리트라고 불린다.

해설_ 전반적으로 헤센이라는 주의 지리에 대해 설명하고 있다. (c) 만 교통 시설에 관한 설명으로 본문의 흐름에 배치된다.

어휘_ border 경계를 이루다

run through 가로지르다

infrastructure 기반 시설

mountain range 산맥

정답_ (c)

2.

해석_ 오늘날 60억이 넘는 세계 인구 중 10억 명 이상이 깨끗한 물을 얻지 못하고 있고 약 26억 명이 향상된 위생의 혜택을 받지 못하고 있으며 그들 중 대부분은 후진국에 살고 있다. 유엔의 아동기구인 유니세프에 따르면, 오염된 물과 기본적 위생의 부족이 매년 150만 명이 넘는 아이들의 생명을 앗아가는데, 대부분은 수인성 질병으로 죽는다. "상당한 진전에도 불구하고 약 4억 2천 5백만 명의 18세 이하 아이들이 개선된 식수를 얻지 못한다"고 유니세프 집행 위원장인 앤 베네만은 말한다. 그렇게 죽는 사람들은 감염된 아이들만이 아니라 "수백만 명 이상이 물과 관련된 질병으로 고통을 겪어왔다"고 그녀는 말했다. 유니세프 보고서는 물과 위생 거의 최고 수준의 보급률을 달성한 선진 공업국가들에 대해서는 합격점을 발부했다.

해설_ 후진국의 많은 사람들이 깨끗한 물과 향상된 위생의 혜택을 받지 못하고 있는 현 상태를 서술한 글이다. (d) 선진국들은 위생과 식수 보급률에서 유니세프에 의해 합격점을 받았다는 내용은 글의 흐름과 맞지 않는다.

어휘_ sanitation 위생

commendable 칭찬할 만한, 훌륭한

undermine (건강 등을) 서서히 해치다

clean bill of health (의사가 발부하는) 건강 증명서

정답_ (d)

3.

해석_ 멕시코의 마약과의 전쟁은 미국에 이주한 멕시코인들의 생활에 깊은 영향을 끼치게 되어 있다. 한편, 세균 전파자로서의 이미지를 갖고 있는 멕시코의 혼돈은 이민을 반대하는 세력에 힘을 실어줄 수도 있을 것이다. 반면, 미국에 갓 이민 온 멕시코인들은 점점 위험에 처해가는 모국을 되돌아볼 때 의식적으로든 무의식적으로든 미국에 더 깊은 뿌리를 내리고자 할 것이다.

해설_ 현재 멕시코가 미국에게 주는 이미지는 매우 부정적인 것이다. 이러한 때문에 미국에 살고 있고 새로 이민을 오고자 하는 멕시코인들에겐 그들의 고국에 대한 이러한 평가가 매우 부담스러울 수 있을 것이다. 이러한 평가를 벗어나기 위해 그들이 미국에서 가장 염두에 두고 있는 일이 무엇일지 추론해보면 정답을 알 수 있다.

어휘_ bound to do 꼭 ~하게 되어 있는

profound 깊은

contagion 세균, 전염병(infection)

consciously 의식적으로

break off relations with ~와의 관계를 끊다

정답_ (a)

Chapter 15
질병

STEP 2 Actual Test

1.

해석_ 몇 년 전 30대 초반의 급성 백혈병에 걸린 젊은 전문직 종사자 티모시 스미스의 진찰 의뢰를 받았다. 치료를 받으면 팀은 25%의 생존확률이 있었고, 치료를 받지 않으면 몇 개월 안에 사망할 것으로 판단되었다. 팀은 충격을 받았다. 그의 반응은 자포자기와 분노 속에 자살에 집착하며 자살하도록 도와달라고 요청하는 것이었다. 그는 남에게 의존하게 되는 것을 두려워했고 그의 병의 증상과 치료의 부작용을 걱정했다. 팀의 요청은 조력 자살의 핵심 문제와 맞닿아 있다. 불치병에 걸린 사람들을 돌보아야 하고 그들의 고통을 덜어주어야 하는 우리의 책무에 비추어 의사에게 환자의 생명을 마감시킬 권리를 주어야 하는가? 안락사라는 이 말 많은 문제는 우리 사회를 분열시킬 수도 있다.

해설_ 논란의 여지가 많은 안락사에 대한 사설을 통해 대의 파악 능력을 측정하는 문제이다. 시한부 인생을 사는 환자의 통증을 줄여주는 안락사에 관한 내용이므로 (d)가 정답이다. (b)는 정반대의 내용이므로 답이 될 수 없다.

어휘_ acute leukemia 급성 백혈병

　　　chronic 만성의

　　　be stunned 깜짝 놀라다

　　　preoccupation with ~에 집착함

　　　side effects 부작용

　　　assisted suicide 조력 자살

　　　be terminally ill 불치병에 걸리다

　　　euthanasia 안락사

　　　tear ~ apart ~를 분열시키다

정답_ (d)

2.

해석_ 체중 감소를 약속하지만 실제 가벼워지는 것이라고는 지갑뿐인 소위 '기적의 알약'에 넌더리가 난다구요? 구석에 방치된 채 먼지만 수북이 쌓여 있는 수백 달러짜리의 운동 기구를 구입하신 적이 있습니까? 만약 이 질문들에 '예' 라고 대답하신다면, 저희한테 여러분에게 딱 맞는 제품이 있습니다. 저희가 새롭게 선보인 간편 조리 음식들은 지방 대체물인 올레스트라로 만들어졌습니다. 올레스트라는 음식 맛을 그대로 유지하면서도 열량이 전혀 들어있지 않습니다. 따라서 체중 증가에 대한 염려 없이 아무 때나 원하는 음식을 드실 수 있습니다.

해설_ 본문에서 필자는 '올레스트라는 음식 맛을 그대로 유지하면서도 열량이 전혀 들어 있지 않습니다.' 라고 하며 올레스트라의 장점을 알리고 있다.

어휘_ line 종류, 품종

　　　substitute 대용품, 대체물

　　　in conjunction with ~과 결합하여

　　　obesity 비만

정답_ (b)

3.

해석_ 미국 고속도로에서 운전자들의 '운전 중 분노' 경험을 입증하는 금요일 발표된 설문조사에 따르면 뉴저지 주에 사는 540만 면허 운전자 중 절반 이상이 운전 도중 화를 내며, 그 중의 반 정도가 도로에서 다른 운전자에게 보복하려 한다는 것이다. 뉴저지 보험 뉴스 서비스 사 전무인 존 틴은 "이것은 매우 우려할 만한 사실입니다. 문제가 생각보다 훨씬 더 심각합니다" 라고 말했다. 뉴스 서비스 사에 의하면 분노한, 즉 공격적인 운전자들은 미국에서 인구 밀도가 가장 높은 뉴저지 주에서 정말 위협이 되고 있다고 말한다.

해설_ 고속도로에서 벌어지는 교통 문제를 다룬 기사문을 통해 대의 파악 능력을 측정하는 문제이다. '화가 난 운전자들이 상대방 운전자들을 응징하려는 욕구를 느낀다' 는 내용이므로 정답은 (d)이다. (a)는 '무의식적으로 화를 낸다' 인데, 바로 앞에 화를 낸다는 말이 있으므로 부적절하다. (b)는 '화가 난 운전자들이 다른 사람을 배려하지 않는다' 는 뜻으로 엉뚱하며, (c)는 '살인' 을 의미하므로 옳지 않다.

어휘_ licensed motorist 면허 있는 운전자

　　　behind the wheel 운전대 뒤에 있는 (즉, 운전하는)

　　　executive director 전무이사

　　　densely populated 인구가 밀집한

정답_ (d)

STEP 2 Actual Test

1.

해석_ 자외선 차단 로션은 아마 피부암을 막지 못할 것이다. 일부 영국 의사들은 선크림이 피부암에 대해 완전하게 보호하지 못하며 거의 최후의 방어막과 같다고 주장한다. 그들은 사람들에게 모자를 쓰고 그늘에 있으라고 충고한다. 그들의 주장에 따르면, 사람들이 선크림을 바르고 있으므로 완전하게 보호된다고 생각해선 안 된다고 한다. 그러나 선크림을 바르고 햇볕에 신경을 쓰는 것은 아무것도 안하는 것보다 훨씬 낫다.

해설_ 선크림이 피부암을 완전하게 방지하지 못하지만 안 바르는 것보다는 훨씬 낫다는 것이다. 빈칸 앞과 뒤의 내용이 상반되므로 빈칸에는 역접의 접속사가 들어간다.

어휘_ cancer 암
sunscreen 자외선 차단제
assume 가장하다
completely 전적으로, 완전하게

정답_ (a)

2.

해석_ 과학자들은 수면과 암의 관계에 대한 연구를 해왔고 수면이 신체의 호르몬 균형을 바꿀 수 있다는 것을 알게 되었다. 호르몬 코티솔은 어떤 사람이 종양을 키우는가를 결정하는 데 중요한 역할을 한다. 좀 더 구체적으로 말하면 코티솔은 신체가 암과 싸우는 것을 도와주는 세포와 같은 면역 시스템을 통제하며 이 호르몬의 수치는 새벽에 최고조에 달하고 낮 동안에는 내려간다. 유방암의 발병 가능성이 높은 여성들은 코티솔 사이클에 변화가 있었다고 연구는 밝혀냈다. 수면장애 때문에 코티솔 리듬이 교란되면 사람이 암에 더 취약해질 수 있다.

해설_ 빈칸 다음의 내용은 빈칸 앞의 내용을 더욱 구체적으로 설명하고 있다. 따라서 빈칸에는 '더욱 구체적으로 말하면' 이라는 뜻을 가진 To be more specific이 적합하다.

어휘_ cortisol 코티솔(부신 피질에서 생기는 스테로이드 호르몬의 일종)
disrupt 분열시키다, 혼란케 하다
demonstrate 증명하다
nevertheless 그럼에도 불구하고

정답_ (b)

3.

해석_ 아이들은 제각각 기본적인 기질을 갖고 태어나며 이것은 생활의 경험에 의해 형성된다. 아이는 부모와 환경이 조화로울 때 잘 자란다. 환경이 맞지 않으면 고통 받게 된다. 어떤 때는 환경 탓이 아니기도 한다. 예를 들어 나는 자폐증을 앓는 한 젊은 여성 예술가를 치료한 적이 있다. 그녀한테는 불행하게도, 그녀는 회계사 집안에서 태어난 것이다. 좋은 부모였지만 그들은 그녀를 어떻게 대할지 몰랐고 그녀는 가족들과 다르고 가치 없게 느껴지는 것을 고민하게 되었다. 더 심각한 예는 어린 남자아이의 경우인데, 그는 15살까지 여러 차례 심장 수술을 요하는 심장 장애를 앓고 있었다. 그의 어머니는 이미 불치병을 겪는 조부모들을 간호해 왔기 때문에 그를 돌보는 것에 진저리를 느꼈다. 그가 처음에 어떤 정상적인 수치심을 가졌든 그것은 이미 삐뚤어졌고, 나를 만났을 때 그는 집안에 틀어박혀 있고 수줍어하며 성난 젊은 어른이었다.

해설_ 환경과 부모 중 환경 자체는 문제가 없는데 부모의 태도가 문제되는 경우를 주로 설명하므로 (b)는 답이 될 수 없으며 본문의 사례는 회계사 집안에서 예술가로 자란 경우와 병을 앓는 아이를 잘 돌보지 못한 어머니 밑에서 자란 비정상적인 성격을 말하므로 (c)와 같이 부모의 유전자와는 상관없다. 하지만 본문의 첫째 문장에서 '아이들은 제각각 기본적인 기질을 갖고 태어나는데 이것은 경험에 의해 형성된다.' 고 한 것은 (a)처럼 '어릴 적 인성과 과거의 경험들이 현재를 형성한다' 는 것과 일맥상통한다.

어휘_ temperament 기질
flourish 무성하게 자라다, 번창하다
instance 사례
surgery 수술
autism 자폐증

정답_ (a)

Chapter 17

환경과 인간/대체의학

STEP 2 Actual Test

1.

해석_ 현대 의학이 수많은 새로운 치료법을 가능하게 만들어 왔지만, 의사들은 일부 전통적인 방식도 역시 유용하다는 것을 깨닫고 있다. 예를 들면, 의사들은 현재 식이요법과 건강 사이의 관계에 더욱 많은 관심을 보이고 있다. 거머리까지도 현대 의학에서 자리를 찾아오고 있다. 특정한 종류의 수술에서, 최신의 외과 의사들은 환자의 동맥이 막히는 것을 방지하기 위해 거머리를 사용하고 있다.

어떤 사람들은 인간 질병의 모든 치료제는 자연에 있다고 믿는다. 다른 사람들은 기술이 더 유용하다고 믿는다. 아마 전통과 기술이 함께 모든 곳의 사람들을 보다 낫고 건강한 삶을 살 수 있도록 도울 것이다.

해설_ 첫 번째 문단은 현대 의학이 전통 의학의 방식을 도입하는 내용을 담고 있고, 두 번째 문단의 마지막 문장 It just might be that, together, tradition and technology will help people everywhere live better and healthier lives.에서 주제를 찾을 수 있다. 따라서 답은 (b)가 적절하다.

어휘_ pay attention to ~에 유의하다
　　　surgery 수술
　　　leech 거머리
　　　artery 동맥

정답_ (b)

2.

해석_ '닥터후'는 장기간에 걸쳐 방영되었으며 수상하기도 한, BBC가 제작한 영국의 공상과학 텔레비전 프로그램이다. 그 작품은 "닥터"라고 알려진 불가사의한 외계인 시간 여행자의 모험을 그리고 있는데, 그는 그의 공간과 시간여행선인 타디스(외형적으로 파랑색의 파출소처럼 생긴)를 타고 여행한다. 이 프로그램은 교육적인 목적으로 만들어졌으며, 토요일 초저녁 시간대에 가족들이 볼 수 있도록 만들어졌다. 그는 동료들과 함께 시간과 공간을 탐험하고, 문제들을 풀어내며 잘못된 것들을 바로잡는다. 이 프로그램은 세계에서 가장 오래 방영된 공상과학 텔레비전 프로로 기네스 기록에 올라 있으며, 영국의 대중문화의 중요한 일부이기도 하다.

해설_ 전반적으로 '닥터후'라는 텔레비전 프로그램의 내용과 의의에 대해 설명하고 있다. 프로그램의 내용을 설명하는 (a)와 (c) 사이에 프로그램의 본래 목적에 관한 (b)가 들어가서 문맥의 흐름상 적절하지 못하다.

어휘_ long-running 장기간 방영된

depict 그리다, 묘사하다
significant 뜻깊은, 중요한
exterior 외관

정답_ (b)

3.

해설_ 농장에서 일하는 사람들에게 살충제 노출이 미치는 건강상 영향에 대한 많은 연구가 있어왔다. 비록 살충제가 올바르게 사용될지라도, 여전히 그것들은 공기 중과 농부들의 몸에 남아 있다. 이러한 연구들을 통해 유기 인산 화합물의 살충제가 피부와 눈 질환뿐만 아니라 복통, 어지러움, 두통, 메스꺼움, 구토와 같은 건강상의 중대한 문제들과 관련되어 왔다. 게다가, 살충제 노출이 호흡기 질환, 기억력 장애, 피부병, 암, 우울증, 신경 장애, 유산 그리고 선천성 결손증 등과 같은 더욱 심각한 건강 문제들과 관련이 있음을 밝혀온 다른 연구들이 많이 있다.

해설_ 전체적으로 살충제 노출이 미치는 건강 상의 해로운 영향에 대한 설명을 하고 있으므로 정답은 (a)이다. (b)는 본문과 배치되는 설명이며, (c)에서 기침은 건강 문제의 하나로 열거되어 있지 않다. (d)는 본문을 통해 알 수 없다.

어휘_ pesticide 살충제
　　　organophosphate 유기 인산 화합물의
　　　abdominal 복부의
　　　dermatologic 피부(병)의
　　　miscarriage 유산

정답_ (a)

Chapter 18
환경 문제

STEP 2 Actual Test

1.

해석_ 지구를 보호하는 오존층은 2000년이나 2001년이면 역사상 가장 얇은 단계가 될 것이라고 세계 기상 기구(WMO)가 월요일 밝혔다. 오존층 감소를 막기 위한 국제적인 조치를 통해 차세기 중반이면 오존층이 두터워지리라는 전망이 있지만, 오존층은 현재 최악의 단계에 와 있으며 상황이 나아지기는커녕 더욱 나빠질 것이라고 WMO는 말했다. 오존층은 태양의 해로운 자외선을 흡수하는 약한 가스 보호 방패인데, 인간이 만들어낸 화학물질로 인해 점점 많은 구멍이 뚫리고 있다. 이 구멍들은 피부암을 일으키는 주범으로 꼽힌다.

해설_ 환경 오염에 대한 기사를 통해 문맥상 가장 적절한 형용사를 고르는 문제이다. 오존층 파괴의 심각성을 다룬 내용이므로, 첫 문장에서 오존층이 2000년이나 2001년에 가장 얇은 단계에 도달한다고 하므로, 빈칸에는 '취약한' 이라는 내용이 적합하다.

어휘_ hit one's all-time+**최상급** 전례 없이 가장 ~하다
meteorological 기상학
measure to do ~하는 조치
things will get worse 상황이 더욱 악화될 것이다
pierce 관통하다, 찌르다
sophisticated 고도로 세련된
vulnerable 상처를 입기 쉬운

정답_ (d)

2.

해석_ 사람들은 항상 쓰레기들을 호수, 강, 강의 어귀 등에 버렸는데, 그것이 쓰레기를 매립하는 것보다 쉽기 때문이다. 많은 양의 물이 더럽거나 위험한 물질들을 희석시키고, 강에서는 물의 흐름이 쓰레기, 화학물질 그리고 오물들을 운반한다. 이것은 미국 인구가 작았을 때는 큰 문제가 되지 않았다. 그러나 수질문제는 그 나라의 인구가 증가하기 시작할 때 표면화된다. 많은 강과 호수들은 회복되고 있지만, 어떤 면에 있어 수질은 항상 관리되어 왔다. 수질 문제는 호수와 강들이 오염 물질들을 흡수·희석시키는 능력을 초과하여 발생한 결과이다.

해설_ 사람들이 지금까지 항상 호수, 강 등에 쓰레기를 버려왔다는 얘기를 하다가 느닷없이 (c)에서 회복된다는 말이 나오기 때문에 (c)가 정답이다.

어휘_ estuary (간만의 차가 있는) 큰 강의 어귀
foul 더러운
dilute 희석시키다
sewage 하수 오물, 오수(汚水)
take off 상승하다

정답_ (c)

3.

해석_ 나무는 개발도상국에서 땔감용으로 많은 수요가 있다. 많은 지역에서 사람들은 그들의 음식을 조리하는 데 나무에 의존하고 있다. 인구가 증가함에 따라 나무에 대한 수요도 또한 증가하였다. 그러나 너무 많은 나무들이 한꺼번에 잘려나가면 숲이 망가진다. 땅이 절박하게 필요한 소규모 농부들 또한 숲에 들어온다. 그들은 잔여 나무들을 잘라내고 불태운다. 이런 식으로 수백만 에이커에 달하는 숲이 매년 파괴된다. 불행하게도 숲의 토양은 농사짓기에 적합하지 않다. 그리하여 이 가난한 농부들은 여전히 가난한 상태로 머무르게 된다. 그 결과 그들은 숲의 자원들도 잃게 된다.

해설_ 농사짓기 위해 숲을 태우는데 숲의 토양이 농사짓기에 적합하지 않다면 가난한 농부들은 여전히 가난한 상태로 남을 것이다.

어휘_ desperate 필사적인, 절박한
resource 자원
destroy 파괴하다

정답_ (c)

STEP 2 Actual Test

1.

해석_ 회오리바람 안의 유체 압력은 속도가 최대인 중심부에서 가장 낮으며, 중심부에서 멀어질수록 점차적으로 올라간다. 이것은 베르누이의 원리와 부합한다. 공기 중의 회오리바람의 중심부는 중심부의 저기압의 응축이 만들어낸 수증기 기둥으로 인해 때로 눈에 보이기도 한다. 토네이도의 기둥은 회오리바람의 중심부가 보이는 가장 고전적이며 무서운 예이다. 열대 사막의 회오리바람도 또한 회오리바람의 핵심인데 지상에서 저기압의 중심으로 향하는 몹시 거친 공기의 기류로 인해 상승하는 먼지에 의해 보이게 된다.

해설_ 열대 사막의 회오리바람도 중심부의 저기압의 응축이 만들어낸 공기 기류로 인해 보이게(visible) 된다는 내용이므로 빈칸에는 열대 사막의 회오리바람도 '회오리바람의 핵심' 이다가 적합하다.

어휘_ fluid 유동체[성]의, 불안정한

vortex 회오리바람

dust devil (열대 사막의) 회오리바람

turbulent 몹시 거친, 사나운

정답_ (a)

2.

해석_ 아스완 댐이 건설되기 전까지, 이집트는 매년 나일강의 범람(1년 주기의 홍수)을 겪었다. 고대 이집트인들은 몰랐지만, 그 홍수는 에티오피아 고원에 내린 여름 폭우 때문이었으며, 인접한 다른 지류들과 다른 강들을 팽창시켜 나일강이 되었다. 이것은 이집트인들이 Akhet, 즉 범람이라 부르는 6월부터 9월까지의 계절에 매년 발생한다. 이것은 이집트인들에게는 지상에 비옥함을 가져다주는 하피 신이 매년 오는 것으로 여겨졌다.

해설_ 이집트인은 그 범람을 지상에 비옥함을 가져다주는 신 Hapi가 매년 오는 것으로 여겼다는 본문의 내용처럼 이집트인들은 그 범람을 상서로운 것으로 보았다.

어휘_ inundation 범람

tributary (강의) 지류

fertility 비옥함

정답_ (a)

3.

해석_ 작은 눈사태라도 생명에 심각한 위험이 되며, 그것은 눈사태를 대피훈련이 잘 돼 있고 좋은 장비를 갖춘 일행과 같이 있어도 위험이 된다. 노지에 있다가 파묻힌 희생자의 55%에서 65%가 죽었으

며 지표면 위에 남아있던 희생자 중 오로지 80%만이 살아남았다. 역사적으로, 생존 확률은 15분 이내에는 85%, 30분 이내에는 50%이며, 1시간 이내에는 20% 정도이다. 결과적으로 눈사태를 면한 사람들은 모두 구조 요원이 도착하기를 기다리기보다는 즉시 희생자 수색 및 구조 작업을 취하는 것이 중요하다. 만약 어떤 사람이 눈사태 속에 파묻히더라도 가벼운 로프가 눈 위에 그대로 있게 되고 그 로프는 색깔때문에 구조 요원들에게 잘 보인다.

해설_ (a)에서 (c)까지는 눈사태가 발생하면 재빨리 구조해야 사람을 살릴 수 있다는 내용이다. (d)에서 로프의 내용이 갑자기 나오는 것은 논리적·순차적으로 오류가 있다.

어휘_ avalanche 눈사태

immediate 즉시의

rescue personnel 구조 요원

정답_ (d)

STEP 2 Actual Test

1.

해석_ 슈퍼컴퓨터의 성능과 공학 기술이 눈부실지라도, 하드웨어만으로는 컴퓨터 과학자들의 최종적인 목표, 즉 인간의 결정 능력을 흉내낼 수 있는 시스템의 창조를 부분적으로만 달성할 것이다. 이 목표는 AI, 즉 인공 지능이라고 하는데, 수십 년 동안 컴퓨터 프로그래머들은 이것을 만들어내지 못했다.

해설_ 문장의 맨 앞에 양보절을 이끄는 Although가 문제 해결의 핵심이다. 즉 컴퓨터가 뛰어날지라도 그와 상반되는 '인간'의 능력을 뛰어넘을 수 없다는 이야기가 된다.

어휘_ virtuosity 묘기, 기교

artificial intelligence 인공 지능

mimic 흉내내다

elude 피하다, 알 수 없다

정답_ (b)

2.

해석_ 구 소련은 세계 최대의 자석을 보유하고 있다고 주장했다. 모스크바 근처의 두브나 소재 합동 핵 연구소에 있는 이 자석은 지름이 60미터에 무게가 36,000톤을 상회한다. 그러나 이 자석이 세계에서 가장 강력한 자계력을 가진 것은 아니다. 가장 강력한 자석은 MIT의 프랜시스비터 국립 자력 연구소에 있는 것으로, 이 자석은 초전도성의 니오브-티타늄 합금으로 만들어졌다. 말할 것도 없이, 이곳을 찾는 사람들이 이 자석 근처에 가기 전에 모든 귀금속들을 떼어놓으라는 권고를 듣는다.

해설_ 세계 최대의 자석은 구 소련에 있으므로 (a)는 틀린 진술이다. 그리고 니오브-티타늄의 밀도에 관해서는 본문을 통해 명시되지 않았으므로 (c)의 진위는 알 수 없다. 또한 구 소련이 문제의 자석을 만든 동기에 대해서도 언급되지 않았으므로 (d)도 답이 될 수 없다.

어휘_ lay claim to ~을 자칭하다, ~에 대한 소유[권리]를 주장하다

diameter 직경, 지름

magnetic field strength 자계력

superconducting 초전도의

niobium-titanium 니오브-티타늄 합금

vicinity 근처

정답_ (b)

3.

해석_ 점화전 설치는 급속히 늘고 있는 가내 정비인이 손수 할 수 있는 가장 간단한 일 중 하나다. 먼저 점화전에서 점화선을 분리한다. 올바른 점화전에 다시 연결할 수 있도록 각각의 점화선에 표시를 해두도록 유의해야 한다. 점화선용 소켓과 4분의 3인치 래치트를 이용하여 낡은 점화전을 제거한다. 엔진 제작업체의 시방서에 맞게 새 점화전들의 간격을 조정한다. 우선 손가락을 이용하여 새 점화전을 넣어 조인 후, 래치트로 반 바퀴 내지 4분의 3바퀴 정도 더 돌려준다. 점화선을 다시 연결하면, 모든 일이 끝난다.

해설_ 점화선에 표를 다는 이유는 본문의 세 번째 문장에 명시된 대로 나중에 제자리에 점화선을 연결하기 위한 것이다.

어휘_ spark plug (내연기관의) 점화전

do-it-yourself 손수 하는

burgeon 갑자기 커지다, 빠르게 성장하다

ignition 점화

socket (전구 따위를 끼우는) 소켓

ratchet 래치트, 깔쭉 톱니바퀴를 이용한 도구

specification 시방서, 설명서

conduction 전도

정답_ (c)

STEP 2 Actual Test

1.

해석_ 물은 모든 음식에 함유되어 있다. 물을 마심으로써도, 우유와 주스를 마시는 것으로도 물을 얻는 것이 가능하다. 어떤 물은 음식이 세포 분열하면서 발생하기도 한다. 대부분의 과일과 야채는 수분은 물론 영양을 얻을 수 있는 좋은 원천이다. 그것들은 소화기관의 근육을 자극할 수 있는 섬유질을 포함하는 거칠고, 소화하기 힘든 섬유소 음식의 좋은 원천이기도 하다.

해설_ 첫 번째 문장이 주제문으로, 물이 모든 음식에 들어 있다는 것이다. (a)는 ~ but 이하의 내용이 틀렸다. 다음 (b)와 (d)는 야채, 과일에 대한 언급으로, (b)는 세 번째 줄 중간에서 답이 아님을 알 수 있고 마지막 줄에서 (d)가 답임을 알 수 있다.

어휘_ roughage 조악한 음식물, 섬유소를 함유하는 음식
coarse 조잡한, 조악한
digestive 소화의
tract 관(管), 도(道), 계통

정답_ (d)

2.

해석_ 약 2억 1천만 년 전인 후기 트라이아스기(紀)에 우리가 현재 알고 있는 대륙들은 존재하지 않았다. 2억 1천만 년 전에 그 대륙들은 그것이 현재 가지고 있는 모양과 위치를 나타내었다. 지구의 표면은 광대한 바다와 하나의 거대한 대륙인 판게아를 포함하였다. 그러나 거의 감지할 수 없게 판게아가 떨어져 나가 독립된 대륙들이 지구를 떠다니게 되었다. 수백만 년 동안, 이 표류는 계속되었고 어떤 면에서는 지금도 계속되고 있다.

해설_ 첫 문장에서 2억 1천만 년 전 트라이아스기 때 우리가 지금 알고 있는 대륙의 모습은 존재하지 않았다고 했는데 갑자기 (a)에서 오늘날의 대륙과 모양과 위치가 비슷하다고 했으므로 (a)가 답이다.

어휘_ Triassic 트라이아스기(紀)의
landmass 광대한 토지; 대륙
Pangaea 판게아(트라이아스기(紀) 이전에 존재했다고 하는 대륙; 그 후 북의 Laurasia와 남의 Gondwana로 분리됨)
imperceptibly 감지할 수 없게
in a sense 어떤 점으로는, 어느 정도까지

정답_ (a)

3.

해석_ 로봇들은 인간을 위해 위험한 일을 하도록 프로그램화된 기계류이다. 그것들은 이미 우주 공간에도 보내져 그들이 그곳에서 발견한 것을 우리들에게 알려주었다. 그것들은 심해에 들어가 인간을 위해 유용한 정보를 수집한다. 그것들은 또한 전쟁과 평화에도 이용된다. 그것들의 일부는 지뢰들을 폭파함으로써, 전쟁터를 농지로 바꾸는 걸 가능하게 한다.

해설_ 빈칸 뒤에서 로봇은 우주 공간이나 심해에서 인간을 위해 인간이 하기에 위험한 일을 한다는 내용을 언급하고 있다.

어휘_ explode 폭발시키다
battlefield 전쟁터
farmland 농지

정답_ (a)

일반 생물학

STEP 2 Actual Test

1.

해석_ 공격은 한 동물이 다른 동물을 강습하거나 습격하는 것을 특징으로 하는 동물 행동 양식이다. 공격은 연관된 요소가 다양함에 따라 여러 가지 모습을 띨 수 있다. 공격의 한 형태는 서로 다른 종 사이의 충돌이다. 이 형태에는 약탈적 공격(먹이 획득)과 방어적 공격, 먹이나 물 같은 자원을 놓고 경쟁자에게 가하는 공격이 포함될 수 있다. 이런 종류의 공격은 분노와 같은 감정의 개입이 없는 게 일반적이며 생존 행위의 구성요소로 인식될 수 있다.

해설_ 동물 행동의 공격성에 대한 설명문을 통하여 대의를 파악하는 능력을 측정하는 문제이다. 여기서 말하는 공격은 감정이 개입되지 않은 생존(survival)을 위한 행위이다.

어휘_ be characterized by ~이 특징이다

derived from ~에서 유래된

predatory 약탈하는, 육식의

be perceived as ~로 인식되다

evolutionary process 진화 과정

aggressive instinct 호전적인 본능

정답_ (a)

2.

해석_ ecology(생태학)라는 용어는 100년 전 독일의 생물학자인 에른스트 헤켈에 의해 만들어졌다. 그리스어 oikos(집)에서 유래한 eco-는 economics(경제학)에서의 eco와 같다. 옛날의 정의에 따르면 생태학자가 연구하는 것은 동물과 식물의 economy(질서)이다. ecosystem(생태계)은 생태학자가 연구하는 지역의 자연에 서식하는 생물군과 물리적 환경을 함께 의미한다. 현대의 표준 정의로 ecology는 유기체와 환경의 관계를 연구하는 학문이다.

해설_ '생태학(ecology)' 이라는 용어에 대한 설명이다. 보통 이런 지문들은 대학교 교양 과목 원서에 잘 나온다. 용어의 기원을 설명하는 (a), 이전의 정의를 설명하는 (b), 현재의 의미를 설명하는 (d) 모두 ecology라는 용어 설명을 위한 진술들인데 여기서 갑자기 ecosystem(생태계)의 의미를 설명하는 (c)는 자연스럽지 못하다.

어휘_ ecology 생태학

coin (신어·신표현을) 만들어내다

definition 정의

정답_ (c)

3.

해석_ 세계에서 유일하게 생존하고 있는 한 마리로 간주되는 흰색 고릴라 한 마리가 피부암으로 죽어가고 있다. 스노우플레이크(눈송이)라는 이름을 가진 그 흰색 고릴라는 1966년 적도 기니에서 한 사냥꾼에 의해 생포되었으며 그 뒤 바르셀로나 동물원에서 지냈다. 수의사들은 그 고릴라가 병을 앓고 있다는 것을 꽤 오래전부터 알고 있었지만 그 병이 갑자기 진행되었다. 그 동물원의 한 수의사는 그들이 고릴라를 보호하기 위해 최선을 다했지만 그 병은 치료할 수 없으며 그들은 고릴라가 자연적 과정을 따르게 놔둘 것이라고 말했다.

해설_ 그 병을 치료할 수 없다면 자연적 과정, 즉 죽게 놔둘 수밖에 없다.

어휘_ snowflake 눈송이

equatorial 적도의, 적도 부근의

vet 수의사 (veterinarian의 축약형)

incurable 불치의

정답_ (b)

STEP 2 Actual Test

1.

해석_ 둥지 만드는 법을 배우는 것은 새들이 번식에 성공하는 데에 중요한 역할을 한다. 예를 들어 스노우 박사는 여러 해 동안 많은 찌르레기의 번식 성공을 기록해왔다. 그는 처음으로 둥지를 지은 새들은 나이가 든 새들에 비해 번식에 덜 성공적이라는 것과 바로 다음 해에 비해서도 덜 성공적이라는 것을 알았다. 이것은 크기나 힘 같은 단순한 문제가 아니다. 왜냐하면 대다수의 새처럼 찌르레기도 완전히 자랐을 때 둥지를 떠나기 때문이다. 결국 새들도 둥지 짓기 경험에 의해 도움을 얻는다는 결론을 피할 수 없을 것이다.

해설_ 글의 하단에서 '크기나 힘 같은 단순한 문제가 아니다' 또는 '새들도 경험에 의해 도움을 얻는다' 는 내용이 있으므로 선택지에서 그것을 언급한 것을 찾으면 된다.

어휘_ blackbird 찌르레기

breed 번식하다

predator 약탈자, 포식자

정답_ (c)

2.

해석_ 생태계에 있어서, 원인과 결과는 시간적으로 또한 공간적으로 현격하게 동떨어져 있는 경우가 많다. 따라서 우리의 개입이 예상하지 못하였던 결과를 낳는 경우가 빈번한 것이다. 수년 동안 곤충을 죽이기 위하여 잘 분해되지 않는 살충제를 뿌리고 나서, 우리는 흰머리수리를 거의 말살해버릴 지경에 이르렀음을 발견한다. 먹이사슬을 통하여 농축된 살충제는 독수리와 어떤 다른 새들의 조직에 번식을 해칠 정도까지 축적된다. 어떤 바람직한 결과를 만들어내기 위해서 복잡한 체계에 개입하면 우리는 반드시 다른 결과, 흔히 바람직하지 않은 결과를 추가로 얻게 돼 있다.

해설_ '우리의 개입이 예상하지 못하였던 결과' 또는 '추가적으로, 흔히 바라지 않는 어떤 다른 결과들' 이란 것은 부작용을 말하는 것이다.

어휘_ consequence 결과

persistent (화학 약품) 분해하기 어려운

impair 해치다, 손상시키다

reproduction 번식

정답_ (b)

3.

해석_ 거북은 거북목의 파충류로서 몸의 대부분이 특별한 뼈나 그들의 늑골로부터 발전된 연골성의 껍질로 뒤덮여 있다. 거북목은 지금도 남아있는 종과 멸종된 종을 모두 포함한다. 최초로 알려진 거북은 2억 1천5백만 년 전으로 거슬러 올라가는데, 거북이 가장 오래된 파충류군 중 하나이며, 도마뱀이나 뱀보다도 오래된 군이다. 대략 300종이 오늘날 살아 있으며, 어떤 것들은 상당히 멸종위기에 처해 있다. 거북은 물에서 숨을 쉴 수 없지만 다양한 시간 동안 그들의 숨을 참을 수 있다. 그리고 거북은 비록 많은 종들이 물 속이나 물 근처에서 살지만, 공기로 숨쉬며 수면 아래에 알을 낳지 않는다.

해설_ 본문에서 거북은 물 속에서 숨을 쉴 수 없고 참는다고 하였으므로 (a)는 옳지 않고, (c) 역시 도마뱀이나 뱀보다 오래된 군이라고 언급되어 있지만 가장 오래된 군인지는 알 수 없다. 또한 거북목은 살아있는 종과 멸종된 종을 모두 포함하므로 (d)도 옳지 않다. 따라서 첫 번째 문장에서 확인할 수 있는 (b)가 정답이다.

어휘_ reptile 파충류

order testudines 거북목(order는 '질서, 명령' 의 의미로 쓰이지만 생물학적 분류로서 '목' 의 의미도 있다.)

cartilaginous 연골성의

rib 늑골

extant 현존하는

정답_ (b)

Chapter 24
교육

STEP 2 Actual Test

1.

해석_ 각 확장 활동의 중요한 부분은 CNN 비디오 자료로부터 얻은 자극적이고, 확실한 영상에 중점을 두었으며, 비디오를 위주로 한 짧은 수업들입니다. 각 비디오 수업은 활동의 같은 순서를 따릅니다. '보기 전에' 활동은 학생들이 자신들의 경험에 바탕을 두었거나, 또는 읽기자료에서 얻은 배경지식을 상기하도록 합니다. '보면서' 활동은 학생들에게 비디오의 주제와 같은 일반적인 정보를 보도록 요구합니다. '보고 난 뒤' 활동은 학생들이 독해 지문, 고유한 경험이나 그들의 생각과 견해와 심화적인 연관을 지음으로써 비디오의 핵심 내용을 확장하도록 합니다.

해설_ Before You Watch encourages students to recall background knowledge based on their own experiences or from information presented in the readings.에서 (b)의 내용을 확인할 수 있다. (a)의 경우 open-ended contexts에 관한 언급이 본문에 없으므로 옳지 않고, (c)도 본문에 제시되지 않은 내용이다. (cnn측의) 비디오 자료영상을 보는 것은 As You Watch활동에만 해당되므로 (d)의 경우도 옳지 않다.

어휘_ highlight 중요한 부분
　　　stimulating 자극적인, 격려하는
　　　authentic 확실한, 진짜의
　　　archive 보관소
　　　sequence 절차, 순서
　　　recall 상기하다

정답_ (b)

2.

해석_ 아이가 태어난 후 첫 해에 동안 겪는 경험이 그 아이의 성격과 개성의 결정에 큰 역할을 한다는 것은 일반적으로 인정되고 있다. 모든 경험이 그 아이에게 무언가를 가르치고 그 효과는 누적된다. '양육' 이라는 말은 보통 집안에서 아이를 다루거나 훈련한다고 할 때 쓰이는 말이다. 아이를 기르는 이상과 관습은 문화별로 다르다. 이것은 학교에서의 아이를 다루는 것과 훈련하는 것에 밀접한 관계가 있는데 이것은 보통 교육이라는 말로 구별된다. 우리가 살고 있는 것과 같은 사회에서는 부모도 교사도 다 아이의 발달을 위해 주어지는 기회에 책임이 있으므로, 양육과 교육은 서로 의존적 관계에 있다.

해설_ 문화별로 아이 양육 방식이 다르다는 것은 아이의 양육, 교육에 관한 본질적인 내용을 담고 있는 본문의 흐름과 맞지 않는다.

어휘_ determine 결정하다
　　　cumulative 누적되는
　　　upbringing 양육
　　　interdependent 서로 의존하는

정답_ (b)

3.

해석_ 내가 내년에 빙스톤 대학에 진학하기로 결정한 데는 두 가지 중요한 이유가 있다. 우선 금전 문제가 있다. 즉 빙스톤 대학의 수업료는 비싸지 않고, 한꺼번에 납부할 필요도 없다. 나의 아버지가 부자가 아니기 때문에 이것은 매우 중요하다. 빙스톤 대학의 '등록금 후불 제도' 덕분에 나의 아버지는 큰 어려움 없이 나의 수업료를 지불할 수 있다. 두 번째 이유는 그곳에서 내가 선택한 분야인 농업에 대한 우수한 교육을 받을 수 있을 것이라 생각하기 때문이다. 빙스톤 대학이 농대에 가장 훌륭한 교수만을 채용한다는 것은 널리 알려진 사실이다. 더욱이 이 대학교는 모든 농업 전공 학생들에게 재학 중에 이 지역의 농장에서 일하여 실기 경험을 얻도록 요구하고 있다.

해설_ 본문의 첫 문장에서 '빙스톤 대학에 진학하기로 결정한 두 가지 중요한 이유' 에 대해 언급하였고, 그 뒤에서 그 두 가지 이유에 대해 상술을 하고 있다.

어휘_ tuition 수업료
　　　reasonable (가격이) 적당한, 비싸지 않은
　　　deferred payment plan 등록금 후불 제도
　　　agriculture 농업

정답_ (b)

Chapter 25
생활 문화

STEP 2 Actual Test

1.

해석_ 급료, 봉급, 혹은 보수를 받으면, 우리들은 만족할 것이다. 왜냐하면 우리가 열심히 일한 대가를 받는 것이니까. 그러나 우리가 벌지 않은 돈, 즉 횡재는 우리 얼굴에 큰 웃음을 안겨준다.

해설_ 빈칸을 포함한 문장 앞에 역접의 접속사인 However가 키포인트이다. However의 앞에서 what we have worked hard가 있으므로 빈칸에는 그와 반대되는 의미인 we have not earned가 들어가야 한다.

어휘_ wage 급료

content 만족한

deserve ~할 만하다

windfall 뜻밖의 횡재

정답_ (d)

2.

해석_ 유기농 식품은 특정한 생산 기준에 따라 생산되는데, 그것들이 재래식 살충제나 인공적인 비료, 인분이나 하수 침전물의 사용 없이 재배된다는 것을 의미하며, 전리 방사선이나 식품 첨가물 없이 가공된다는 것을 뜻한다. 동물들에게는, 항생제의 일상적인 사용이나 성장 호르몬의 사용 없이 사육된다는 것을 의미한다. 대부분의 나라에서 유기 농산물은 유전적으로 조작되어서는 안 된다. 유기농 식품 생산은 법적으로 규제된다. 현재 미국, 유럽연합, 일본 그리고 다른 많은 국가들이 생산업자들에게 유기농 식품을 판매하려면 유기농 증명을 획득할 것을 요구하고 있다.

해설_ 유기농 식품의 전반에 대해 설명하고 있는 글이므로 답은 (b)이다.

어휘_ organic food 유기농 식품

conventional 전통적인, 재래식의

pesticides 살충제

artificial 인공적인

sewage 하수

sludge 침전물

ionizing radiation 전리 방사선

antibiotics 항생제

certification 증명서

정답_ (b)

3.

해석_ 저는 작가나 편집자 같은 직업을 결코 계획하지 않았지만, 제가 해온 마케팅 일의 상당 부분은 좋은 글솜씨와 창의적인 편집기술에 의존했습니다. 저는 대학 때 시간제로 일한 신문사에서 컴퓨터 출판과 효과적인 지면 배치법, 그리고 짧은 글로 최대의 효과를 낼 수 있는 방법 등에 대해 많이 배웠습니다. 모든 마케팅 일에서 저의 목표를 그래픽 디자이너들에게 분명히 설명할 수 있었고 그 때문에 디자인을 바꿀 때 비싼 돈을 들이지 않았습니다. 이러한 전문 기술들은 현재 저의 중요한 자산이 되었습니다.

해설_ 직장을 얻고자 하는 자기 소개서이다. 자신의 경력에 대해 자신감있는 태도를 보이고 있다.

어휘_ layout (신문, 광고 등의) 지면 배치

maximum impact 최대의 효과

costly design revisions 돈이 많이 드는 디자인 수정

asset 자산

solemn 엄숙한

정답_ (d)

Final Test 1

1.

해석_ 한국의 회사 문화에서 전통적으로 전해오는 관습대로, 온라인 게임 회사의 38세인 한 매니저는 일을 마치고 10여 명의 팀원들을 데리고 일주일에 두 번씩 술자리를 만들었다. 그는 그의 부하 직원들에게 술 마시기를 권했다. 거기엔 맥주 2잔이 한계여서 마시기를 거부한 29세의 여성 그래픽 디자이너도 포함된다. "마시든가 아니면 나한테 혼날 줄 알아." 그 상사는 그녀에게 어느 날 저녁 그렇게 이야기했다. 그녀는 거절했다가는 경력에 해가 될 것을 두려워해서 마셨다. 결국 더 이상 술자리를 견딜 수 없었던 그녀는 (회사를) 그만두었고 (그 회사를) 고소했다.

해설_ 거절하는 여직원에게 술을 마시라고 강제로 권하는 상사의 말이므로 (b)가 적절하다.

어휘_ exhort 간곡히 타이르다, 권하다
　　　subordinate 부하직원
　　　refuse 거절하다
　　　eventually 결국
　　　sue 고소하다

정답_ (b)

2.

해석_ 일본인 연구자들은 아이슈타인의 방정식 E=mc2을 박테리아의 일종인 고초균 DNA에 접목시켜 그들의 주장을 뒷받침했다. 게이오 대학 고등 생명 과학 연구소의 분자 생물학자인 요시아키 오하시는 자외선, 탈수, 산소와 영양 부족, 유기용매에 저항력이 강한 포자를 생성하는 토양에 무해한 박테리아인 고초균을 연구하기로 했다. 그는 상대성 방정식을 택했다. 왜냐하면 20세기의 가장 중요한 유산 중에 하나이기 때문이다. 그러나 그렇게 말하면서도 "우린 아이슈타인 박사의 광적 찬양자는 아니다."라고 덧붙였다.

해설_ 빈칸 앞에 although라는 접속사가 있으므로 그 접속사 앞의 내용과 상반되는 내용이 빈칸에 들어갈 것을 추측할 수 있다.

어휘_ Bacillus subtilis 고초균(枯草菌)(박테리아의 일종)
　　　molecular 분자의
　　　spore [균류(菌類)·식물의] 포자(胞子), 아포(芽胞)
　　　dehydration 탈수

정답_ (a)

3.

해석_ 오늘날 사람들은 신분도용범죄에 대해 광적인 반응을 하는데, 거기에는 그럴 만한 이유가 있다. 컴퓨터 해킹과 판매인들의 부정행위, 쓰레기 속에서 정보 찾기, 그리고 메일 절도 같은 기술은 사회보장번호와 신용카드 프로그램 도둑들에게는 금광과도 같은 것이다.

그래서 서류 분쇄기를 구입하거나 우편함을 갖게 되는 좋은 이유가 된다! 우리는 자신의 사생활을 지키는 데 신경을 써야 한다. 남의 신분을 도용하는 행위는 해결되기까지 몇 달에서 몇 년까지 걸릴 수 있기 때문이다!

해설_ 문맥상 개인 정보 도난 문제를 해결하는 데 시간이 많이 걸린다는 내용이므로, (b) straighten out(해결하다)가 답이 될 수 있다.

어휘_ straight out 명료하게 하다, 정리하다, 해결하다
　　　figure out 계산하다, 생각해내다, 이해하다
　　　phase out (단계적으로) 철수하다, 폐지하다
　　　sweep out 일소하다

정답_ (b)

4.

해석_ UCLA의 심리학자 매튜 리버만과 그의 동료들은 주어진 순간에 뇌의 활동적인 부분과 비활동적인 부분을 나타내기 위해 뇌를 스캔하는 기계인 fMRI로 30명을 실험했다. 그들은 피실험자들에게 남성과 여성이 감정 표현을 하고 있는 사진들을 보라고 요청했다. 일부 사진 밑에는 '분노'나 '공포'처럼 감정을 표현하는 단어나 사진 속 인물을 나타내는 두 이름-하나는 남자 이름이고 또 하나는 여자 이름을 넣은 보기를 넣었다. 잊고 싶은 나쁜 기억이나 과거의 골칫거리가 있는가? 하버드와 몬트리올의 맥길 대학 연구자들은 나쁜 기억을 막거나 지우는 기억 상실증 약을 연구하고 있다. 이 기술로 정신의학자들은 기억을 되살리는 생화학적 통로를 확장할 수 있는 것 같다.

해설_ 나쁜 기억을 막거나 지우는 것은 기억 상실증에 관한 것이다.

어휘_ biochemical 생화학의
　　　articular neuralgia 관절 신경통
　　　amnesia 건망증, 기억 상실증
　　　psychiatrist 정신의학자
　　　pathway 통로

정답_ (a)

5.

너무 많은 사람들이 단지 칼로리에만 집중하고 자신들이 먹는 음식 칼로리의 원천에 대해선 신경 쓰지 않습니다. 음식의 영양소는 인간 몸을 관할하는 내분비기관에 직접적인 효과를 미칩니다. 건강한 음식이 섭취되느냐 아니면 많이 가공된 음식이 정기적으로 섭취되느냐에 따라 인간의 내분비 기관은 반응을 합니다. 더 건강한 식이요법을 취할수록 더 빠른 실행의 결과가 보일 겁니다.

해설_ 빈칸 뒤의 내용은 음식이 인간의 몸에 미치는 영향에 대해 언급하고 있다. 따라서 빈칸에는 칼로리의 원천이 적합하다.

어휘_ endocrine system 내분비 기관

ingredient (혼합물의) 성분, (요리의) 재료

정답_ (d)

6.

해석_ 옛날에 사람들은 자연을 지배할 힘이 없었다. 기계적 에너지를 얻는 오직 유일한 도구들은 시계태엽 장치, 물로 움직이는 바퀴와 풍차 정도였다. 모든 교통수단은 발 또는 말에 의한 것이었으며, 모든 해상 운송은 노를 젓거나 돛을 이용한 것이었다. 사람들은 계절 음식 부족의 희생양이 되었으며 이유도 알 수 없었고 대항할 합당한 수단도 없어 주기적인 풍토병에 희생되었다.

해설_ 빈칸 뒤에서 '이유도 알 수 없었고 대항할 합당한 수단도 없어 주기적인 풍토병에 희생되었다' 는 내용이 있으므로 빈칸에는 음식이 부족한 것으로 희생을 당했다는 내용이 적합하다.

어휘_ clockwork 시계[태엽] 장치

windmill (제분소 · 양수기 따위의) 풍차

decimate 10명에 1명꼴로 제비뽑아 죽이다, (전염병 등이) 많은 사람을 죽이다

at the mercy of ~의 희생으로

rational 합리적인

lookout 감시, 망보기, 경계

정답_ (b)

7.

해석_ 인간은 살아있는 모든 생물체 중에서 가장 공격적이고 잔인함에 틀림없다. 만약 난폭한 사람을 가리켜 '야수와 같이' 행동한다고 한다면, 우리는 동물들을 중상모략하는 것이다. 왜냐하면 어떠한 야수들도 인간만큼 난폭하지 않기 때문이다. 토착 동물 또는 텃새가 같은 종의 다른 동물의 영역을 침범할 때, 침범을 당한 쪽은 침입자들에게 경고를 하는 의례적인 적대 신호만을 표한다. 그럼에도 불구하고 어느 측도 많이 다치지 않는데, 패배자가 항복의 제스처를 표함으로써 자신을 구하기 때문이다. 보통 한 동물은 오직 먹이를 얻기 위해 다른 동물을 죽이며, 같은 종의 구성원을 죽이는 일은 거의 없다.

해설_ 빈칸 앞의 문장에 나온 동물들은 같은 종끼리 심하게 싸우지 않는다는 내용이 힌트가 된다.

어휘_ slander 중상모략하다

territorial 영토의, 특정 영역[관할구]의

encroach 침입하다

intruder 침입자

submission 항복

정답_ (a)

8.

해석_ 지구상에서 과학을 연구하는 종족은 인간밖에 없다. 과학은 완전하지 않다. 그것은 분명히 오용될 수 있다. 그것은 단지 도구일 뿐이다. 그러나 그것은 우리가 가지고 있는 단연 최고의 도구이며, 자기 교정적이고 모든 것에 적용될 수 있는 것이다. 그것은 두 가지 규칙을 가지고 있다. 첫째, 신성한 진실이란 존재하지 않는다. 모든 가정들은 비판적으로 검토되어야 한다. 권위에서 나오는 주장이란 가치가 없다. 둘째, 사실과 일치하지 않는 것은 무엇이든 폐기 또는 교정되어야 한다. 우리는 우주를 있는 그대로 이해해야 하며 우리가 바라는 것과 혼동해서는 안 된다. 확실한 것이 때로는 틀릴 수 있다. 예상치 못한 것이 때로는 진실이다.

해설_ 빈칸 뒤에서 '예상치 못한 것이 때로는 진실이다' 라고 언급한 것이 힌트가 된다.

어휘_ misuse 오용하다; 학대[혹사]하다

cosmos (질서와 조화의 구현으로서의) 우주, 천지 만물

by far 훨씬, 단연.

obvious 분명한

정답_ (c)

9.

해석_ 매우 오랫동안 수맥 찾기는 많은 사람들에게 회의와 의심의 눈초리를 받아 왔거나 논리적 설명이 안 되는 초자연적인 것으로 여겨져 왔다. 두 관점 모두 비록 과학적으로 알 수 없는 기술이지만 보통 사람의 이해의 범위 내에 있는 하나의 기술로 인정받고 있는 것에 대한 올바른 평가가 아니다.

해설_ 문맥상 사람들의 편견으로 올바른 평가를 받지 못하고 있다는 내용이 적합하다.

어휘_ dowsing 수맥 찾기

skepticism 회의

suspicion 의심

do little justice to 올바로 평가하지 못하다

paranormal 과학적으로 알 수가 없는

정답_ (c)

10.

해석_ 1847년 가난에 찌든 17살의 농장 근로자인 마이클 무어는 아일랜드를 떠나 미국으로 갔다. 그 앞에 펼쳐진 미래를 그는 알지 못했다. 하지만 그는 과거보다 더 나쁠 수 없다는 것을 알고 있었다. 그는 아일랜드의 대기근 기간에 자랐고 매우 굶주린다는 것이 무엇인지를 알고 있었다. 그는 그의 엄마가 한 달 전에 티푸스로 죽는 것

을 보았다. 그의 아버지는 마이클이 태어난 지 1년 후에 죽었다. 그가
아일랜드에 남을 이유는 없었다, 그래서 6월의 어느 맑은 날 아침, 그
는 미국으로 향하는 배에 몸을 실었다.

해설_ 문맥상 빈칸 앞에서 '미래를 그는 알지 못했다'고 했으므로
빈칸에는 과거에 대한 내용이 적합하다. 그 뒤에 비참했던 과거에 대
한 내용이 연결된다.

어휘_ poverty 빈곤

typhus 발진(發疹)티푸스

bound for ~로 향하는

정답_ (b)

11.

해석_ 많은 사람들이 TV를 보며 자라난 어린 세대에게 TV가 끼친
영향에 대해 걱정한다. 첫 번째로, 최근에 TV가 창의적인 상상력을
질식시킨다는 연구 결과가 나왔다. 일부 선생들은 TV가 아이들의 마
음속에 정신적인 그림을 만드는 능력을 앗아가 아이들이 시각적인
그림 없이는 간단한 이야기도 이해하지 못한다는 것을 느끼고 있다.
두 번째로, 너무 어린 나이에 너무 많이 TV를 본 아이들이 실생활의
경험에서 움츠러드는 경향이 있다. 그리하여 그들은 삶에서 무엇을
시작하지 못하고 그저 바라만 보는 수동적인 방관자로 자라게 된다.

해설_ 문맥상 주도적으로 참여하지 못하고 '그저 바라만 보는' 수동
적인 방관자가 적합하다.

어휘_ initiate 시작하다, 가입[입회]시키다, 제안하다

withdraw 움츠리다

illustration 삽화, 예해(例解), 실례

stifle 숨 막히게 하다, 질식시키다

정답_ (b)

12.

해석_ 17세기의 헌법적 안정의 파생적 효과 중 하나는 헌법이 의회
역할을 두드러지게 했다는 것이다. 오늘날 우리는 법률을 의회의 창
조물로 간주한다. 우리가 입법을 이야기할 때 의회에서 여왕에 의해
통과된다고 수사적으로 표현한다. 하지만 사실상 왕실의 역할은 단
지 형식적인 것이며 도장 찍는 것에 불과하다. 원래 법률은 단지 법
령에 불과했으며, 그 단어는 '세우다', '명령하다'란 의미를 가지는
라틴어의 statuere에서 온 것이다.

해설_ 빈칸 뒤에서 단어의 어원에 대해 언급했으므로 빈칸에는 '원
래는'이라는 originally가 적합하다.

어휘_ spin-off 파생의, 부가적인

constitutional 헌법적

rhetorical 수사적인

rubber-stamping 고무도장을 찍는

decree 법령, 포고

정답_ (b)

13.

해석_ 스스로 달 대사관의 헤드치즈라고 선언한 데니스 호프는 당신
에게 달을 약속할 것이다. 아니면 적어도 한 부분만이라도 말이다.
1980년부터 호프는 에이커당 19.99달러에 달의 부동산을 팔아서 현
재 9백만 달러 이상을 긁어 모았다. 바바라 월터스, 조지 루카스, 로
널드 레이건과 심지어는 부시(1세) 대통령 같은 유명인을 포함하여
지금까지 425만 명이 달의 일부분을 구매했다. 호프는 국가가 달을
소유하는 것을 금지한 1967년 유엔 우주 협약의 허점을 이용했다고
말한다.

해설_ 문맥상 '~를 포함하여'란 의미를 갖는 것이 빈칸에 들어가야
하며 그러한 의미를 가진 것은 including이다.

어휘_ proclaim 선언하다

celebrity 유명인, 명사

exploit a loophole 허점을 이용하다

prohibit 금지하다

정답_ (c)

14.

해석_ 걸프 지역은 아랍 반도가 남쪽으로 향하는 거대한 모래 폭풍
을 만드는, 특히 예민한 시기에 돌입하려 한다. 올해의 폭풍은 기름
불에서 나온 검댕과 폭발에 의해 분해된 많은 양의 먼지를 빨아들일
수 있다. 화재로부터의 열기로 인해 더 강화된 그 폭풍은 사우디아라
비아와 인도에 걸친 지역에 검댕과 기름의 분자를 뿌릴 수 있다. 해
당 지역 사람들의 건강에 해를 입히는 것 외에도, 그 오염은 야생, 농
업, 어업에 해를 끼칠 수 있다. 최악의 경우엔 기름불의 분진이 그 지
역의 연간 몬순 비를 교란시킬 수 있다.

해설_ 문맥상 '~외에도'가 적합하므로 빈칸에는 apart from이 적
합하다.

어휘_ soot 검댕

fishery 어업

fallout 낙진

agriculture 농업

정답_ (a)

15.

해석_ 인류학은 데이터의 정확성에 신경을 써야 한다. 인류학은 인간이 주요 연구 대상이며, 다른 인간들이 대부분의 데이터를 제공한다는 점에서 학문 중에서도 독특하다. 최소한 연구의 초기 단계에서 인류학자들은 많은 부분을 정보 제공자와 더불어 그들 데이터의 관찰에 의존해야 한다. 정보 제공자들은 그들 자신의 문화에 대해 깊은 지식을 가지고 있으며 이 지식을 인류학자에게 전달할 의사와 능력이 있는 사람들을 말한다.

해설_ 문맥상 '~라는 점에서, ~측면에서' 라는 것이 적합하므로 빈칸에는 in that이 들어가야 한다.

어휘_ anthropology 인류학

　　　 accuracy 정확성

　　　 informant 정보 제공자

　　　 initial 초기의

정답_ (d)

16.

해석_ 초등학교 선생들에 의해 자주 제기되는 가장 심각한 문제 중 하나는 아이들이 배움의 어려움에 대해 낮은 인내심을 보인다는 것이다. 그들은 TV에서 30분 내지 60분 안에 모든 문제가 해결되는 것에 길들여져있기 때문에, 즉각적인 욕구 충족이 이루어지지 않는 어떠한 활동에 의해서도 쉽게 풀이 죽는다는 것이다. 하지만 가장 심각한 결과는 TV 폭력이 아이들에게 끼치는 영향인데, 아이들은 이미 그것을 일상적인 일로 여기고 있다. 대부분의 전문가들은 특정 상황에서 일부 아이들은 TV에서 본 반사회적인 행동을 따라할 것이라는 사실을 인정한다.

해설_ 빈칸이 있는 문장의 구조가 원인, 결과의 형태이므로 빈칸에는 because, since 등의 접속사가 들어가야 한다.

어휘_ tolerance 인내

　　　 frustration 좌절

　　　 violence 폭력

　　　 concede 인정하다

　　　 antisocial 사회를 어지럽히는, 반사회적인

정답_ (b)

17.

해석_ 확실히 돈의 첫 번째 의미는 음식, 의류 그리고 집 같은 기본적인 심리적 욕구의 충족을 구매하는 힘에 있다. 담배처럼, 심리적 동기에서 나온 일부 후천적 욕구들도 이러한 기본적 욕구와 밀접하게 연관돼 있다. 이러한 기본적인 충동들이 비교적 잘 충족된 다음에야 상당한 돈이 다른 물품에 유용될 수 있다.

해설_ 기본적 욕구에 대한 돈의 역할을 '담배에 대한 욕구와 같은 심리적 기반을 두고 생겨난 일부 욕구' 에 빗대어 설명하고 있다.

어휘_ physiological 심리적인

　　　 shelter 쉼터, 집

　　　 fundamental 기본적인

　　　 divert ~으로 전환하다, 딴 데로 돌리다

정답_ (d)

18.

해석_ 정력적인 운동 프로그램을 정규적으로 수행하는 수백만의 미국인과 같이, 나도 운동이 나의 기분을 좋게 한다는 것을 알고 있다. 하지만 당신이 알지 못하는 또 다른 매력이 있다. 건강을 유지하면 보험료도 절약된다는 것이다. 당신은 어떻게 1파운드의 살과 1온스의 현금을 거래할 수 있는가? 우선, 당신의 위험 수준이 평균이어야 한다. 위험한 직업이나 취미를 가진 사람들은 자동적으로 탈락된다. 게다가 가장 기본적인 보험료 할인에는 어떠한 육체적인 노력이 필요 없다. 비흡연자의 생명 보험 할인이 그것이다.

해설_ 가입자의 건강 관련 사항과 보험료 등 보험 정책과의 상관관계에 관한 글이다.

어휘_ vigorous 활발한, 강성한

　　　 enticement 유혹, 매력

　　　 exertion 노력

　　　 premium 보험료

정답_ (c)

19.

해석_ 세상에는 수백 가지의 와인이 있다. 특히 좋은 포도주가 생산되었던 해에 나온 제품일 수도 있고 과소평가되는 부류나 이름없는 지역, 잘 알려지지 않은 품종을 대표할 수도 있고, 혹은 재고품이거나 경기 침체기에 거래된 물량일 수도 있지만 모두 팔리고 있는 것들이니, 그런 와인들도 들여놔야 한다. 내 생각에는 선택의 폭이 좁지만 6종의 와인과 6개의 화이트 와인이 놓치면 안 되는 가치를 가진 열 두 가지 와인이라고 보는데, 모두 15달러 이하로 적당히 만족스럽고 정직한 맛으로 너무 과하지 않아 믿을 만한 것들이 좋다. 일단 화이트 와인으로 시작해보자. 지금은 봄철이니, 이런 것들로는 대개 오크통 숙성을 거치지 않아 가벼운 봄철 식사를 돋보이게 해줄 가볍고, 신선하고, 허브향이 나는 와인들이 주로 선택된다.

해설_ 특정 브랜드의 와인을 거론하지 않은 것으로 보아 광고성 글이 아님을 알 수 있다. 와인 전문가 혹은 애호가가 쓴 싼 값에 좋은 와인 고르는 방법에 대한 글이다.

어휘_ vintage 포도가 수확된 특정 연도

overreach 너무 뻗다, 도를 지나치다

herbaceous 와인에서 허브의 향과 맛이 있을 때 사용하는 표현

devoid of ~이 없는

정답_ (b)

20.

해석_ 콘트라 코스타 교통당국은 2백억 달러 규모의 카운티 교통 발전과 성장 경영 프로그램을 담당하는 공공기관이며, 현재 최고 재무책임자를 맡아줄 인재를 찾고 있습니다. 우리는 우선적으로 공공 부문에서 검증된 많은 재정 및 행정 경험을 가지고 계신 분을 모십니다. 후보자는 반드시 공공 행정과 비즈니스, 재정 또는 회계 그리고 예산 발전과 분석, 재무제표의 준비, 투자 관리, 일반 원장 조정, 그리고 감사관들과의 작업을 포함하여 최소 7년 이상 공공 기관에서 근무하신 경력과 인문학 학사학위를 소지해야 합니다. 만약 귀하가 이 조건에 맞고 도전해볼 만한 일의 경험에 관심이 있으시다면 커버레터와 이력서를 headhunter @contracosta.com으로 보내주십시오.

해설_ 특정 직위에 적합한 인물을 찾기 위한 구인 광고(job offer)이다.

어휘_ BA degree 문학사(Bachelor of Art)

candidate 후보자

ledger 원부(原簿), 원장

reconciliation 조정, 조화, 일치

resume 이력서

정답_ (d)

21.

해석_ 그것은 첫 번째 시험관 아기가 탄생했던 15년 전 이래로 의학 윤리에 관한 가장 치열했던 과학적 논란의 시작이었다. 윤리학자들은 아기 농장의 악몽판을 떠올렸다. 정책 입안자들은 미국에서 생명 윤리 지도력의 공백을 꼬집었다. 비평가들은 생식 기술의 상업화를 비판했으며 성난 시위대들은 거리를 점거하여 인간 배아 복제를 즉시 금지할 것을 요구했다. 실제로 TIME/CNN 여론 조사에서 3/4이 반대하였는데, 이것은 미국인들이 인간 복제의 개념을 매우 골치아픈 문제로 보고 있다는 것을 보여준다.

해설_ 인간 배아 복제는 15년 전 이래로 의학 윤리에 관한 가장 치열했던 과학적 논란의 시작이었다고 언급하는 등 이 글은 인간 복제에 관한 윤리적인 문제에 관한 글이다.

어휘_ ethicist 도덕가, 윤리학자

fertility 비옥, 다산(多産), 번식[생식]력

decry 공공연히 비난하다, 헐뜯다

human-embryo 인간 태아

ban 금지(하다)

정답_ (d)

22.

해석_ 크고 강한 것들이 작고 부드럽고 약한 것보다 훨씬 덜 위험하다는 것이 사실이라고 생각한다. 죽기 전에 보다 번식하지 않는 것들은 사멸한다. 하지만 사소한 실수, 사소한 고통, 사소한 걱정들은 어떠한가? 궤양은 큰 고장에서 발생하는 것이 아니라 사소한 염증으로 생긴다. 한 사람은 잔소리, 소액 청구서, 전화, 무좀, 꽃가루, 흔한 감기, 권태로 무너진다. 그러한 모든 것들은 모두 사소한 결함, 좌절이지만 어느 누구도 그것들을 그다지 중시하지 않는다.

해설_ 크고 강한 것들보다 작고 사소한 것이 더 위험하다는 내용이다.

어휘_ reproduce 재생하다

athlete's foot 무좀

ragweed 호그위드(꽃가루는 알레르기의 원인)

nagging 잔소리

정답_ (c)

23.

해석_ 거리 설교는 그 분파(종교)에 대한 개인적 헌신을 증명하는 것이다. 이 책무의 완수가 그 그룹 내에서 지위를 수여한다. 정렬적인 유형의 거리 설교자들은 매우 신중하다. 그들은 사람들이 그들의 이야기를 듣기 위해 멈추지 않는다는 것을 안다. 결과적으로 그들의 스타일은 그들의 이야기를 듣는 사람들이 미래에 언젠가 "주님께 다가가리라" 는 희망으로 "씨앗을 뿌리도록" 계획된다.

해설_ 첫 번째 문장의 '거리 설교는 그 분파(종교)에 대한 개인적 헌신을 증명하는 것' 이라는 내용과 하단의 미래에 언젠가 "주님께 다가가리라" 는 희망으로 "씨앗을 뿌리도록" 계획된다는 내용에서 거리 설교가 미래의 교화를 목적으로 한 헌신적인 활동임을 알 수 있다.

어휘_ manifestation 증명

commitment 충성, 헌신

impassion 깊이 감동[감격]케 하다

sow the seed 씨를 뿌리다

정답_ (c)

24.

해석_ 게임을 하지 않는 친구들에 비해, 학교를 가는 날에 비디오 게

임을 하는 소년들은 책 읽는 시간이 30% 정도 적고 소녀들은 34%가 숙제하는 시간이 적다고 미국 연구자들이 월요일 말했다. 하지만 비디오 게임이 가족이나 친구들과 함께 보내는시간을 심각하게 방해하지는 않는 것 같다고 그들은 말했다. "게이머들은 책 읽기와 숙제하는 시간을 줄이지만 부모와 친구들과 함께 보내는 시간 그리고 스포츠나 여가 활동 시간은 그렇지 않다"고 미시간 대학의 호프 커밍스는 말했다. 이 연구는 비디오 게임의 장기적인 효과들에 대해 염려하는 미국 의사들의 목소리가 커지면서 나온 것이다.

해설_ 글의 하단에 '이 연구는 비디오 게임의 장기적인 효과들에 대해 염려하는 ~' 의 내용으로 보아 게임의 부정적 효과에 대해 언급할 것을 예상할 수 있다.

어휘_ interfere 방해하다
　　　　 significantly 중대하게
　　　　 interact 상호 작용하다, 서로 영향을 주다
　　　　 concern 염려

정답_ (b)

25.

해석_ 최근 광고주들이 그들 제품에 대한 평판을 제고하기 위해 과학과 의학의 권위를 빌리는 일이 더욱 관례가 되어왔다. 어떤 것을 팔거나 어떠한 것을 믿게 하려 할 때 그런 사람들의 인정은 상당한 힘을 부여한다. '의료계의 최고 권위자들이 말하기를' 이나 '독립 연구소의 테스트 결과는' 이라는 문구들은 과학의 권위를 치약 또는 시리얼에 부여하도록 고안된다. 그러나 그 단순한 문구들은 비판 능력이 없는 사람들에게 강력한 설득력을 발휘할 수 있다.

해설_ 마지막 부분, '과학계가 ~라고 말한다' 라는 문구들은 비판 능력이 없는 사람들에게 잘 받아들여진다는 내용에서 답을 찾을 수 있다.

어휘_ prestige 권위, 위신
　　　　 alleged ~라고 하는, ~로 알려진
　　　　 uncritical 비판력이 없는, 맹종하는
　　　　 credulous 쉽게 믿는
　　　　 trustworthy 믿을 만한

정답_ (a)

26.

해석_ 많은 흡연가들은 회사의 금연 운동을 은밀하게 환영할지 모른다. 그들 중 많은 이들이 회사의 운동을 영원히 담배를 끊을 자극으로 받아들인다. 흡연에 대해 제약을 가하는 더 많은 회사들은 그들의 직원들이 담배를 끊는 것을 도와주는 시도를 하고 있다. 애보트 연구소는 흡연자를 고용하지만 그들에게 금연 방법을 가르쳐주는 회사

지원의 워크숍에 참석하겠다는 서약서에 서명하도록 요구한다. 변화가 일어나고 있음에도 불구하고 반 흡연 로비스트들은 직장 내 흡연에 대해 더 가혹한 제약을 가하도록 지속해서 압박하고 있다.

해설_ 이 글에 따르면 흡연자들은 금연 운동을 환영하고 그것을 자신들이 금연을 하는 계기로 삼고 싶어한다.

어휘_ crusade 십자군; (종교상의) 성전(聖戰); 강력한 개혁
　　　　 embrace 포옹하다, 받아들이다
　　　　 pledge 서약(서)
　　　　 limitation 제한

정답_ (b)

27.

해석_ 화성의 바위 샘플들은 콘드라이트라 불리는 원시 유성에서 발견되는 것과 동일한 실리케이트의 가벼운 형태, 즉 "아이소토프"를 포함하고 있다. 과학자들은 콘드라이트를 지구로 떨어진 행성을 구성하는 원래의 구석체에서 떨어져 남은 조각으로 생각한다. 실리케이트는 실리콘과 산소 그 밖의 요소가 섞여 만들어진 복합물이다. 화성과는 달리 지구의 실리콘은 두 종류로 나뉜다. 첫 번째 부분은 금속 상태로 녹아 있는 지구 중심부의 가벼운 요소가 된 것이고 더 큰 부분은 지구의 맨틀과 크러스트의 규산염에 붙어있는 산화 실리콘의 형태로 된 것이다.

해설_ 화성과는 달리 지구에는 두 부분으로 나눠져 있고 하나는 가벼운 부분이고 하나는 무거운 부분임을 유추할수 있다. 그러나 가벼운 부분은 제일 첫 문장에서 화성에서도 있다고 서술하고 있다.

어휘_ remnant 잔존물, 나머지
　　　　 compound 복합물
　　　　 dissolve 용해하다
　　　　 silicate 규산염
　　　　 isotope 동위체

정답_ (d)

28.

해석_ 여성권리 운동은 1820년대 이후 발전했고, 약간의 변화를 초래했다. 1833년 오버린 대학 재단은 미국 내 최초의 남녀 공학 대학으로서 문을 열었다. 몇몇 남자 대학교들은 곧 여성들을 받아들이게 되었고, 여자 대학교들이 신설되었다. 1848년 루크레티아 모트와 엘리자베스 캐디 스탠턴은 뉴욕의 세네카 폴즈에서 여권 회회를 조직하였다. 회회에서 여성 참정권(투표할 수 있는 권리)을 위한 최초의 공식 청원서를 발표하였다. 하지만 전국적인 참정권은 1920년에 와서야 가능해졌다.

해설_ 미국에서의 여성들의 권리 신장에 관해 1820년대, 1833년,

1848년, 1920년까지 연대기적으로 설명하고 있다.

어휘_ collegiate 대학의, 대학생의[다운]; 대학 정도의

coeducational 남녀 공학의

convention 총회

suffrage 참정권

정답_ (c)

29.

해석_ 중국 중부의 한 마을 주민들은 다량의 공룡 뼈를 파내어 끓여서 수프로 만들거나, 전통 약으로 만들기 위해 갈아서 가루로 만들었다. 그들은 이 뼈들은 용의 것이며 치료의 효과가 있다고 믿었다. 칼슘이 풍부한 뼈들은 때때로 다른 재료들과 함께 끓여졌으며 다리에 쥐나는 것과 현기증을 치료하기 위해 어린이들에게 먹여졌다. 어떤 때에는 주민들이 그것들을 갈아서 고약으로 만들어 골절상이나 다른 상처에 발랐다. 이런 행위는 적어도 20년 동안 지속되었다.

해설_ 글의 중간 부분에 '어떤 때는 갈아서 고약으로 만들어 골절상이나 다른 상처에 직접 발랐다.' 는 내용이 힌트가 된다.

어휘_ dinosaur 공룡

dragon 용

leg cramps 다리에 쥐가 남

dizziness 현기증

정답_ (a)

30.

해석_ 자연에서는 한 동물이 다른 동물을 잡아먹는데 이것은 생존에 필수적인 부분이다. 살생을 거부하는 불교신자들은 정말로 어리석은데, 만약 그가 매일 단지 쌀알 두개를 먹는다면, 그것은 그 두 낟알의 생명이다. 우리는 창조하지도 않았고 우주의 창조자도 아니다. 그리고 만약 전체의 창조가 하나의 생명의 다른 생명을 잡아먹는다는 사실에 기반을 두어 창조된다는 것을 안다면, 존재의 한 순환은 다른 존재의 순환을 정복함으로써 존재하게 된다는 것을 안다면, 그렇지 않은 척한들 무슨 소용이 있는가? 단 한 가지의 할 일은 존재의 순환에 있어 더 높고 더 낮은 것을 인식하는 것이다.

해설_ 불교신자들이 어리석은 것은 그들이 어떤 생명도 파괴할 수 없기 때문이 아니라, 자연에서는 하나가 다른 하나를 취하는데 이것은 모든 존재들에게 있어 필수적이기 때문이다.

어휘_ devour 게걸스럽게 먹다, (질병·화재 등이) 멸망시키다

essential 필수적인

grain 낟알, 곡물

subjugate 정복하다, 복종[예속]시키다

정답_ (c)

31.

해석_ 전자 범죄자는 일반적 도둑이 갖고 있는 것보다 뚜렷한 이점이 있다. 우선 컴퓨터 횡령 범죄자들은 다른 횡령 범죄자보다 범죄당 훨씬 많은 돈을 번다. 그리고 컴퓨터 절도는 위험이 적다. 가정용 컴퓨터를 가진 사람들은 누구나 시스템 접속을 위한 전화 접속을 이용할 수 있다. 그러한 사람들은 집을 떠날 필요 없이 수백만 불의 돈을 벌 수 있다. 또 다른 이점은 훔친 물건을 처리하기 위해 다른 범죄자들에게 의존할 필요가 없다는 것이다. 이러한 범죄들은 혼자 진행하므로 수익을 나눌 공범도 없다. 또 다른 이점은 사법 당국에 컴퓨터 범죄에 관한 전문가가 별로 없다는 것이다. 따라서 지금이 컴퓨터 범죄자에게는 전성기이다.

해설_ 주로 절도 범죄와 다른 범죄의 차이점에 대해 설명하고 있다. 갱생에 관한 이야기는 없다.

어휘_ hookup 접속, 중계

heyday 전성기

rehabilitation 사회 복귀, 갱생

정답_ (d)

32.

해석_ 내가 왜 폭스바겐을 사고 싶어하냐고? 나는 1,700달러의 견적을 받았고 그 가격은 내가 원하는 모든 옵션을 포함한다. 일단 내가 폭스바겐을 가지면, 운영비는 매우 낮다. 그것은 1갤런에 32마일을 달리며 공기 냉각식이므로 부동액도 필요없다. 차량 보험료도 미국 차에 비하면 반도 안 된다. 수리비는 훨씬 저렴하며 타이어 위치 교환을 잘 해주고 공기압을 적절히 유지한다면 타이어는 차량의 수명만큼 지속될 것이다. 차량 번호판 가격은 큰 차 가격의 1/3에 불과하다. 이러한 수치는 사실이며 거짓이 아니다.

해설_ 미국 차보다 폭스바겐의 수리비가 더 저렴하다는 내용이 본문 중간에 있다.

어휘_ antifreeze 부동액(不凍液)

air-cooled 공기 냉각식의

inflate (공기·가스 따위로) 부풀리다

license plate 차량 번호판

정답_ (b)

33.

해석_ 가까운 미래에 170억 명의 인구가 북적거리는 지구의 모습을 상상해 보라. 마지막 남은 열대우림이 방목지를 만들기 위해 희생되었다. 먹을 물은 너무 귀해 수백만 명이 갈증으로 죽는다. 전쟁은 석유가 아니라 밀밭을 확보하기 위해 발생된다. 이러한 종말이 촉발되

는 데는 많은 시간이 걸리지 않을 것이다. 세계 인구는 매년 9,300만 명씩 늘어나 1994년에 56억 명에 달했다. 인구통계학자는 현재와 같은 비율로 진행된다면 2050년이면 쉽게 두 배로 늘어날 것이라 예상한다. 어떤 나라도 뒤따르는 황폐한 환경으로부터 자국을 보호할 수 없을 것이다.

해설_ '인구통계학자는 현재와 같은 비율로 진행된다면 2050년이면 두 배로 늘어날 것이라 예상한다' 라는 언급이 힌트다.

어휘_ thirst 갈증, 목마름

apocalypse 천계(天啓), 계시, 종말

demographer 인구통계학자

devastation 유린, 황폐

정답_ (b)

34.

해석_ 인간의 희망은 항상 두 종류이다. 인간은 자기 자신에 대한 희망, 즉 개인적이고 사적인 희망을 가지고 있다. 동시에 그는 인류 또는 그것의 작은 부분, 즉 그의 부족, 가족 아마도 그의 교회 등에 대한 초이기적 희망을 가지고 있다. 이러한 인간의 두 가지 희망은 항상 서로 명확하게 구분되는 것이 아니다. 자기중심주의는 너무 강력한 힘이어서 심지어 우리의 초이기적 희망까지 침범하기도 한다. 한편, 우리의 개인적 희망은 자기중심주의에 대항하는 도덕적 반응과 그것을 전달하려는 노력의 형태를 취할 수도 있다.

해설_ 중간 부분에 '이러한 인간의 두 가지 희망은 항상 서로 명확하게 구분되는 것이 아니다' 라는 말에서 힌트를 얻을 수 있다.

어휘_ superpersonal 초이기적인

self-centeredness 자기중심주의

distinguishable 구분할 수 있는

transcend 초월하다, 능가하다

정답_ (c)

35.

해석_ 레이건의 솔직한 행동은 미국에서 알츠하이머에 대한 사회적 인식을 증진하고 연구지원에 강력한 추진력을 줄 것이다. 그렇게 함으로써 그는 또 다시 유명인들과 나란히 걸을 것이다. 자신의 심장병에 대한 드와이트 아이젠하워의 솔직함은 세계가 이 병을 다루는 태도를 바꾸었다. 베티 포드와 낸시 레이건의 유방암에 대한 공개적인 투병은 수많은 여성들이 유방 촬영 사진을 찍게 하였다.

해설_ 첫 번째 문장에서 '레이건의 솔직한 행동은 미국에서 알츠하이머에 대한 사회적 인식을 증진하고 연구의 지원에 강력한 추진력을 줄 것이다' 라고 하였으며 이것은 (b)의 내용과 일치한다.

어휘_ affliction 고통, 고뇌, 병

bout 한 판 승부, (권투 따위의) 시합

mammogram 유방 촬영 사진

disclosure 공개

정답_ (b)

36.

해석_ 몇 년 전까지만 해도 국제 '음반점의 날' 에 대한 평가는 음악을 취급하는 독립적인 상점들이 음악에 끼치는 영향력에 대한 경축이라기보다는 거의 장례식처럼 느껴졌었다. 음반의 배급이 인터넷의 영역으로 옮겨가면서 타워레코드 및 전국의 많은 음반 소매상들은 파산했다. 그러나 두 번째 '음반점의 날' 이 토요일에 열릴 때 음악가들과 음반사들은 대대적으로 행사를 벌이기로 하였다. 최근 독립 음반 상점의 수가 현격히 감소했음에도 불구하고, 아직 남아있는 상점들은 잘 견디고 있다. 그리고 그 중 몇몇은 침체된 경제 상황에도 불구하고 매출이 늘고 있다. 비닐 레코드에 대한 관심의 부활은 이러한 독립 운영자들이 여전히 사업을 할 수 있게 도움을 주었다.

해설_ 이러저러한 어려움에도 불구하고 여전히 비닐 레코드에 대해 수요가 있을 뿐더러, 이에 관련된 비즈니스가 없어지는 상황에서도 몇몇 사업들이 명맥을 이어가고 있다는 것이 글의 요지이다. 비닐 레코드의 수요가 인터넷 세대들의 복고풍 취향에서 나왔다고는 볼 수 없으며(d), 이들 산업을 새로이 하는 게 인터넷에 의한 것이라고도 볼 수 없다(b).

어휘_ go belly up 끝나다, 파산하다

in force 일제히, 대대적으로

sluggish 기능이 둔한, 활발하지 못한

vinyl record (LP등) 비닐 레코드, 레코드판

정답_ (a)

37.

해석_ 신화는 학생들이 처음에 모순되게 보일 수 있는 상황을 맞닥뜨리게 한다. 한편으로, 신화의 과정에서는 어떠한 것들도 발생할 수 있는 것처럼 보인다. 논리도 일관성도 없다. 신화에서는 모든 것이 가능하다. 하지만 다른 한편으로는 이처럼 명백한 임의성이 멀리 떨어져 있는 다양한 지역에서 수집된 신화들 사이에서 보이는 놀랄 정도의 유사성과 배치된다. 여기서 문제가 생긴다. 만약 신화의 내용이 우연이라면, 전 세계를 통틀어 신화들이 서로 매우 닮았다는 것을 어떻게 설명할 수 있을까?

해설_ 일반적으로 글 중간에 역접의 접속사가 있다면 그 뒤에 글의 포인트가 있다. 글의 중간에 But on the other hand라는 표현이 있

는데 그 뒤의 내용은 '신화들 사이의 놀라운 유사성' 또는 '신화는 전 세계를 통틀어 서로 매우 닮았다' 는 내용으로 보아, 신화는 내재적인 구조가 있다는 것을 알 수 있다.

어휘_ contradictory 모순된, 양립하지 않는
  arbitrariness 임의성
  contingent 우발적인, 우연의
  apparent 분명한, 명백한
  astound 놀라게 하다

정답_ (b)

38.

해석_ 고대 중국 황제들이 누렸던 사치의 으뜸가는 예로, 위진시대에 살았던 호랑이란 별명의 호왕의 비정상적인 생활 양식을 들 수 있을 것이다. 그는 〈스타워즈〉에 나오는 엄청나게 추악하고 매우 거대한 'Jabba the Hut'을 떠올리게 한다. 그는 너무 뚱뚱해서 왕실 사냥이라도 나갈라치면 가마꾼이 스무 명이나 필요했다. 그의 주요 관심사는 백성의 안위였다. 그는 회전의자를 만들어 사람들이 그것을 돌려 자신이 원하는 어떤 방향으로든 활을 쏠 수 있도록 했다.

해설_ 중국 황제들의 사치스러운 생활 방식의 예로 한 왕의 일화를 들고 있다. Age of Division은 위진시대와 전국시대를 가리키는 말인데, 여기에 나오는 왕은 실제 인물이라기보다는 신화 혹은 우화 속의 가상 인물일 가능성이 크다. 뚱뚱하고(b), 게으른(d) 생활방식을 이야기하는 중에 (c)와 같이 백성의 안위를 걱정하는 내용이 나오는 것은 맥락에 벗어난다.

어휘_ extravagance 사치, 무절제
  ancient 고대의
  outrageous 터무니없는
  revolving couch 회전의자

정답_ (c)

39.

해석_ 1700년대 중반까지 신문은 크기와 종류에 있어 성장을 해왔다. 전에는 모든 광고가 신문의 뒤에 배치되었다. 하지만 이제 일부는 앞면에 나타난다. 그 신문들의 발행인은 추가적인 돈의 필요성이 커질 때까지 지면에 광고를 싣는 것을 거부했다. 1784년 일간신문이 된 첫 번째 신문은 그것이 많은 광고를 게재했기 때문에 일간지가 될 수 있었다.

해설_ 신문 지면의 광고 거부에 대한 내용은 글의 전체 내용과 맞지 않는다.

어휘_ previously 전에(는), 본래는
  advertisement 광고

appear 나타나다
resist 저항하다, 거부하다

정답_ (c)

40.

해석_ 좌익과 우익의 극단주의자들이 신경증 환자들에게서 일반적으로 발견되는 것과 같은 성격 장애를 갖고 있다는 사실은 매우 분명하다. 하지만 정치적 개성이라는 전체 개념에서 빠져 있는 것은 확고하게 인식되는 정치 이론이다. 신경질적인 성격이 파시스트나 공산주의자와 같은 극단주의 정치 운동에 이끌릴 것이다. 이러한 특정 정치적 선택에 영향을 미치는 요소는 개인의 사회적 및 지적 성격이다. 하지만 설명이 되지 않는 것은, 다른 사람들은 술을 마시거나, 성적 난교 또는 이혼을 하는데 왜 일부 신경증 환자들이 그들의 내적 갈등에 대한 해결책으로 극단주의자 정치 노선에 관심을 갖는가 하는 것이다.

해설_ 정치적 극단주의자와 신경증 환자들의 성향에서 나타나는 공통점 및 상관관계대해 서술하고 있는 글에서, 정치적 개성이 정치이론에 대한 확고한 인식이 부족하다는 (a)는 흐름과 어긋나는 문장이다.

어휘_ neurotic 신경증 환자; 신경증의
  promiscuity 뒤범벅, 난잡
  maladjustment 부적응, (조절) 불량
  divorce 이혼

정답_ (a)

1.

해석_ 타이 대중문화와 민속에 대한 가이드이자 동시에 반세기 이상 커다란 논쟁거리로 국가의 정체성에 대하여 소개하는 '타이다움' 라는 제목의 독특한 가이드북이 발간되었다. 2차 대전 당시, 피번송캄 군사정부는 '타이인들을 위한 타일랜드' 라는 슬로건 아래 모였다. 오늘날 이 나라는 민족주의에 다시 최면이 걸린 듯하다. 교육부는 국기를 더 잘 보이는 곳에 게양하고 국가를 더 큰 소리로 부르도록 학교와 대학들에 명령하였다. '타이다움' 이란 다시 한번 유용한 정치적 개념이다.

해설_ 타이의 민족주의로의 회귀를 비판하는 글이며, '타이인들을 위한 타일랜드' 는 곧 민족주의를 뜻한다.

어휘_ regime 정권, 정부

    rally 모이다, 집결하다

    nationalism 민족주의

    euphemism 완곡어법

정답_ (c)

2.

해석_ 왜 명상이 효과가 있는지를 추측하는 새로운 연구에 따르면 만약 당신이 당신의 감정에 이름을 붙인다면 당신은 그 감정들을 다스릴 수 있다고 한다. 뇌 스캔은 말에 부정적인 감정을 넣으면 뇌의 감정 센터가 조용해진다는 것을 보여준다. 그것은 명상의 감정적 이점으로 알려진 것들을 설명해주는데, 명상하는 사람들은 종종 (안 좋은 기억들을) 잊기 위하여 부정적 감정을 분류해내기 때문이다. 심리학자들은 자신의 감정을 이야기하는 사람들이 그 감정을 조절할 수 있다고 오랫동안 믿어왔으나 어떻게 그렇게 되는지는 몰랐다.

해설_ 부정적 감정을 넣으면 뇌의 감정 센터가 침묵하므로 어떤 것을 잊거나 없애기 위해 부정적 감정을 붙어넣는다.

어휘_ meditation 명상

    purported ~라고 알려진

    benefit 이점

    label (라벨을 붙여) 분류하다

정답_ (b)

3.

블루 오션이란 용어는 새로운 것임에도 불구하고 그것의 존재는 그렇지 않다. 그것들은 과거 그리고 현재의 비즈니스 생활의 한 특징이다. 백 년 전을 돌아보고 스스로에게 물어보자. 얼마나 많은 오늘날의 산업이 알려지지 않았었는가? 답은 이렇다. 자동차, 음악 녹음, 항공, 석유 화학, 건강 보험, 경영 컨설팅 같은 기본적인 업종들은 당시 알려지지 않았거나 막 시작된 것들이었다. 이제 30년 전으로 시계를 돌려보자. 다시 넘쳐나는 수백억 달러의 산업들이 터져 나왔다. 조금만 꼽아 봐도 뮤추얼 펀드, 핸드폰, 가스 화력 발전소, 생명 공학, 할인 소매점, 익스프레스 배송, 미니밴, 스노보드, 커피 바, 그리고 홈비디오 등이 있다. 불과 30년 전만 해도 이러한 산업은 의미 있게 존재하지 않았다.

해설_ 새로운 시장을 뜻하며, 현재의 비즈니스 생명의 한 형태는 블루 오션이다.

어휘_ aviation 항공

    petro-chemical 석유화학

    biotechnology 생명공학

정답_ (a)

4.

해석_ 지난주 펩시에서는 고과당 옥수수 시럽 대신 진짜 설탕을 사용한 새로운 콜라 두 종류를 미국 시장에 출시했다. '펩시 내추럴' 은 12온스의 유리병에 담겨져 나오며, 탄산수, 설탕 그리고 사과와 콜라 추출물을 함유한다. '펩시 쓰로우백스' 는 미국 음료 시장에 고과당 옥수수시럽이 홍수를 이루기 전, 우리가 70년대에 알았던 복고풍의 진짜 설탕이 담겨져 있다. 겉보기에는 펩시에서 자연식품 팬들과 옛날 펩시 제조법에 대한 향수를 가지고 있는 사람들에게 어필하는 새로운 음료를 만들었다. 펩시는 고과당 옥수수 시럽에 어떠한 문제가 있어서 (새로운 음료를) 만든 것이 아니라고 말한다. 물론 아니다. 그러나 이유가 어떻든 간에, 일부 펩시에서 진짜 설탕을 사용한 것을 보니 기분이 좋다.

해설_ 맨 마지막 줄에서 '펩시에서 진짜 설탕을 사용한 것을 보니 기분이 좋다' 라고 한 것이 힌트가 된다.

어휘_ release 출시하다

    fructose 과당(果糖)

    formula 제조법

    extract 추출물

정답_ (a)

5.

해석_ 최근의 연구 결과에 따르면 침술 치료를 받은 만성적인 허리 통증 환자들은 오직 기존의 치료만 받은 사람들보다 (치료가) 더 진전되었다고 한다. 재미있게도 가짜 침술 — 바늘 대신에 이쑤시개를 맞은 — 치료를 받은 사람들도 기존의 치료를 받은 사람보다 더 나은 결과가 나타난 것으로 연구에서 드러났다. "이로써 침술 치료 중 실제로 침을 찌르는 행위 외에 어떠한 의미 있는 것이 이루어지고 있다는 것을 검증하는 증거가 하나 더 늘어난 셈입니다. 앞으로 이러한 반응을 유발하는 것에 대한 보다 깊은 연구가 필요합니다." 라고 국립 대체의학 센터 소장인 조세핀 P. 브리그스 박사가 말했다.

해설_ 빈칸 뒤에서 나타났듯이 '바늘 대신 이쑤시개' 로 침술 치료를 받았다면 그것은 가짜 침술 치료(simulated acupuncture)라는 것을 알 수 있다.

어휘_ fare 대우받다, 진척되다

　　　toothpick 이쑤시개

　　　delve 탐구하다, 정사(精査)하다

정답_ (d)

6.

해석_ 여가는 단순히 시간의 문제가 아니라 정말로 분위기와 운치의 문제이다. 그것은 시간적인 사건이 아닌 영적인 상태이다. 그것은 한 사람의 본래의 열정 사이에서 서두르지 않는 여가의 삶이다. 여가는 자극과 휴식이 혼합될 때 우리의 삶에서 휴지(休止)를 구성한다. 진정한 여가는 우선 활기찬 감정과 평화로운 느낌을 우리에게 준다. 그것은 너무나 명확하고 즐거운 순간으로 구성되어 있어 우리는 그것들이 영원하길 바라게 된다.

해설_ 문맥상 그러한 즐거운 감정이 '영원하길' 바란다는 것이 적합하다.

어휘_ chronological 연대기적인

　　　enthusiasm 열정

　　　fusion 혼합

　　　stimulation 자극

정답_ (d)

7.

해석_ 우리들 중 더 많은 사람들이 환경적으로 적극적인 사람으로 변모하지 않는다면, 개인이나 조직된 그룹으로서 모두 환경 혁명은 성공하지 못할 것이다. 성공은 인간의 타성과 사회의 일부 구조적인 장애물을 극복하는 데 달려있다. 회사에서 리더의 행태는 단기 수익 창출의 압박에 의해 형성된다. 정치인들은 재선을 위한 단기적 이해와 특정 이해집단에 의해 영향을 받는다. 하지만 환경그룹은 장기적 안목을 취하며 다수를 대변할 수 있다.

해설_ 빈칸 앞에나온 회사 리더의 단기적 이해, 정치인의 단기적인 대한 관심과 달리 환경운동가들은 그 반대의 행태를 보여야 한다.

어휘_ overcome 극복하다

　　　inertia 불활발, 타성

　　　impediment 장애물

　　　profit-making 이익 창출

정답_ (a)

8.

해석_ 경쟁은 비윤리적인 사업 관행의 원인이 되기도 한다. 일부 회사들은 경쟁자들을 따라잡기 위한 방법으로 문제가 있는 사업 관행을 이용하기도 하는데, 그 경쟁자들은 많은 주요 고객을 끌어들이기 위해 뇌물을 사용하여 그들의 지배적인 시장 지위를 확립했을지도 모른다. 파산 위기에 와 있는 회사들은 생존과 재무적 실패 사이에서 중요한 역할을 할 수 있는 사업을 소유한 고객들을 잡거나 유지하기 위해 의심스러운 수단을 이용하기도 한다.

해설_ 문맥상 빈칸에는 경쟁자를 '따라잡다' 라는 내용이 들어가야 한다.

어휘_ dominant 지배적인; 유력한

　　　under-the-table 뇌물의, 은밀히

　　　bankruptcy 파산

　　　dubious 의심스러운, 수상한

정답_ (a)

9.

해석_ 흡연과 심장질환, 폐암과 같은 주요 치명적인 질병과의 의학적 연관으로 인해 보험회사들은 20년 동안 비흡연자들에게 낮은 보험료로 보상해 주었다. 오늘날 5개 중 4개의 보험회사들이 평균 10%에서 15%에 이르는 (보험료) 할인을 제공한다. 국내 제2위 보험회사인 메트로폴리탄 생명보험과 같은 회사는 어떤 건강 기준에 부합하는 사람들을 위해 가장 좋은 조건의 보험료율을 마련해 놓고 있다. 흡연자들은 자동적으로 탈락된다.

해설_ 빈칸 뒤에 '흡연자들은 자동적으로 탈락된다' 라는 내용이 있고 글 상단에서 '비흡연자들에게 낮은 보험료로 보상해 주었다' 라는 내용으로 보아 빈칸에는 보험회사에서 '어떤 건강 기준에 가장 잘 맞는 사람들' 을 위해 좋은 조건을 따로 준비해 놓고 있다는 내용이 문맥상 적합하다.

어휘_ life insurance company 생명보험회사

　　　criteria (판단) 기준

　　　reward 보답[보상]하다

　　　reserve (특정인을 위해) ~을 마련해 두다

정답_ (d)

10.

해석_ 컴퓨터 범죄 건수가 빠르게 증가하고 있다. 컴퓨터 범죄로 인한 손실이 매년 수십억 달러에 이르기 때문에, 업계는 컴퓨터로 절도를 저질렀던 전직 도둑들을 채용하고 있다. 대기업들은 컴퓨터 시스템에 침투할 수 있는 이러한 전문가들의 기술을 원하고 있다. 그 시스템에 들어가는 방법을 아는 바로 그 사람들이 다른 사람들이 그런

짓을 하는 걸 더 잘 막을 수 있다. 그들의 기술이 수요가 매우 높기 때문에 컴퓨터 시스템을 뚫을 수 있는 컴퓨터 범죄자들은 복권되어 유급으로 채용 될 수 있다. 아이러니하게도 그들은 성공적인 사업가와 컨설턴트가 된다.

해설_ '컴퓨터로 절도를 저질렀던 사람' 이라면 전직 도둑을 말하는 것이다.

어휘_ rehabilitate 원상태로 되돌리다, 회복시키다

gainful 이익이 있는, 유리한

commit theft 도둑질을 하다

prevent 막다

정답_ (b)

11.

해석_ 연구자들이 인간 배아를 복제해 기술이 도를 넘었다는 목소리를 촉발시키고 있다. 인간 배아가 복제되었다는 소식이 위성을 통해 단신으로 전 세계에 퍼져나갔다. 그날 오후 조지 워싱턴의 전화 교환대는 언론사로부터 250통의 전화가 연결되었다. 그 다음날은 스페인, 남아공화국 그리고 호주 등의 지역에서 더 많은 전화와 팩스들이 홍수처럼 밀려왔다. 바티칸의 L'Osservators Romano는 그러한 행위가 인간을 '광기의 터널' 로 전락시킬 수 있다고 일면 사설에서 경고했다.

해설_ 빈칸의 내용에 대한 힌트는 본문의 마지막 부분, 즉 '바티칸의 L'Osservators Romano는 그러한 행위가 인류를 '광기의 터널' 로 전락시킬 수 있다' 는 내용에서 얻을 수 있다.

어휘_ embryo 태아, 배아

provoke 촉발하다

sound bite (뉴스에서) 사건을 짤막하게 전하는 영상

humanity 인류

madness 광기

정답_ (d)

12.

해석_ 1970년대에 의학 연구자들은 전염병에 대한 인간의 승리가 시간의 문제였는지에 대해 토론을 하였다. 소아마비 바이러스는 소크와 세이빈의 백신에 의해 기세가 꺾였다. 천연두는 사실상 사라졌다. 말라리아를 발생시키는 기생충은 퇴치되었다. 한때 치명적인 병이었던 디프테리아, 백일해, 파상풍 등은 무성영화와 같은 흘러간 시대의 기묘한 잔상으로 남아있다.

해설_ 빈칸 뒤에 한때 치명적인 질병이었던 것들이 퇴치되었다는 내용이 있으므로 그것이 시간의 문제인가 하는 내용이다.

어휘_ polio 소아마비

smallpox 천연두

parasite 기생충

diphtheria [의학] 디프테리아

pertussis 백일해

tetanus 파상풍(균)

quaint 기묘한, 기이한

정답_ (b)

13.

해석_ 안드레오티 수상이 대형 횡령 음모에 연루되었는지는 아직 확실하지 않지만, 그가 마피아와 악명 높은 관계를 맺고 있는 정치인들의 출세를 조직적으로 후원했다는 많은 증거가 있다. 그는 공직을 남용한 혐의에서 벗어날 수 없다. 법적 범행이 아직 증명되지 않았지만 지금 현재 그가 마피아와 연계되었다는 것은 의심의 여지가 없다.

해설_ 빈칸 앞의 그가 마피아와 연계되었다는 내용이 힌트가 된다.

어휘_ Prime Minister 수상

embezzlement 횡령

notorious 악명 높은

beyond question 의심의 여지가 없는

정답_ (a)

14.

해석_ 영어를 주로 두 번째 언어로 사용하는 많은 나라들 중에서 남아프리카 공화국은 영어를 제1언어로 구사하는 사람 - 180만 명이 넘는다 - 이 가장 많은 나라이다. 이 글을 쓰는 지금 11개의 공식 언어가 있는데, 영어, 네덜란드 관련 언어인 아프리칸스 어, 그리고 9개의 아프리카 언어들이 그것이다. 네덜란드인들의 정착은 1652년부터 시작되었고 영국인들이 1795년에 도착했을 때 네덜란드인들은 모두 잘 정착했고 1814년 케이프를 합병했다. 네덜란드 말을 하는 많은 보어인들은 그들만의 공화국을 세우기 위해 이주해 나갔다. 하지만 두 번의 전쟁에서 영국에 패하면서 보어인들이 세운 공화국들은 1910년 대영 제국의 자치령인 남아프리카 공화국 유니온에 흡수되었다.

해설_ 문맥상 '영국인들이 1795년에 도착했을 때 네덜란드인들은 모두 잘 정착했다' 가 적합하므로 빈칸에는 '~할 때' 를 나타내는 when이 들어가야 한다.

어휘_ settlement 정착, 이주

annex 합병하다

dominion 자치령

정답_ (b)

15.

해석_ 연방과 주의 자금지원 규정 및 실무에 대한 지식, GASB 재무제표의 이행, 공채 발행과 투자에 관련된 재무 서류의 분석과 관련된 경험이 필요합니다. 표준 표 계산 소프트웨어, 워드 프로세싱 그리고 인터넷 소프트웨어의 능숙한 활용과 더불어, 훌륭한 조직 및 커뮤니케이션(구두와 작문)과 프레젠테이션 기술은 필수입니다. 우리는 전문직 작업 환경과 좋은 보너스 혜택들을 제공합니다.

해설_ 문맥상 '~와 더불어' 라는 의미를 가진 along with가 빈칸에 적절하다.

어휘_ implementation 이행, 실행
investment 투자
proficiency 능숙, 숙련
as far as ~하는 한

정답_ (b)

16.

해석_ 세계로 과감하게 진출하기 위해서 젊은이는 어린 시절의 집이 여전히 무조건 그의 것이라는 것을 느낄 필요가 있는데 그것은 유아가 자기의 침대를 벗어나는 모험을 할 때 안전함을 느끼기 위해 엄마의 앞치마 끈이나 나중에 테디베어를 잡아야 하는 것과 매우 비슷하다. 어린 아이들이 잡아야 하는 물리적 물체가 필요하다면, 젊은이에게는 가정이 주는 안전을 언제든지 누릴 수 있다는 느낌이 필요하다.

해설_ 문맥상 빈칸에는 '~하는데', '~하는데 반해' 라는 내용의 접속사가 들어가야 하는데 when은 문어체에서 대조·범위 등의 부사절을 이끌어 위와 같은 의미로 사용된다.

어휘_ adolescent 청춘기의 사람(남녀), 청년, 젊은이
toddler 아장아장 걷는 사람, 유아
unconditionally 무조건적으로
apron 앞치마

정답_ (b)

17.

해석_ 연구에 의하면 사람들은 다른 색깔에 대해 다르게 반응한다고 한다. 예를 들면 사람들은 붉은 빛에 노출되었을 때 더욱 흥분하며 파란 빛에는 수동적으로 되는 경향이 있다. 재미있는 것은 파란색보다 빨간색에 더 가까운 핑크색은 모든 색 중에서 가장 진정 효과가 강한 것으로 보인다. 이 발견은 특히 병원과 교도소의 벽을 어느 색으로 칠할 것인지를 결정하는 인테리어 장식가들에게 암시를 준다.

해설_ 첫 번째 문단의 '사람들은 다른 색깔에 대해 다르게 반응한다' 는 내용이 힌트가 된다.

어휘_ reveal 드러내다; 알리다

soothing 달래는 듯한, 마음을 진정시키는
decorator 장식가, 장식업자

정답_ (b)

18.

해석_ 미국인들이 믿는 것과 그들의 생활과의 관계를 이해하는 데 있어, 이상과 현실을 구분하는 것이 중요하다. 기회 균등과 자립 같은 미국의 가치들은 반드시 미국 생활의 실상을 보여준다고 할 수는 없는 이상들이다. 예를 들어 기회 균등은 항상 실현되지는 않는 이상이다. 현실적으로, 어떤 사람들은 다른 이들보다 더 나은 성공의 기회를 갖고 있다. 부잣집 아이들은 가난한 집 아이들보다 기회를 더 많이 갖는다. 모든 인종에 똑같은 기회가 부여되도록 만들어진 법에도 불구하고 많은 흑인들은 평균적인 백인들보다 더 적은 기회를 갖는다.

해설_ 부잣집 아이와 가난한 집 아이, 백인과 흑인을 비교하며 기회 균등이 이루어지지 못하고 있다는 내용을 예로 들어 미국적 이상과 현실의 괴리를 설명하고 있다.

어휘_ idealism 이상
self-reliance 자립
equality 균등
promote 증진하다, 장려하다

정답_ (a)

19.

해석_ 주요 지역인 런던, 뉴욕, 도쿄뿐만 아니라 전 세계의 도시에 사무소를 운영하고 있는 국제적 기업인 네이처 출판 그룹(NPG)은 전 세계에 채용의 기회를 드립니다. NPG 사는 포트폴리오를 개발하고 확장함에 따라, 편집, 제작과 디자인, 영업, 마케팅, 광고, IT, 웹 출판, 비즈니스 개발, 그리고 관리를 포함하는 모든 부서에 취업기회가 생기고 있습니다. 현재 공석이 있는 부서를 확인하고 지원하려면 웹사이트를 방문해주십시오. NPG 사의 직원들은 경쟁력 있는 보수와 혜택을 누리고 있으며, 가장 중요한 것은 직원들이 자기 소질을 개발하고 성과를 내면 인정 받고 보상을 받는 사내 문화 속에서 일한다는 만족감을 만끽한다는 점입니다..

해설_ NPG 사의 채용에 대한 글이다. 글은 먼저 NPG 사가 전 세계적으로 사무소와 직원을 갖고 있다는 약간의 자사 홍보성 글로 시작하지만, 이는 지원자들의 구미를 당기기 위한 역할을 할 뿐이다. To view and apply for current vacancies에서 이 글의 목적을 파악할 수 있다. 이 문장을 직역하자면, '결원이 생겼는지 확인하고 그 자리에 지원하려면' 정도가 되겠다.

어휘_ expand 확장시키다, 넓히다

vacancy 결원, 빈 자리

compensation 보상, 보수, 월급

nurture 양육하다, 기르다

정답_ (d)

20.

해석_ 의회는 오랫동안 순수한 자문의 기관이었으며 왕이 정기적으로 소집해야 할 어떤 의무도 없었다. 헨리 5세의 통치 기간인 1414년이 되어서야 의회의 동의 없이 새로운 법이 만들어지지 않는다는 것을 공식적으로 왕이 승인하게 되었다. 강력한 왕의 재위기에 의회의 영향력이 증가한 이런 부조화적인 현상은 헨리 8세 시대에도 반복되었다. 헨리의 해결책은 로마 교회와 분리하여 자신을 수장으로 한 영국 국교회를 설립하는 것이었다. 하지만 일반인에게는 심각한 격동일 수 있는 이 종교개혁에서 왕국의 중요한 사람들의 도움이 절실했다. 그의 전임 왕들이 했었던 것보다 협조를 확보하기 위해 헨리 8세는 그의 결정 과정에 의회를 훨씬 많이 끌어들여야 했다.

해설_ 의회와 왕국의 종교개혁의 관계에 관한 글이다.

어휘_ parliament 의회

advisory body 조언 기관

obligation 의무

summon 소환하다, 소집하다

정답_ (d)

21.

해석_ 캘리포니아 주 중부 연안에서의 야생동물들에 대한 실험의 초기 결과에선 치명적인 2006년 사건에서 시금치를 오염시킨 유독성 박테리아에 감염된 866개의 동물 샘플에서 사소한 흔적만을 발견할 수 있었다. 캘리포니아 주의 야생동물 관리국은 그 결과가 사슴과 그 밖의 야생동물들을 문제의 중심에서 빼주기를 바라고 있다. 중부 연안의 농장주들은 샐리나스의 동쪽 목장의 가축 및 멧돼지와 연관된 2006년의 사건 이후 농장에 있는 야생동물과의 전쟁을 선포하였다. 그들은 사슴에게 총을 쏘고, 개구리를 제거하기 위해 연못에 독을 풀고, 나무와 관목들을 없애버렸다. 만약 도매업자들이 사슴이 어느 농장에 있었다는 증거를 발견하면, 그들은 그 농작물을 구입하지 않을 것이기 때문이다. 그러나 검은꼬리사슴으로부터 추출된 311개의 샘플들에서 박테리아에 대한 양성 반응은 없었다. 캘리포이아 주 야생동물학자 테리 팔미사노 씨는 말한다. "야생동물들은 일부 사람들이 생각하듯이 장티푸스의 숙주가 아니다."

해설_ '야생동물들은 장티푸스의 숙주가 아니다' 라는 인용이 글의 마지막에 배치된 것은 글쓴이의 주장이 바로 이와 같기 때문이다. 얼핏 설명문 같지만 글쓴이의 주장이 들어가 있는 글이므로, 이를 염두에 두고 제목을 골라야 한다. (c)는 너무 포괄적인 제목으로 알맞지 않다.

어휘_ fraction 파편, 조각

contaminate 오염시키다

virulent 유독한, 맹독성의

spinach 시금치

deer 사슴

정답_ (d)

22.

해석_ 연구를 하기 위해서 철학자들은 관찰자로 남아 행동에 참여하지 않아야 한다. 그는 게임의 관객처럼 경기장 바깥에서 바라봐야 한다. 하지만 그 장면에 대한 철학자의 숙고가 요구하는 객관적 판단은 공간적 거리에 의해서만 유도되는 것이 아니다. 시간적인 거리도 똑같이 필수적이다. 그 사건으로부터 떨어져 숙고할 수 있는 시간은 그가 사람이 인생에서 갖는 열정들을 평가하고 동기들을 인식할 수 있게 한다.

해설_ '철학자들은 관찰자로 남아 행동에 참여하지 않아야 한다' 는 등 현상을 평가, 조사하는 철학자의 태도에 관한 이야기이다.

어휘_ spectator 관객, 구경꾼

arena 경기장, 활동무대

contemplation 숙고

spatial 공간적인

appreciate 평가하다

정답_ (d)

23.

해석_ 화재가 '핵겨울' 을 야기시켜 지구 기후를 교란시킬 수 있다는 초기의 두려움이 사라진 반면에, 일부 과학자들은 재앙적인 결과들이 쿠웨이트의 국경에서 수백, 수천 킬로미터 떨어진 곳에서도 감지될 수 있다는 새로운 예상을 하고 있다. 과학자들은 매일 매일 대기로 뿜어지는 기름, 가스, 연기의 거대한 검은 구름의 크기에 대해 아는 것이 별로 없다. 그러나 다음 몇 주 동안 이 유독 물질 덩어리에 일어날 일이 앞으로 수억 명의 생명에 영향을 줄 것을 우려하고 있다.

해설_ '매일 매일 대기로 뿜어지는 기름, 가스, 연기의 거대한 검은 구름의 크기' 등을 언급하고 있는 것으로 보아, 환경적 문제에 관한 글임을 알 수 있다.

어휘_ disrupt 교란시키다

noxious 유해한

prediction 예언, 예보

정답_ (a)

24.

해석_ 지구는 인구 과잉 상태이다. 우리의 기술은 40억을 상당히 초과하는 인구를 적절하게 유지할 수 있을 것으로 여겨진다. 지구는 심리적 의미에서도 과잉 상태이다. 그 동안 우리 인류를 위해 새로운 길을 개척해 온 그 소수의 야심에 사로잡힌 인간들 때문에 우리에게는 이제 더 나아갈 새로운 장소가 없다. 해양 유역이 있긴 하지만 우리는 아직 그것들을 진지하게 개발할 생각이 없다. 우리의 역사에서 지금 이 순간은 우주의 이웃 세계를 개발할 가능성이 다가오고 있다.

해설_ 우주의 이웃 세계를 탐험한다면 태양계가 그 중 하나가 될 수 있다.

어휘_ overcrowded 인구 과잉의
　　　 blaze (길을) 내다, 개척하다
　　　 psychological 심리적인

정답_ (c)

25.

해석_ 엄청나게 많은 컴퓨터 범죄들이 보고되지 않기 때문에 그것들에 대한 문서도 없다. 보고된 것은 모든 컴퓨터 범죄 중 15% 정도에 불과하다. 회사들은 그것들을 널리 알리면 컴퓨터 범죄의 수가 더 증가할 것을 염려하고 있다. 그들은 야심만만한 도둑들이 컴퓨터 시스템으로 들어가는 새로운 기법을 언론을 통해서 배우지 않을까 걱정한다.

해설_ 중간 부분에 '회사들은 그것들을 널리 알리면 컴퓨터 범죄의 수가 더 증가할 것을 염려하고 있다' 는 내용이 힌트가 된다.

어휘_ unreported 보고되지 않은
　　　 documentation 문서(화)
　　　 aspire 열망하다, 포부를 갖다
　　　 victimize 희생시키다

정답_ (c)

26.

해석_ 보조 도구 없이 인간의 눈으로 볼 수 있는 가장 먼 곳의 물체는 안드로메다 은하계이다. 이것은 안드로메다 성운에서 희미한 빛 조각으로 보인다. 만약 당신이 나선형의 팔을 달고, 먼지선과 빛나는 성운을 가진 안드로메다의 환상적인 망원 사진을 보았다면 현혹되지 말라. 우리의 태양만큼이나 밝은 별들은 너무 희미해서 그렇게 멀리 있으면 우리 눈에 어떠한 인상도 줄 수 없다. 당신이 맨 눈으로 안드로메다에서 볼 수 있는 모든 것은 이 은하계의 중심부에 있는 가장 밝은 별들만이 내뿜는 작고 희미한 빛뿐이다.

해설_ 하단에 '당신이 맨눈으로 안드로메다에서 볼 수 있는 모든 것은 ~ 작고 희미한 빛뿐이다' 라는 내용이 힌트가 된다.

어휘_ galaxy 은하, 은하수(the Milky Way)
　　　 constellation 별자리, 성운
　　　 nebula 성운
　　　 fuzzy 희미한, 분명치 않은

정답_ (a)

27.

해석_ 어떤 사람들은 개의 진화와 사회적 역사에 관한 퍼즐을 풀려는 시도해왔다. 요즘 개의 외모에 나타나는 가장 큰 차이점은 여러 유전적 근원의 차이점으로 나타나는 결과가 아니라 지난 500년간 인간에 의한 강력한 품종 개량의 결과이다. 인간이 어떻게, 왜 개를 길들여왔는가 하는 것은 완전히 밝혀지지는 않았지만, (개의 개체가) 증가하고 (품종이) 다양화되는 속도는 개가 인간 역사에 중요한 역할을 해왔다는 것을 보여준다. 인간의 사냥을 도와줬던 개가 매우 성공적인 품종이 되어 전 세계에 퍼진 것은 좋은 예이다.

해설_ 윗글의 두 번째 문장, '요즘 개의 외양에 가장 큰 차이점은 유전적 근원의 차이점으로 나타나는 결과가 아니라 지난 500년간 인간에 의한 강력한 품종 개량의 결과이다' 가 힌트이다.

어휘_ intensive 강한, 격렬한
　　　 multiply 늘다, 증가하다
　　　 diversify 다양화하다
　　　 breed 유형, 품종

정답_ (c)

28.

해석_ 납부하신 다른 세금이나 부채가 없는 한 이 통지를 받은 날로부터 8주 안에 귀하에게 환급금이 보내질 것입니다. 8주 내에 환급이나 해명서를 받지 못하셨다면 위에 적힌 번호로 연락 주세요. 환불 지연으로 인해 불편을 끼쳐드렸다면 죄송합니다. 귀하의 이해를 돕기 위해 납세자로서의 권리가 적혀 있는 공지문 한 통을 동봉합니다. 협조해주셔서 감사합니다.

해설_ 첫 번째 문장에서 '납부하신 다른 세금이나 부채가 없는 한 이 통지를 받은 날로부터 8주 안에 귀하에게 환급금이 보내질 것입니다' 라고 했으므로 만약 납세자가 다른 미납금이나 부채가 있다면 환불액을 8주 안에 못 받을 수 있다는 것이다.

어휘_ refund 환급금
　　　 notice 통지(서)
　　　 enclose 동봉하다
　　　 taxpayer 납세자

정답_ (d)

29.

해석_ 역사가들은 유럽이 19세기에 세계에서 중심적 지위를 유지했다는 것에 동의한다. 그 주된 이유로 세 가지를 들 수 있다. 첫 번째는 유럽의 경계 안에 세계 농지의 많은 부분이 있었다는 것이다. 결과적으로 유럽 국가들은 그들의 국민들을 어려움 없이 먹일 수 있었고 무역을 번영시킬 수 있었다. 두 번째 요인은 제해권이었다. 유럽인들은 자국에서 전멸하지 않으면서 다른 대륙을 공격할 수 있었다. 유럽인들이 누렸던 세 번째 이점은 유럽인들이 과학과 기술의 놀라운 발전을 이루었다는 점을 들 수 있다.

해설_ 유럽이 성공한 두 번째 요인이 유럽인들의 바다를 지배한 것이라고 글의 하단에서 언급하고 있다.

어휘_ farmland 농(경)지
　　　adversity 역경
　　　thriving 번영하는, 번화한
　　　annihilation 전멸, 완패

정답_ (d)

30.

해석_ 아프리카 최강의 경제 국가로서 가장 밝은 운명을 갖고 있는 남아공화국은 그 대륙을 21세기로 이끌기 시작할 것이다. 그러나 동시에 모든 사람들의 마음은 경제 재앙과 부족 전쟁 등 분열의 장면으로 어두워졌다. 20세기 말, 세계 사람들은 혼란스럽고 종종 위험한 민주주의로의 이동을 보았다. 종족 대립은 확실히 그 과정에서 가장 뼈아픈 장애물이다. 남아공화국은 이제 공식적으로 그 장벽을 허물었다. 그러나 물론 더 무서운 장벽은 인간의 마음이다.

해설_ 글에 의하면 남아공화국은 공식적으로 그 장벽을 허물어왔지만 더 무서운 장벽인 인간의 마음까지는 허물지 못했다는 것은 결국 아직 종족 대립을 극복하지 못했다는 것이다.

어휘_ disintegration 분해, 분열
　　　antagonism 적대(관계), 대립
　　　dismantle 제거하다
　　　formidable 무서운, 만만찮은
　　　obstruct 막다
　　　hatred 적대, 증오

정답_ (d)

31.

해석_ 팔레스타인인의 자유를 위한 투쟁을 비판하는 사람들은 때때로 '팔레스타인의 만델라'의 부재를 안타까워한다. 나는 이스라엘의 F.W. 드 클럭이 없음을 애석해하고 있다. 실은 두 사람 모두가 필요하다. 왜냐하면 이스라엘은 자기네 지역에 살고 있는 1천2백만의 팔레스타인인의 평등을 억제하고 점령지에 살고 있는 팔레스타인인들을 잔인하게 폭력으로 억압하고, 인종 청소된 팔레스타인 피난민의 고향으로 돌아가려는 권리를 60년 동안 거부함으로써 인종차별의 극심한 변종임을 스스로 점점 더 드러내고 있기 때문이다.

해설_ 필자는 이스라엘 쪽에 좀 더 비판적인 눈을 가지고 있다. 이스라엘이 거의 의도적으로 민족분리의 정책을 고수하고 있기 때문이다. (c)에서처럼 팔레스타인 난민들이 60년 동안 점령을 받았다는 내용은 지문에 없다. 또한 이스라엘이 난민들에게 이전의 고향으로 갈 수 있는 기회를 주지 않았다고 했으므로 (d)도 아니다. 남아공에서 만델라와 드 클럭이 한 일에 대한 배경 지식이 있다면 좀 더 쉽게 접근할 수 있을 것이다.

어휘_ lament 한탄하다, 애석해하다
　　　absence 부재(不在), 없음, 결석
　　　withhold 억누르다, 억제하다
　　　refugee 피난자, 난민
　　　apartheid 남아공의 인종분리정책

정답_ (a)

32.

해석_ 위험한 사람들이 총기를 소지할 수 없게 하는 국가적 차원의 법은 딱 세 개뿐이다. 금주법 시대가 끝날 즈음까지 소급되는 총기와 다른 자동화기 소지에 대한 제한법이 있다. J.F. 케네디와 마틴 루터 킹 목사가 암살당한 이후 통과된 1968년의 총기 제한법과 연방으로부터 인가 받은 총기 판매자들이 총기 구입 금지자의 기록을 확인할 수 있게 하는 브래디 법안에 명시된 것처럼 흉악범들과 정신적으로 위험한 질병을 가진 사람과 같은 총기 구입 금지자들은 주에 의해서 임의로 분류되었다.

해설_ 관련법이 단지 세 개밖에 없다는 첫 문장에서부터 필자의 논지를 가늠할 수 있다. 그나마 있는 법들도 너무 오래 전에 만들어졌거나, 엄연히 연방법이라 할 수 없다는 주장을 통해 이 문단에서 필자가 주장하고자 하는 바가 무엇인지 파악해야 한다.

어휘_ date back 소급시키다, 거슬러 올라가다
　　　the Prohibition era 미국에서 1920년부터 33년까지 발효된
　　　금주법 시대
　　　felon 중죄인; 흉악한, 잔인한
　　　licence 면허; 인가, 허가를 주다

정답_ (c)

33.

해석_ UCLA에서 개최되는 2009년 로스앤젤레스 타임즈 북 페스티벌 자원봉사에 관심을 가져주신 여러분께 감사드립니다. 이 축제

의 14번째 연례 행사가 4월 25일 토요일과 26일 일요일에 열립니다.
우리는 여러분들이 자원 봉사자로 참여해 주시기를 바랍니다.
자원봉사의 세부 요건:
- 봉사 단원들은 무료 주차와 주차장의 셔틀버스 서비스, 그리고 점
  심식사를 제공 받을 수 있습니다.
- 행사 이후에도 입을 수 있는 자원봉사자용 티셔츠를 드립니다. (카
  키색이나 베이지색 바지 또는 반바지를 착용해주세요.)
- 자원봉사의 주된 활동은 주로 발로 뛰는 데 있습니다. 편안한 신발
  을 착용해 주세요.
- 봉사 단원은 만 18세 이상입니다. 봉사 활동 중에 18세 미만의 아
  이들과 함께 다니실 수 없습니다.

해설_ 자원봉사 단원의 주 업무는 행사장을 감시하는 게 아니라 on
your feet for most of your shift에서 알 수 있듯이 주로 돌아다니
거나 그와 유사한 업무를 하는 것이다. 나이에 대한 제한만 있을 뿐
사는 지역이나 국적에 대한 제한은 없으므로 (b)가 답이다.

어휘_ hold 개최하다
    volunteer 지원하다, 지원자
    khaki 카키색의, 황갈색의
    beige 베이지색의
    shift 변화, 이동, 교대

정답_ (b)

34.

해석_ 기회 균등과 자립 같은 미국의 이상들이 실제 생활에서는 부
분적으로만 실행된다는 사실이 그것들의 중요성을 감소시키지 않는
다. 대부분의 미국인들은 여전히 그것들을 믿으며 일상생활에서 강
하게 영향을 받고 있다. 우리가 미국인들의 기본적인 가치와 미국에
서 그것들이 어떻게 거의 모든 일상생활에 영향을 미치는지를 이해
한다면 미국인들의 생각과 감정을 더 잘 이해할 수 있다.

해설_ 내용을 간추려 보면 미국의 가치들이 미국인들의 모든 일상생
활에 영향을 미친다는 것을 알 수 있다.

어휘_ diminish 감소시키다
    affect 영향을 미치다
    influence 영향

정답_ (b)

35.

해석_ 정치적 행태가 깊은 인격 특성의 기능이라고 믿는 사람들은
우연한, 그럼에도 불구하고 실재적인 경험, 학습 그리고 사회적 상황
같은 요소들을 고려하지 않는다. 바로 그 성질에 의한 일원론적인 심
리적 설명으로는 정치적 현상의 복잡성과 다양성을 설명하기 어렵

다. 게다가 특정 종류의 정치로만 배타적으로 규명될 수 있는 성격
타입은 존재하지 않는다. 같은 성격적 경향들은 극좌 또는 극우의 이
데올로기와 연관될 수 있으며 온건한 민주적 이데올로기와도 공존할
수 있다.

해설_ 정치적 행태 또는 현상은 너무 복잡해서 한두 가지의 요소로
규명할 수 없다는 내용의 글이다.

어휘_ make no allowance for ~을 참작하지 않다
    accidental 우연의
    personality 개성, 성격, 인격
    coexist 공존하다

정답_ (c)

36.

해석_ 문학 분석에 과학적 원리를 도입하는 것을 반대하는 또 하나
의 매우 유명한 주장이 있다. 우리는 그 경우 과학은 객관적이어야
하지만 반면에 문학의 해석은 항상 주관적이라고 배웠다. 내 생각에
이런 노골적인 반대는 지지할 수 없다. 비평가의 일은 주관성에 있어
다양할 수 있다. 만약 그가 주어진 환경의 기간 동안 그것의 중요성
을 찾기보다 그 작품의 성격을 확인하려 한다면 이 정도는 매우 낮아
질 것이다. 게다가 그가 같은 작품에 대해 다른 측면을 검토한다면
그 주관성의 정도는 달라질 것이다.

해설_ 학문 분석의 한 종류인 문학적 분석에 대해 독자에게 소개하
듯이 덤덤하게 분석하는 글이다.

어휘_ untenable 지킬 수 없는, 지지할 수 없는
    subjectivity 주관성, 자기 본위
    ascertain 확인하다

정답_ (c)

37.

해석_ 개인들은 사회적 관계에 관한 맞물리는 세트 안에서 특정한
공간을 부여받는다. 그러나 사회적 인간으로 자신을 인식하는 것은
고정적이고 변하지 않는 위치를 점유하는 것이 아니다. 그것은 발전
목표를 만들어내는 것이며, 인생을 살아가는 것은 주어진 끝을 향해
나아가는 것이다. 그리하여 완전한 인생은 성취이며 죽음은 어떤 사
람이 행복하거나 불행한 것으로 평가받을 수 있는 시점인 것이다. 고
대 그리스 속담에 이러한 것이 있다. '그가 죽기 전까지 어떤 사람도
행복하다고 할 수 없다.'

해설_ 행복이란 인생을 살아가는 과정에서 생성되는 것이라는 내용
을 언급하고 있다.

어휘_ inherit 상속하다, 부여받다
    interlock 맞물리다

occupy (시간 · 장소 따위를) 차지하다

proverb 격언

정답_ (c)

38.

해석_ 위험 허용 수준은 개성과 실용성의 혼합이다. 당신이 긍정적인 성향이라면 하락세가 결과적으로 상승할 것이라고 확신할 것이며, 당신은 단기간의 시장 유동세에 그리 당황하지 않을 것이다. 따라서 시장은 당신이 투자를 다변화하기를 원한다. 하지만 시장의 혼란에 의해 좌초될 수도 있는 단기간의 목표를 갖고 있다면, 실용적인 필요성이 우선이다. 당신의 현실적인 위험 허용 수준을 평가하기 위해서는, 단기적 필요성을 충족시키는 데 얼마의 돈이 필요할지, 즉 다음 3년 안에 돈을 투입해야 하는 목표들을 잘 따져봐야 한다.

해설_ 주식 투자에 대한 조언을 하고 있다. 시장이 요구하는 것보다 자신의 자산 상태와 시장의 상황을 실용적인 관점으로 판단하여 투자하라는 내용이므로 (b)의 내용은 문맥에서 벗어나 있다.

어휘_ risk tolerance 위험 허용수준

disposition 성격, 기질

diversify 분산시키다

junker (미국 속어) 털털이 자동차, 고물 자동차

practicality 실용성

정답_ (b)

39.

해석_ 더 젊은 지원자들을 고용하는 데 대한 고용주들의 선호는 새로울 게 없는 일이다. 자격이 완전히 일치할 때조차 그간의 실험은 고용주들이 더 젊은 사람을 선호한다는 것을 보여왔다. 이 전체적인 선호에 대한 합당한 이유가 없다. 계속된 연구는 나이든 노동자들이 새로운 직업을 구하는 데 젊은 경쟁자들보다 더 긴 시간이 걸린다는 것을 보여준다. 나이든 사람들은 더 나은 기술, 특히 대인관계의 기술, 더 성실한 근태, 더 양심적인 것 등 관련된 성과 지표의 전 영역에 걸쳐 더 잘 해낸다. 나이 든 직원들을 쓰는 게 돈이 더 들 것이라고 생각할 수 있으나, 사실 나이 든 직원이 누리는 우대 조건은 그들의 경력 때문이며 경력은 업무 성과에 영향을 끼친다. 그리고 나이든 사람들이 더 높은 임금을 요구할 것이라 짐작하지 말고 오히려 그들에게 조건을 제시하고 그들 스스로 결정하게 해야 한다.

해설_ (a)의 앞에서 젊은이들에 대한 고용주들의 선호에는 합당한 이유가 없다고 했으므로 그 이후에는 나이든 이들을 고용해야 하는 합당한 이유에 대한 언급이 바로 뒤따라와야 한다.

어휘_ candidate 후보자, 지원자

credential 신임장, 자격, 적성

relevant 관련된

indicator 지표

conscientious 양심적인, 성실한

정답_ (a)

40.

해석_ 빨래 건조기가 미국 가정에서 사용되는 전기량의 최소 6%를 차지한다는데, 빨랫줄 건조가 다시 이용되고 있다는 게 놀랍지 않은가? 이웃에게 흉물스럽다는 이유로 이러한 행위가 금지된 곳에서는, 건조할 수 있는 권리를 위한 운동가들과 블로그 애호가 어머니들은 동맹을 형성하고 있다. 그들이 이런 운동을 하는 이유는 에너지 소비를 줄이고 흰 세탁물을 더 희게 한다고 표백제를 쓰는 것보다 자연광으로 말리는 것이 더 좋기 때문이다. 그리고 그들은 바람에 날리는 하얀 천의 이미지에서 가난을 보기를 싫어하기 때문이다. 2001년 미국 에너지부의 한 보고서는 전기 세탁 건조기가 미국 가정에서쓰는 총 전기 사용량의 5.8%를 차지한다고 추정하였다. 같은 보고서에서 미국 가정의 실내외 조명이 단지 전기 사용량의 8.8%밖에 차지하지 않는다는 사실에 비추어보면 놀라운 사용량이다. 게다가, 5.8%의 사용량은 가스 건조기의 모터를 켜기 위해 소요되는 동력을 포함하고 있지 않다는 점이다.

해설_ 줄에 널린 빨랫감이 바람에 날리는 모습을 통해 가난한 이미지를 보기 싫다는 내용은, 에너지 소비를 줄이고 환경 보호에도 앞장서기 위한 이 운동의 취지에 맞지 않다. 따라서 정답은 (c)이다.

어휘_ account for 차지하다

nuisance 성가신 것

startling 놀라운

constitute 구성하다

정답_ (c)

고득점을 위한
Advanced Voca

Advanced Voca

☐ abdomen 배, 복부

☐ accidentally 우연히, 뜻밖에

☐ accomplishment 성취

☐ account for (~의 비율을) 차지하다

☐ administer (약을) 투여하다, (치료를) 해주다

☐ adornment 장식품

☐ a good day's work 꼬박 하루가 걸리는 일

☐ airborne 공중에 떠서

☐ alliance 동맹, 연합

☐ anti-rollover 전복 방지

☐ assure 보증하다, 보장하다

☐ atrocity 흉악, 잔인

☐ attribute A to B A를 B의 탓(덕분)으로 돌리다

☐ automated teller machine 현금 자동 입출금기

☐ avaricious 탐욕스러운

☐ aviation 비행, 항공

☐ award 상, (손해 배상의) 재정액

☐ backfire 기대에 어긋나다

☐ backing 안감 (재료)

☐ balance 잔액

☐ balancing act 양쪽을 만족시키는 행위, (위험한) 줄타기

☐ be condemned to ~할 운명이다

☐ bedbug 빈대

☐ billion 10억

☐ bleach 표백제

☐ Blue State 민주당 지지 주

☐ bowel 내부

☐ brotherhood 형제간, 형제애

☐ call upon 이용하다

☐ catastrophic 파멸의, 비극적인

☐ catchall 일괄하는, 포괄적인

☐ category 부문, 종류

☐ caterer 출장 연회업자

☐ cease 멈추다, 중단하다

☐ cerebellum 소뇌

☐ charge 혐의

☐ coax (물건을) 잘 다루어 뜻대로 되게 하다

☐ coddle 상냥하게 다루다, 응석받이로 기르다

☐ coincide 동시에 일어나다, 일치하다

☐ collision 충돌

☐ congestion 혼잡

☐ compliment 칭찬

☐ comply with ~에 따르다

☐ compile 집계하다

☐ concentration camp 강제 수용소

☐ consensus 일치된 의견, 합의

☐ consent 동의하다, 승낙하다

☐ correspond to ~에 일치하다, 부합하다, 상응하다

☐ crash 충돌

☐ crawl 기어가다

☐ creed 신념, 주의

☐ cuddle 껴안다, 껴안고 귀여워하다

☐ curb 억제하다

☐ day-to-day 일상의

☐ deadly 치명적인

- [ ] deficit 적자
- [ ] demographic 인구의
- [ ] depositor 예금자
- [ ] description 기술, 서술
- [ ] diarrhea 설사
- [ ] dictate 명령하다, 지시하다
- [ ] dip 내려가다, 감소하다
- [ ] dire straits 곤경
- [ ] disparity 상이, 격차
- [ ] distribute 살포하다, 배포하다
- [ ] docile 온순한
- [ ] docility 유순함, 온순함
- [ ] doldrums 침체
- [ ] dominate 지배하다
- [ ] downturn 침체, 하락
- [ ] dub 이름을 붙이다

- [ ] entangle oneself in ~에 빠지다, 말려들다
- [ ] erect 세우다
- [ ] escalation 상승
- [ ] extreme 극심한

- [ ] fad 일시적 유행
- [ ] fare well 잘 되어가다
- [ ] fawning 아양 부리는, 아첨하는
- [ ] feel 분위기
- [ ] feline 고양이
- [ ] flashy 번지르르한
- [ ] flush 붉게 물들이다
- [ ] foliage 무성한 잎

- [ ] folklore 민간 전승(傳承)
- [ ] forklift 지게차
- [ ] framework 틀, 구조
- [ ] frill 겉치레, 과잉 서비스
- [ ] frustration 좌절

- [ ] get an earful from ~로부터 잔소리를 듣다
- [ ] getaway 휴양지
- [ ] get the credit for ~에 대한 공을 인정받다
- [ ] gist 요점
- [ ] glaring 번쩍이는, 눈에 띄는
- [ ] grapple 맞붙어 싸우다
- [ ] greenery 녹색 식물[잎]

- [ ] hail 환영하다
- [ ] hammer 되풀이하여 역설하다, 주입시키다
- [ ] hand-off 통화 채널 전환
- [ ] hangar 격납고
- [ ] heretofore 지금까지, 이전에는
- [ ] hideous 가증스러운, 끔찍한
- [ ] high-flying 고가의
- [ ] homicide 살인
- [ ] hospitalization 입원, 병원 치료
- [ ] humble 겸허하게 하다, 낮추다

- [ ] impaired 손상된
- [ ] in a bid to ~하려고 하여, ~할 목적으로
- [ ] in all likelihood 아마, 십중팔구
- [ ] in an instant 눈 깜짝할 사이에, 즉시
- [ ] inaugural 취임(식)의

- [ ] in parallel 병행으로, 동시에
- [ ] intuition 직관
- [ ] in captivity 사로잡혀, 감금되어
- [ ] induce 일으키다, 야기하다
- [ ] infamous 악명 높은
- [ ] infrared 적외선(의)
- [ ] infrastructure 기반 시설
- [ ] in more ways than one 여러 가지 의미로, 여러 면에서
- [ ] inscription 비문
- [ ] insectivore 식충 동물
- [ ] instruct 지시하다, 명령하다
- [ ] intoxicated 술 취한
- [ ] intuitive 직관[지각]에 의한

- [ ] jittery 신경과민의
- [ ] juice 전기, 전류

- [ ] kidney 신장
- [ ] kinase 키나아제 《효소의 일종》
- [ ] knockout KO

- [ ] lethal 죽음에 이르는, 치명적인
- [ ] level off 안정되다
- [ ] levy 부과하다
- [ ] live out 이룩하다, 현실화시키다
- [ ] log 기록하다
- [ ] lot 운, 운명
- [ ] low 최저 수준
- [ ] limestone cave 석회동, 종유굴

- [ ] liposuction 지방 흡입(술)
- [ ] locust 메뚜기

- [ ] malpractice 의료 과실, 부정 치료
- [ ] make an appeal against ~에 대해 항소하다
- [ ] massive 대규모의
- [ ] meaningfully 의미심장하게
- [ ] measles 홍역
- [ ] medical examiner 검시관
- [ ] mobile switching center 이동 통신 교환기
- [ ] molecule 분자
- [ ] mollusc 연체동물
- [ ] moratorium 지불 유예[정지]
- [ ] mortality rate 사망률
- [ ] multi-potent 다양한 효능이 있는

- [ ] naive 순진한
- [ ] negation 부정
- [ ] nocturnal 야행성의
- [ ] no doubt 필시, 아마도
- [ ] non-partisan 초당파적인, 객관적인
- [ ] nuisance 폐, 남에게 폐가 되는 행위
- [ ] numerical 수의, 숫자로 표시된

- [ ] ochre 황토색
- [ ] ostentation 겉치레, 허식
- [ ] outrageously 지나치게, 터무니없이
- [ ] outstanding debts 미불 채무

- [ ] pediatric 소아과의

- [ ] **pending** 미결정의, 현안의
- [ ] **penetrate** 스며들다, 침투하다
- [ ] **perforated** 구멍이 뚫린
- [ ] **perilous** 위험한
- [ ] **pervasive** 퍼지는, 스며드는
- [ ] **pest** 해충
- [ ] **photovoltaic** 광전지의
- [ ] **pick up** 회복하다, 속도를 내다
- [ ] **pit A against B** A를 B와 싸우게 하다
- [ ] **plunge A into B** A를 B로 몰아넣다
- [ ] **point out** 지적하다, 가리키다
- [ ] **pop the question** 청혼하다
- [ ] **potassium** 칼륨
- [ ] **preceding** 선행하는, 앞선, 이전의
- [ ] **premium** 보험료
- [ ] **pronounce** 공식으로 발표하다, 선고하다, 발음하다
- [ ] **proportions** 크기
- [ ] **propose** 청혼하다
- [ ] **protectionism** 보호 무역주의
- [ ] **provided** ~을 조건으로 하여, 만일 ~라면

- [ ] **racism** 인종차별주의
- [ ] **ramshackle** 넘어질 듯한, 흔들거리는, 약한
- [ ] **recall** 상기하다, 생각해내다
- [ ] **recipe** (요리의) 조리법
- [ ] **Red State** 공화당 지지 주
- [ ] **rental** 임대
- [ ] **replica** 모사, 복제
- [ ] **reproduction** 재현, 복원
- [ ] **reserve** 저축, 적립금

- [ ] **retreat** 퇴각, 도망(치다)
- [ ] **reverse** 바꿔 놓다, 전환하다
- [ ] **rooftop** 지붕의, 옥상의
- [ ] **ruling** 판결, 결정
- [ ] **ruthless** 무자비한

- [ ] **sanatorium** 요양소
- [ ] **sanction** 제재, 처벌
- [ ] **scrap** 폐기하다
- [ ] **seat-of-the-pants** 직감적인, 반사적인
- [ ] **segregation** 인종 차별
- [ ] **separate** 분리된, 독립된
- [ ] **sequence** 순서
- [ ] **Sin City** 라스베이거스
- [ ] **size up** 평가하다, 판단하다
- [ ] **skewing** 비대칭
- [ ] **slow-witted** 우둔한
- [ ] **snap** 갑작스러운, 즉석의
- [ ] **sober** 술 취하지[마시지] 않은
- [ ] **solely** 다만, 오로지
- [ ] **solemn** 엄숙한, 근엄한
- [ ] **sophistication** 복잡화, 세련화
- [ ] **special session** 임시 회의
- [ ] **squeak** 찍찍 우는 소리
- [ ] **stab** 찌르다, 찔러 죽이다
- [ ] **stain** 얼룩
- [ ] **straight** 호모[동성애자]가 아닌
- [ ] **stratosphere** (물가의) 최고가
- [ ] **stretch the truth** 진실을 왜곡하다
- [ ] **strip down** 니스·페인트 등을 벗겨내다

- ☐ structured 구조화된
- ☐ stunning 기절할 만큼의, 근사한
- ☐ subject 피실험자
- ☐ subsidy 보조금
- ☐ swallow 삼키다
- ☐ synonymous with ~와 동의어의, 같은 뜻의

- ☐ take ~ into custody ~을 구속[체포]하다
- ☐ take steps 조치를 취하다
- ☐ take the wraps off 공개하다
- ☐ tall tale 터무니없는 이야기, 믿기 어려운 사실
- ☐ terminate 끝내다, 마무리하다
- ☐ therapeutic 치료의
- ☐ the short end of the stick 불리한 입장, 손해
- ☐ time span 기간
- ☐ toss out 제거하다, 버리다
- ☐ trade off 번갈아[교대로] 하다
- ☐ transaction fee 거래 수수료
- ☐ transition 변화, 추이
- ☐ treacherous 불안정한, 위험한
- ☐ Treasury Secretary 재무 장관
- ☐ triumphal arch 개선문
- ☐ turnover 전환, 재편성
- ☐ twig 작은 가지

- ☐ Uncle Sam 미국 정부
- ☐ unconscious 무의식(의)
- ☐ unsightly 보기 흉한, 눈에 거슬리는
- ☐ unveil 발표하다, 공개하다
- ☐ uprising 봉기

- ☐ upwards of ~ 이상, 거의, 약

- ☐ varnish 니스, 광택제
- ☐ verbally 말로, 구두로
- ☐ verbal rose 입에 발린 칭찬
- ☐ vicious 사악한
- ☐ victimize 희생시키다
- ☐ virtual 가상의
- ☐ vouch 증명하다, 입증하다

- ☐ zero in on ~에 목표를[초점을] 맞추다
- ☐ zoom 급등하다, 급상승하다